D0462820

Spending Time

Spending Time

The Most Valuable Resource

Daniel S. Hamermesh

OXFORD
UNIVERSITY PRESS

OXFORD

UNIVERSITY PRESS

Oxford University Press is a department of the University of Oxford. It furthers
the University's objective of excellence in research, scholarship, and education
by publishing worldwide. Oxford is a registered trade mark of Oxford University
Press in the UK and certain other countries.

Published in the United States of America by Oxford University Press
198 Madison Avenue, New York, NY 10016, United States of America.

© Oxford University Press 2019

Library of Congress Cataloging-in-Publication Data
Names: Hamermesh, Daniel S., author.
Title: Spending time : the most valuable resource / Daniel S. Hamermesh.
Description: New York : Oxford University Press, [2018] |
Includes bibliographical references and index.
Identifiers: LCCN 2018027022 (print) | LCCN 2018028064 (ebook) |
ISBN 9780190853846 (UPDF) | ISBN 9780190853853 (EPUB) |
ISBN 9780190853839 (hardcover : alk. paper)
Subjects: LCSH: Time—Social aspects. | Time management.
Classification: LCC HM656 (ebook) | LCC HM656 .H36 2018 (print) |
DDC 650.1/1—dc23
LC record available at https://lccn.loc.gov/2018027022

1 3 5 7 9 8 6 4 2

Printed by Sheridan Books, Inc., United States of America

33614081460288

CONTENTS

Preface vii

1. You Can't Always Get What You Want *1*

2. What We Do When We're Not Working *15*

3. How Much Do We Work? *33*

4. When Do We Work? *45*

5. Women and Men *55*

6. Togetherness *73*

7. "The Last of Life, for Which the First Was Made" *87*

8. The Perennial Issue and an Old/New Concern *103*

9. E Pluribus Unum? *117*

10. The Rich Are Different from You and Me *133*

11. Kvetching about Time *151*

12. Do We Have More Time Now? Will We Get More Time? *163*

13. What Is to Be Done? *177*

Notes 197
Index 213

PREFACE

Scholarly articles about time are abundant: in the economics literature since 2000, over 6,700 published articles include the word "time" in the title.[1] Many books deal with time already, some with attractive titles that I might have used here. That made finding a title for this book difficult. There are also a few scholarly monographs that deal with specific aspects of people's time use.[2] Given all these efforts, why yet another book on time? The best answer is that how we use time and why we make choices about time should be fundamentally interesting questions for everyone. Time and money are the two scarcest things in everyone's life, and in most countries incomes have grown greatly over the past fifty years. Time has not.

No book has discussed the panoply of ways that we use time and how those differ among countries, and none has tried to explain why people differ in their use of time.[3] Economic thinking can explain patterns of time use and do so in ways that are totally comprehensible to any adult. They are even comprehensible to teenagers (as discussions with my fifteen-year-old grandson demonstrate). While the issues may be complex, they are readily understandable because they affect us all: we can empathize with the behavior of people making decisions about time, because we make them ourselves all the time. Deciding when to wake up, how much to sleep, how many meals to have, and when to have them are just a few examples of the decisions about time that we all make. We base these decisions on the incentives that we face because of the scarcity of time, even though we rarely consider why or how we are making those decisions. "Time itself is neutral; it can be used either destructively or constructively," so that our decisions about time affect our well-being and that of other members of our society.[4]

The US now has what is in many ways the best information in the world about how its citizens spend their time. Before 2000, many other countries, and the US too, had very occasional surveys in which respondents kept diaries that were completed on the next day and recorded what they were doing at each point of the previous day. These time-diary surveys were useful indicators of what people did. But they were not produced on a continuing basis; intervals between them were irregular; the few produced at irregular intervals were not always comparable within the same country, including the US; and most, including the few American studies, did not cover many people.[5]

When I began working on time use I remarked that the US was in the *derrière garde* in the creation of data that allow chronicling how people spend time. That is no longer true. In 2003, the American Time Use Survey (ATUS), a product of the US Bureau of Labor Statistics (BLS), began collecting time diaries each month that are completed by about a thousand randomly chosen Americans ages fifteen or over, in which they record their activities on the previous day. With this survey the US has created a continuing record of Americans' spending their time. No other country has done this, so today the US is clearly in the *avant garde* in its provision of the information with which to analyze its citizens' decisions about spending time. I use the ATUS for the years 2003–2015, about 170,000 diaries, throughout this study, so that original calculations based on the ATUS underlie many of the statistics presented, obviating the need in these cases to refer to the underlying set of data. I am extremely grateful to the Minnesota Population Center and the Maryland Population Research Center for producing the ATUS data sets based on the raw BLS data.

American scholars are remarkably ethnocentric in their concentration on domestic issues, in far too many cases basing general conclusions about people's behavior solely on results produced using American data. And because of the predominance of American scholarship worldwide, especially in economics, scholarly research too often gives the impression that we have learned something about people's behavior generally, when in fact we have only learned about the behavior of the less than 5 percent of the world's population that resides in the US.

If Americans' use of time were representative of time use worldwide, or at least of that in other rich countries, there would be no problem. As I show throughout the book, though, along some dimensions Americans use time much differently than do citizens of other wealthy countries. To demonstrate these differences, and to understand how people generally spend time, on most of the topics that I discuss I also present evidence based on time diaries kept by people elsewhere. While I use information from many countries, including Australia, Canada, Italy, Japan, Korea, the Netherlands, Portugal, and Spain, most of the comparative analysis relies on original calculations using time diaries collected in three large wealthy European countries: France (*Enquête emploi du temps*, 2009–2010, about 24,000 diaries); Germany (*Zeitverwendungserhebung*, 2012–2013, about 25,000 diaries), and the United Kingdom (*Time Use Survey*, 2014–2015, about 16,000 diaries). In some cases, I use these data instead of the American data because the latter lack information on some crucial aspects of time use. I thank the Centre Maurice Halbwachs in Paris, the Statistiches Bundesamt in Wiesbaden, and the Multinational Time Use Survey of Oxford University for providing these data sets. Here too, when I refer to calculations for each of these countries, I am referring to calculations based on these particular sets of data.

With much of the discussion based on previous analyses of data or on new analyses using these four sets of data, the question is how to present the results in an interesting and readable way. From my experience teaching more than 25,000 undergraduates over the past fifty years, I'm convinced that figures—pictures—work better than tables of numbers. For that reason, there are thirty figures in the text but no tables at all. There are also none of the equations that are so beloved by economists. The figures are completely self-explanatory, and the reader should be able to infer the message of each figure at a glance. Because of my technological incompetence, the figures were drawn by other people, with Yonah Meiselman offering tremendous help.

I began working on questions about people's use of time in the late 1980s, publishing in 1990 two scholarly articles on the subject, both based on US time-diary information from the mid-1970s. Since then I have been continually studying questions related to time use, increasingly in conjunction with other economists. Many of the ideas in this book and much of the information presented come from these joint efforts. The volume would not have been possible without the ideas and labor that these scholars have supplied over the years. Thus Jeff Biddle, Hielke Buddelmeyer, Michael Burda, Ana Rute Cardoso, Katie Genadek, Reuben Gronau, Daiji Kawaguchi, Jungmin Lee, Caitlin Myers, Gerard Pfann, Mark Pocock, Joel Slemrod, Elena Stancanelli, Stephen Trejo, José Varejaõ, Philippe Weil, and Mark Wooden have all published scholarly work with me that provides the basis for some of the arguments here. While it wouldn't be fair to implicate any of them as coauthors, their work and inspiration clearly made this book possible.

Other people too can be thanked as "unindicted co-conspirators." A Barnard student, Mia Lindheimer, made a useful suggestion; and our New York neighbor, Kevin Hyams, made a very helpful point. George Borjas offered help on Chapter 8, and Pierre Cahuc provided good comments on chapter 10. David Pervin, who has shepherded this book from its inception, commented in detail on every chapter and greatly improved the book's organization. My sister, Deborah White, caught some errors in the final draft. My wife, Frances Witty Hamermesh, read every word in the first and second drafts and greatly improved the logic of the exposition and the arrangement of the ideas.

Throughout the discussions I motivate the issues by anecdotes, things that I have observed that illustrate in daily life how we spend our time and help us to understand why we make the decisions that we do. Many of these come from my wife's and my experiences and interactions. Others stem from the behavior of our daughters-in-law Amy and Hannah Hamermesh, and our six grandchildren, Jonathan, Samuel, Miriam, Yonah, Noah, and Raphael Hamermesh, all of whom also offered suggestions about the book's title. Many more come from things that our two now middle-aged sons did as children and from activities that they have engaged in as adults. It is to our sons, David J. Hamermesh and Matthew A. Hamermesh, that I dedicate this book.

Daniel S. Hamermesh
Austin, June 2018

Spending Time

CHAPTER 1

✧

You Can't Always Get What You Want

Time and numbers have intrigued me since I was a little kid. When I was four my parents bought me a watch—analog, of course, as digital didn't exist in 1947. They taught me how to tell time, which got me "hung up" with concerns about time. That same year my maternal grandmother taught me to play the card game Casino. I learned how to add (at least up to ten) and became fascinated by numbers at an early age. This interest grew into complete nerdiness by my teen years: when I was fourteen my sister (also a nerd—now a college math instructor) and I spent one month of summer vacation tabulating the frequency of given names in the local telephone directory.

Those two concerns (my wife calls them obsessions) play out regularly in my life. Today I had a lunch appointment with someone across Manhattan. I spent $2.75 in subway fares, only for the other person not to show up. That small amount of change was a minute fraction of the cost of this fiasco, which took an hour of my time. If I could get work at the US minimum wage for that hour, I would have made $7.25. And even if I couldn't have found work, I could have used the time to do something that I value more highly than subway travel and waiting for someone—which is almost everything. Quite literally, I was spending time, and the time spent cost me much more than the $2.75 subway fare. Because time is scarce, using it costs us money. We *spend* time.

But how much time do we really have? Most people in wealthy countries are born with an expectation of eighty plus years of life. When we are young, most of us feel that time is endless. Who can't remember sitting around in summer vacation from grade school trying to find something to do? Yet as we age, time seems to accelerate: on my forty-fifth birthday I remarked to my sixteen-year-old son, "Time is going faster and faster than it used to." His response was, "Yeah, Dad, that's because you're going downhill." We can ignore the wise-guy nature of his comment, but he was correct about my accelerating physical deterioration.

My son only hit on half the story, though. There are also fundamental changes in our attitude toward time that occur throughout most of our adult lives, and these changes condition much of what we do with our lives. They arise from the changing incentives that we all face as we grow older, and these in turn result from changes in the amount that we can earn for each hour of work, how much our partners can earn for their work, and the growing scarcity of time because we have fewer years of life left to us.

Everything is scarce—we want more of everything, including love, money, recognition, and power. Someone who denies being interested in at least one of these is laboring under self-delusion. Among these things that are essential to our satisfaction, time is the one that we are least conscious of, yet it is scarcest of all. Everything we do eats up time, and this scarcity is something economists can provide useful insights about. One purpose here is to demonstrate how that scarcity affects what we do—how we split our time among different activities—and when we undertake them.

We think that certain ways of spending time are beyond our control: we must sleep eight hours per day; we must eat three meals per day; we must work eight hours per weekday. No doubt there are other "natural" requirements that we have in mind. But this is just wrong: we have choices to make even in these activities, and those choices arise from our subconscious efforts to get the best outcomes in terms of making ourselves as happy as possible. Those outcomes depend on the limits that the available time imposes on us, on our opportunities for earning money to finance our activities, on the choices that those with whom we associate—family, friends, fellow workers, and others—make, and on the resources at our disposal for making these choices. The Mick Jagger and Keith Richards 1969 song "You Can't Always Get What You Want" made these limits very clear.

The economic approach to thinking about time (and everything else) conceives of people making decisions, either consciously or more often unconsciously, that are designed to make themselves as well off as possible. We are limited in our choices by the time available to us each year and by the remaining length of our lives. We are limited by the income that we can earn, the amount of other income we and our partner—if we have one—can contribute, the family circumstances that we have chosen to create, and the prices of the things we might want to buy.

Whenever we choose to buy a Big Mac we are choosing *not* to use our income to buy something else, perhaps a Whopper with cheese. The same is true for time: when we choose to spend two hours attending a concert we are choosing *not* to use those two hours to get some more sleep or to go for a long run. Just as we face trade-offs in the things we buy, we also face them in the time that we spend in different activities. We "trade off" one activity for another.

IS TIME REALLY SCARCE?

How can I claim that time is scarce? It is true that there are only 24 hours in a day and 365 1/4 days in the average year, but most people know that over the last century or so, people in today's wealthy countries have been living longer. And people in countries that have not achieved the same level of wealth as Western democracies are also living a lot longer.

Despite these gains, the amount of time that we can expect to enjoy over our lives—a total of about forty-two million minutes—is not that much higher than it was even fifty years ago. Look at Figure 1.1, in which the

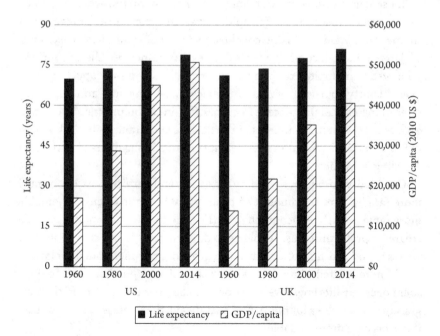

Figure 1.1 Gross Domestic Product (GDP) Per Capita (2010 US$) and Life Expectancy, US and UK, 1960–2014.

Source: http://data.worldbank.org/indicator/SP.DYN.LE00.IN; http://data.worldbank.org/indicator/NY.GDP. PCAP.KD

solid bars show the expected length of life for the average person born in each year in the United States or the United Kingdom, two wealthy countries, between 1960 and 2014. In both countries average life expectancy has risen—but by "only" 13 percent in the US, and by only 14 percent in the UK. On a per-year basis, longevity increased by 0.2 percent in both countries on average.

These are remarkable increases in life expectancy, but compared to the increases in spending power per person, they are tiny. The striped bars in Figure 1.1 show the level of income, after accounting for inflation, that has been available to the average citizen of each country. This income level is the actual amount of command over available goods; it shows how much we could buy if we spent every dollar or every pound that we had. This disposable income rose by 198 percent in the US and by 193 percent in the UK over this fifty-four-year period, on average at a rate of nearly 2 percent per year. After inflation spending rose at about the same rate as after-inflation incomes in both countries. This change means that our spending power per year of life has nearly tripled during this roughly half-century. Put another way, our time is now worth more—it is more valuable—and increasingly scarcer than the incomes we use to buy things.

These comparisons are not unique to rich countries, where we know that incomes rose unusually rapidly over this period. A similar set of comparisons yields the same conclusions for Brazil and Mexico, examples of large middle-income countries. Life expectancy in these countries improved more rapidly than in the rich countries—in Brazil by 37 percent over this fifty-four-year period, in Mexico by 34 percent—annual average rates of increase of 0.6 percent in each. After-inflation incomes also rose in each country, but much more rapidly than life expectancy—by 244 percent in Brazil and 155 percent in Mexico, more than tripling in Brazil, more than doubling in Mexico.

Our ability to purchase and enjoy goods and services has risen much more rapidly than the amount of time available for us to enjoy them. The more rapid growth in income than in the time that we have at our disposal creates a problem for us: it makes it difficult to stuff all the things that we want *and* can now afford into the growing, but increasingly relatively much more limited, time that we have available to purchase and to enjoy them over our lifetimes. We have more dollars per minute of life than our grandparents did—a lot more. And that means that time is scarcer for us— it has become more valuable.

With higher incomes and only a bit more time, we can engage in more different activities in each hour of time than our predecessors. Even if we spend no money, the cost of an hour of time itself is higher for us than it was for our grandparents. Even if we do nothing, an hour of time is costly—it has an "opportunity cost"—because we could use it for something other than just lying around. The idea of opportunity cost is illustrated to me every day when I walk by the empty parking place that we own in our building's garage. We could rent it out for seventy dollars a month, but we don't; even though we pay no money for the spot, leaving it empty—not using it—effectively costs us that seventy dollars every month.

WHAT DOES THIS SCARCITY MEAN IN OUR LIVES?

We think of credit cards as saving our time—no need, for example, to write monthly checks for utility and other bills. Not always the case: in the 2010s, perhaps because I had published economic research about how people use time, US government attorneys asked for my help as an expert witness in two lawsuits. One was against a company that had allowed security breaches enabling incorrect charges to be billed to customers' credit cards.[1] My initial reaction was, "Why me? What do I know about credit cards?" The attorneys pointed out that it takes time for credit-card users to correct an incorrect billing. In the other case, repeated security lapses at a company caused credit-card providers to shut down consumers' accounts. This forced the company's clients to arrange for new credit cards. Anyone who has ever lost a card or had one stolen or shut down knows that starting a new card takes time. If the card is used to pay recurrent bills that are charged directly, such as telephone service, cable service, and other bills, the time spent in getting the credit-card problem rectified is even greater.

The question in both cases was how to value the time that customers spent getting their credit-card bills corrected. Ignoring the fact that you incur the pain and suffering of spending fifteen minutes listening to dreadful music while waiting to spend two minutes with a "customer-service representative," your time on the phone could have been spent doing something else. And that alternative might at least yield a bit of enjoyment; also, it would be something that you chose to do, not something that was imposed on you by some company's negligence. Because the time could have been used for some alternative activity, it has value. And its value exists because it is scarce; the time you have at your disposal to enjoy an alternative becomes more limited because of the offending company's carelessness. The court recognized the validity of this argument in the one case that went to trial and ordered the company to pay damages—a small amount per plaintiff but tens of millions of dollars in total—to the large class of people who had been damaged by the company's behavior.

The importance of the scarcity of time exists in every aspect of our daily lives. Last night my wife and I were walking home from a restaurant and had to detour across a street because a large construction project had closed the sidewalk. This detour added an extra minute to our homeward journey—obviously a tiny burden on us. But these snippets of time add up. If one hundred people per day are forced to take the detour, and the project runs for two years, over twelve hundred hours of time are wasted. Valuing their time at even only half of the US minimum wage, that is nearly four thousand dollars of cost that the construction company foisted off on the public. We bear the cost of the project—our time could be better used (from our own points of view) than in needlessly crossing the street. We are essentially being forced to use our time to save the construction company the cost of creating a setback while the project is underway.

Just as companies' activities can cost us time, so their and governments' activities can bestow more time on us and reduce the time scarcity that we face. One of the main arguments for such projects as bridges and highways is that they will save their users time. And in each case that time should be valued, precisely because the time that the project has freed up is valuable to us. It is a benefit that the construction project creates for all of us. The necessity of valuing the time saved is why the US government explicitly requires its agencies to include calculations of the value of the time that will be saved as a way of justifying a newly proposed project.

Many research studies have used estimates of how people respond to changes in their commuting time—their willingness to pay for reductions in time spent sitting in cars—to value public projects that will ease commuting. As anyone who has sat in a traffic jam on the way to or from work will attest, this valuation makes sense. The recent addition of express lanes with toll charges on a freeway in Austin, Texas, for example, showed that some people are willing to pay as much as five dollars to speed up their ten-mile commute. This switch of autos to the toll lanes—this willingness of people to spend a little money to spend less time—validates thinking about the value of time in this activity too.[2]

Whenever a company's or a government's negligence costs us time, or a company's or government's activity yields us some unexpected free time, the scarcity of time changes for us. With less time at our disposal, we need to give up some lower-value activities that we might otherwise have undertaken. With a "time gift," we can indulge ourselves in uses of time that we otherwise would not have enjoyed. If we understand how the world that we face—the changing incentives imposed by time, and especially the growing scarcity of time compared to spending power—will affect how we spend our days, we can make ourselves better off and even happier.

ARE WE AWARE OF ALL THIS?

We could pay attention to the value of time if we are aware of the rising incomes and less rapidly rising longevity that we face, and the increasing relative scarcity of the time available to us. If we are not aware of these changes, we are unable to plan how to spend our money and how to use our time in a way consistent with making ourselves as happy as possible. We might wind up with a huge amount of income left over late in life, the result of our failure to account for the relative increase in income compared to the smaller rise in length of life. There is nothing wrong with having a huge amount of our lifetime earnings remaining when we die—if we planned on that. But as much as we love our children and grandchildren, it does seem like a waste to leave them money simply because we are not aware how rapidly our income will have grown over our lifetime. The existence of the large industry of retirement advisors and financial planners suggests that these concerns matter to us greatly—that we are willing to spend so that we can choose the best combinations of spending of our time and incomes.

Given the importance of "getting it right" to make ourselves as happy as we can, it shouldn't be surprising that people have pretty good information about what will happen to their incomes and to the years available to them. Take expectations about their incomes. A few studies have asked young people whether and to what extent they are aware that their earnings will rise as they age into their careers. Their expectations tracked the actuality quite closely: as a simple example, teenagers seem to know that their first full-time job will not be their highest paying.[3]

Most young people are also keenly aware of the higher incomes that they can expect if they obtain a college degree. They know that college grads earn more than high school grads; they even know very well which college majors will yield higher earnings throughout a career. They recognize, for example, that liberal-arts majors typically earn less than students specializing in accounting or finance.

People are clearly aware that getting additional education and moving up a career path raise their incomes. But it's a subtler question whether they also know that the average college graduate at age forty in 2030, for example, is likely to earn more after-inflation dollars than her friend who was born ten years earlier will earn in 2020, just because living standards on average are rising over time. The US Federal Reserve conducts regular surveys of random samples of Americans about how they expect their incomes to change over the next year.[4] Except during the Great Recession, large majorities believe that their incomes will grow, a belief that reasserted itself in the mid-2010s. People are aware that they are likely to do better in the future than similar Americans have done in the past or are doing now.

People's expectations about how long they will live are also pretty accurate, despite the sharp increases in longevity that have occurred over the past hundred years. In the early 1980s I surveyed a random sample of economics professors, getting information on their age and gender, and asking them how long they expected to live.[5] The older people knew that they would survive to a later age on average than the younger economists—they understood that, having survived the risks of young adulthood, their expected age at death was greater than it had been earlier in their lives. More important, they were able to forecast, based on the increases in longevity that occurred between 1950 and 1980, that they would live to a greater age than those born before them.

It is no surprise that economists can forecast well—that is supposed to be part of their expertise. But another survey, sent to a random sample of residents in a mid-size Midwestern metropolitan area, showed the same thing. These typical middle Americans understood that, having survived thus far, they could expect to live to a later age than they would have expected earlier. They were even aware that life expectancy had been increasing over their lifetimes, and they were able to project that increase into the future.

People have a good understanding that the incomes and time available to them will change over time. Whether they can account for these changes when deciding how to spend their time and money is another question, one that I examine throughout this book. In doing so I examine all the ways that we spend time, how they have changed over the years in response to the changing incentives generated by the changing incomes and time available to us, and how they differ because of differences in characteristics and preferences among individuals. Disentangling the importance of personal characteristics and economic conditions, whether of individuals or of the national economy, and such factors as unemployment, and their effects on work opportunities, is important: without doing so we can't determine how purely economic changes, such as growing inequality of earnings opportunities, will affect how we choose to spend time.

We are clearly aware of our growing incomes and rising life expectancies; since our expectations track both incomes and life expectancies closely, implicitly we are aware that we face a rising relative scarcity of time. More important is whether we know that this scarcity changes our incentives to use time—whether we act upon the information that we apparently have. Answering this question—examining how the scarcity of time and the incentives that scarcity generates alter how we spend time—underlies much of the discussion in this book.

WHAT ARE THE DIFFERENT WAYS WE SPEND TIME?

Ask yourself: What do I do with my time? What are the different things that I spent yesterday doing? Imagine you are asked: How much did you sleep yesterday? How much did you work (for pay) yesterday? How much TV did you watch yesterday? There is a good chance you would give answers that total much more, or much less, than twenty-four hours, which is not physically possible, except on that one day each year when your country starts or leaves Daylight Saving (Summer) Time, giving you twenty-three or twenty-five hours on that day. To measure correctly how people's time is spent, it is necessary to limit their answers—to force them to provide estimates that add up to the twenty-four hours at their disposal on most days. For one hundred years, researchers have been doing this—collecting "time diaries"—asking people to record, typically on the next day, what they were doing at each moment of the previous day. Much of the focus, including that of what was the first professionally collected set of diaries, has been on accounting for and valuing time spent outside the workplace.[6]

These diaries have been collected in substantial detail in at least forty countries, with much of the pioneering research being done in Communist Eastern Europe in the 1960s. For many years the US was a laggard in obtaining information on how its citizens spend their time. No more. Since 2003, a monthly federal government survey of roughly a thousand randomly chosen individuals has allowed us to get a detailed picture of how Americans spend time. Each person in these samples records on the next morning what they were doing at each time between 4:00 a.m. of the previous day and 3:59 a.m. of that morning. They write down descriptions of their activities, and government researchers code these into over four hundred very specific categories of time use. These data are now available for over 190,000 people. Similar but less extensive data for many other rich countries, and even diaries for many less-wealthy countries, underlie research by economists and others who study time—and the bulk of the calculations, data, and discussion in this book.

While I pay special attention to how Americans spend time, I also present many analyses and snapshots of how people in France, Germany, and the United Kingdom use their time. Information on time use in Australia, Italy, Japan, Korea, the Netherlands, Portugal, and Spain also forms the basis for some of the discussion. Looking at so many wealthy countries has the advantage of indicating how the ways that people spend time—the decisions we all face—are nearly universal. But it also demonstrates the extent to which Americans use their time differently from people elsewhere.

A serious difficulty with discussing time use is that it is not easy to classify time. What we call "work" might be a mix of different activities that add to what we or our employers produce, or it might be goofing off, exercising, or socializing with our co-workers. Sleep might be uniform, or time reported as "sleeping" might consist of sleeping, tossing and turning, having sex, or going to the bathroom. The over four hundred categories of time use recorded in the US data contain very detailed information on the kinds of activities that people do. The US surveys divide "sleep" into sleep and sleeplessness, and "work" into regular work, exercising at work, leisure at work, and clean-up at work. Other countries' surveys, including the French, German, and British surveys, go into varying lesser amounts of detail on these and other activities. Regardless, in discussing any use of time we need to think first about how finely we want to divide the activities that we consider.

We spend much of our time multitasking. We eat and watch TV; eat, watch TV, and care for a young child; exercise and listen to music; surf the web and telephone a retailer. Indeed, almost all activities that we undertake, if we think about them carefully, are done simultaneously with one or even several other activities. If we are asked which *single* activity we are engaged in at some point in time, how we answer depends on what we view as the most important (to us, at that point in time) of the several things that we are doing simultaneously. For the preceding examples, my guess is that most people would list eating ahead of watching TV, caring for a child ahead of watching TV, reading ahead of listening to music, and telephoning ahead of web surfing. Any diary that lists a single activity at a point in time is reflecting only one of the things that a person is doing at that time, the single activity deemed most important, even though the person may be doing other things simultaneously.

If we keep these caveats in mind, time diaries give important insights into what people consider to be the major activities in their lives. Most of us don't spend much time thinking about the things that we spend the most time on. On the most time-consuming activity—sleep—the average American does just about the eight hours that conventional wisdom suggests, reporting sleeping 8 1/3 hours on weekdays, but there are huge differences across the population. Ten percent of American adults report sleeping six or fewer hours in their diaries, while another 10 percent say they slept ten hours or more on the day for which they kept a diary. The US is typical in sleep being the single most important activity that people spend time on. In the UK the average adult sleeps only slightly less on weekdays than the average American. There too, large fractions of the population report sleeping six or fewer, or ten or more hours. Our stereotype about a "normal" sleeping time of eight hours is correct for the average American and for the average person elsewhere, but it masks the huge amount of variation among adults in the amount of z's that they typically get.

That people behave differently does not demonstrate that their behavior arises from different responses to the incentives that time scarcity produces. But with this much variation in the amount of time that people spend sleeping, the scope for scarcity and incentives to be generating some of the differences is huge. And later I show that some of the differences in how much people sleep can be attributed to differences in the incentives that they face—the fact that sleeping an extra hour involves a trade-off against other activities, including working, which might make us happier than another hour of sleep.

The second most common activity that Americans undertake is work for pay—over four hours per weekday by the average American adult. That figure seems low, but on many days even people who think of themselves as workers are not working, and only a little more than half of all American adults report doing any work at all on any particular weekday. The average Briton works only slightly less per weekday, and work for pay is the second most time-consuming activity for the average individual in all rich countries. Later I examine how much of differences among people in the amounts they work is determined by the incentives that they face, and how much by their country's culture and their personal characteristics.

Another 2 2/3 hours of the average American's time are spent watching television, whether television shows or movies rented or streamed. The time devoted to this leisure activity is typically less on average in other rich countries—in the UK, for example, it is "only" 2 1/3 hours. Still, taken together, sleeping, working for pay, and television watching, just three of the myriad activities that people might engage in, account for nearly two-thirds of the time that Americans have at their disposal, and for only slightly less in other rich societies.

When we perform different things matters and is the complicated result of our preferences, social pressures, biological effects, and the incentives that the changing scarcity of time over the day, across the week, and even over a lifetime, creates.[7] Spending an hour on an activity at 9:00 p.m. is different from spending an hour on the same activity at 3:00 a.m. In the case of TV, watching *Monday Night Football* is much better live than in a rerun in the middle of the night. Sleeping during the day may be biologically difficult; worse still, sleeping then certainly means that we are out of action when most of our fellows are active—we are out of sync with most of society. It would also mean that, if we work for pay, we are doing so at a time when most of our fellow workers are not on the job.

In addition to how much and when we do things, demographic differences, including differences by gender, race, ethnicity, or geographic location, in how we spend time are important. The news media, and presumably the customers who are devoted to them, are interested in how people in different demographic groups behave, how they live, and what they do. Those differences occur not just because people belong to different cultures. They arise in part from the incentives generated by variations in the scarcity of time across groups as they age, when they are partnered and/or have children, and other circumstances independent of the value of their time. They illustrate how our personal characteristics affect the choices that we are free to make about how we use our time.

One of the most salient characteristics in our lives is our age. You might think that time seems less scarce when you are twenty than when you are forty-five, since you have so many more years to live. It probably does, but personal experience tells me at age seventy-five that time also seems less scarce than when I was forty-five, even though I am very aware that I have fewer remaining years of life now than I did thirty years ago. In societies where an overwhelming majority of citizens can expect to live into old age, societies that represent a growing share of the world's population, the role that age has in affecting how people choose to spend their time has increased in importance.

Most of us do not make decisions about how we use time by ourselves. Instead, we make them at least partly in conjunction with our partner, with other family members, and/or with friends. Being a social animal requires being with other animals in our species. And unless we have total control over others' uses of time, our choices about how we spend our time must in part be determined by the preferences and incentives facing those with whom we want to associate. This seems obvious in the case of activities that require two or more people—such as most sexual activities, a tennis game, or a football match. It is also true for eating and, most important, for working. It means that decisions about time use are essentially social decisions, if "social" means involving at least two people.

Money—the amount we earn, the amount our partner earns, and the amount we can receive from interest or dividends on our wealth—is what people associate most with economics. And income is crucial in determining how we spend our time. That makes it essential that we examine all the ways that differences in incomes affect the kinds of things we spend time on and the time of the day, week, and year when we spend that time. Moreover, spending income takes time. You can't enjoy an instant vacation or a sixty-second Mahler symphony; you can't sleep or shower instantly; and even some activities for which you might hire someone are often more pleasurable, or done more efficiently, if you do them yourself. Think of reading *Hippos Go Berserk* to your two-year-old (at least on the first twenty readings!). That means that differences in income will alter not just the amounts that we purchase but also the kinds of things we buy—and when we buy and consume them.

While time is real, our ways of measuring time are an artifice. Citizens of most countries that are spread widely from east to west, like the United States, have chosen to divide the land into time zones with artificial demarcations, leading to what are really time borders. Time zones affect the ability of a country's citizens to interact efficiently. And, just as both partners in a couple or all friends in a social group must make decisions about how to spend time, some activities require that citizens in different time zones at least implicitly make decisions together. The effect of time zones on our use of time is something we ignore, but the impacts on sleeping, working, and TV watching—the "Big Three" uses of time—may be large. Being in Boston, in the US eastern time zone, may by itself lead us to behave differently than if we were in San Francisco, in the Pacific time zone.

Given the importance of time in our lives, we might paraphrase Charles Dudley Warner (not his coauthor Mark Twain, who usually gets credit for this line): "Everybody complains about time [the weather], but nobody *does* anything about it." In fact, we do more than just complain about the weather—we seed clouds and alter climates by our activities. Similarly, we complain a lot about time. We alter time's impacts on our lives by changing technology in ways that, without our expecting them, affect how we spend time. We as individuals have the power to make choices that will alter how the scarcity of time affects our lives. We cannot stop the flow of time, but we can limit the impacts of its scarcity on our everyday lives. Both individually and as societies changing our policies, we need to know how we can do this.

CHAPTER 2

cﬣﻭ

What We Do When We're Not Working

There are two dimensions to thinking about how much time people spend on each of the Big Three—sleeping, working for pay, and watching TV. One is their incidence—how many of us spend any time at all on these activities during the day. Another is their intensity—the amount of time that we spend on the activity if we do it at all. To understand the distinction between incidence and intensity, think about rainfall. Both Detroit, Michigan, and Austin, Texas, average 32 inches (810 millimeters) of rain per year. But there are 135 rainy days in an average year in Detroit, and only 88 in Austin. The incidence of rain is less in Austin; it rains less frequently, but when it rains, the rainfall on the rainy day is heavier—more intense.

Except for sleep, which nearly all of us do each day, there is tremendous variation in the incidence of nonwork activities—in the percentage of people engaged in them—and the intensity of time spent by those who do them. And this is important: if all of us spend ten minutes per day engaged in religious devotions, the total time spent would be the same as if one-twelfth of us spent two hours per day in those activities. The average amount of time is the same per person, but in the first case the country would be considered uniformly somewhat religious, while in the second a small minority of the population would be viewed as devoutly religious, with the majority being viewed as nonreligious. The first society would be more socially cohesive than the second—people would be doing more similar things.

When we do something is also important. Watching a sporting activity with few other fans, because it is a workday, is less fun than being in a packed stadium on a Saturday cheering on the home team. Many religious activities cannot take place unless sufficient other devotees participate. This means that the same activity can become inherently different depending on whether it is undertaken on a weekday or a weekend, or at daytime or nighttime. For that reason, we need to look at when various activities are performed as well as how many people are doing them and how much time the doers spend on them.

We think in categories—the human mind organizes knowledge into pigeonholes. With the myriad possible ways of spending our time, we need some principle for organizing our thinking about time use. For nearly one hundred years, economists have viewed our activities as falling into four broad categories: 1) work for pay, 2) home production, 3) personal care, and 4) leisure. Work for pay is obvious; it's the activity that—for most of us—finances all our other activities. Home production, sometimes called household production, includes activities that we could pay others to do for us.[1] The category includes such common activities as caring for our kids or aged parents; shopping, cooking, or cleaning up the dishes; and walking the dog. The crucial distinction here is that these are things that we could "outsource"—they meet what economists call "the third-party criterion,"—we could pay others to do them.[2] Whether we do these things ourselves or instead outsource them depends on how much we enjoy doing them, how good we are at doing them compared to a person whom we might hire, how much and what it costs us to pay others, and what it costs us to do them ourselves—that is, the time that we could have devoted to doing something else. We may not outsource any of these, but we could. Either way, it's a choice that we must make.

Personal care includes activities that are human biological necessities, such as sleeping, eating, or having sex. It makes sense to include such activities as washing up and grooming as personal care, since nearly all of us spend some time doing them. Moreover, we cannot usually pay people to do personal care for us—to benefit from them, we must be physically present. You can pay someone to comb your hair or apply makeup to your face; you can pay somebody to have sex *with* you. But your own time must be spent being groomed, and you cannot pay somebody to have sex *for* you. The old Russian line referring to a place where "even the tsar goes on foot" demonstrates this. Although some tsars may have had servants carrying them there, they still had to spend their time getting there.

The fourth and most diverse category of activities is leisure, which essentially includes anything that we typically do not *have* to do, that we enjoy, and that we cannot outsource—that is, something for which we must be present and perform ourselves. This catch-all category includes

TV watching, playing sports and exercising, reading, listening to a concert, attending a sporting event, and many others. That one cannot outsource them seems clear in many cases: cartoonist David Sipress showed the impossibility of contracting out leisure activities, depicting a grumpy man on a couch reading a book, with another man pointing to him and saying, "That's the guy I hired to read Proust for me."[3]

But there are many other leisure or personal activities that we can contract out. Even though it seems a bit weird, for a small financial contribution I can pay someone to say *kaddish* (the Jewish prayer reaffirming belief in God after a relative's death) in Jerusalem on my mother's behalf rather than doing it myself at a religious service. Roman Catholic priests in poorer countries will offer Masses in memory of the departed relative of some Western parishioner. As with any mechanism for accounting, it is not always clear how to categorize some activities.

PRODUCING AT HOME

There are many things that we could find someone else to do for us. A personal shopper, a laundry service, and a personal accountant could remove some of the burdens of spending time on home production. There are nannies to relieve us of time spent in childcare, cooks to relieve us of time spent in food preparation, and maids to clean for us. One can even imagine being sufficiently wealthy that a butler and her minions could relieve us of all tasks so that we would have to spend none of our own time on any of these activities. How much time would that save us? Would it free us up to do more fun things?

Consider the basic activities of food preparation and cleanup, purchasing/shopping, managing the household, and caring for kids. Not surprisingly, their incidence and intensity vary tremendously, as Figure 2.1 makes clear. On a typical day a bare majority of Americans spend any time at all preparing food and cleaning up.[4] And since most of us eat at least one meal a day, this means that a lot of us are relying on other people to prepare that meal. Either a spouse, a roommate, or a restaurant's staff is using their time to save us the time of cooking and cleaning up afterward. Even those who do prepare food or clean up themselves do so for only one hour per day. This is a remarkable contrast to the situation of women in human prehistory or even through the early twentieth century, when preparing meals took up a large fraction of women's time.

Shopping is also not something that most people do on a randomly chosen day: only 44 percent of Americans report shopping on any given

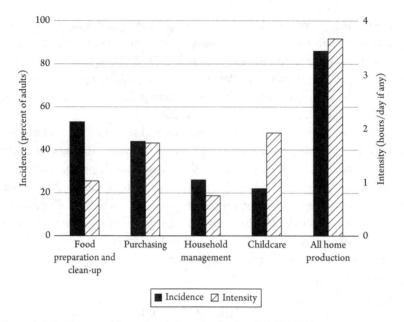

Figure 2.1 Incidence and Intensity of Home Production, US, 2003–2015

day, and if they do, they spend fewer than two hours at it. The low incidence is even more pronounced for managing household activities (such as figuring income taxes, paying bills, and looking over bank accounts). Three-fourths of Americans do none of these activities on a typical day, but if they do, they spend nearly an hour on them.

Nearly 80 percent of Americans spend no time taking care of kids on a typical day—for the simple reason that the majority of Americans do not have kids at home. But if they do report time caring for their kids, engaging in such things as reading to them, taking them to lessons, changing diapers, and so on, they still spend a bit less than two hours doing all these things on that day. Even people who have children under age three at home still average only two hours and forty minutes spent in childcare. And, not surprisingly, that amount declines steadily as the children get older: only one-fourth of parents with teenage children report any time caring for them, and those who do say it takes them less than an hour.

Taking the myriad of household activities together, an overwhelming majority of Americans (nearly seven-eighths) spend at least some time in one or more home production activities on a typical day. And those who do devote 3 hours 40 minutes to household production. This means that the average American is spending a bit less than four hours each day engaged in activities that could be contracted out. Even if we were able to find contractors, could afford to pay them, and wanted to pay them, we would save fewer than four hours to switch to activities that we might enjoy more.

If we are wealthy enough to afford to outsource activities—to substitute someone else's labor for our own, paying others to do things that count as home production—most of us would still not avoid all home production activities. Hiring someone to do one of these tasks takes time—these are what economists call the "fixed costs" of outsourcing the activity. Before paying a tax preparer the seventy-five dollars per hour that her services would cost me, I would have to search for someone whom I could trust to do a good job, and I'd have to spend time getting my paperwork together. To find a nanny, I would have to contact a service that would set up several time-consuming interviews with candidates for the job. Incurring these fixed costs might make sense for a major purchase of a service that I could repeat over and over, such as nanny care, but it wouldn't make any sense if I were going to use this service to substitute for my time just once.

A second reason for doing the activities ourselves is that some of them give us tremendous pleasure and are among the most enjoyable things that we do. Many people would rather cook at home than be cooked for. Some people enjoy shopping for its own sake, for the pleasure of searching over goods and checking out what is available. My older son clearly enjoys time spent walking his dog. Perverse as it might sound, I enjoy doing my own taxes, and in over fifty years of filing what are often complex federal tax returns I have never paid an accountant.

Perhaps most important, there are some household activities that we could outsource but don't because we view doing them ourselves as being more productive or more beneficial. We can pay someone to read to our little kids, which might be more enjoyable for us than having to read the same book for the fifteenth time. But we don't hire anybody, because the time spent reading to the child is a bonding experience that benefits the child in a way that would not occur if someone else read the book. With older children, the same applies: we can hire a tutor to help with a twelve-year-old's algebra homework, but working with her ourselves demonstrates that we care about her getting her homework finished and done well; it also reinforces the parent-child bond created when she was a toddler.

Even if we discount these bonding issues, we might also believe that we can do a better job tutoring our child than someone hired to reduce our burden. Consider the remarkable increase in time spent by college-educated Americans with their teenage kids in the last fifteen years as compared to the 1970s and 1980s. College-educated mothers are spending four hours more per week in childcare than they did forty years ago, and college-educated fathers are spending two more hours per week. Parents with only a high school education have not made a similar increase.

Better-educated parents are investing more in their children because they believe that this will enhance their children's chances of acceptance to first-rate universities—and the potentially resulting higher incomes over their adult lives. This is especially important in a country like the United States, where the quality of university education is so diverse. The contrast between American parents and those in Canada is stark: there has been no such increase in time spent with teenage kids among college-educated Canadian parents. This is not because Canadian parents love their children less. Rather, the costs of and returns from higher education are less than those in the United States. The teenage children of college-educated American parents have responded to these changes: they are spending decreasing amounts of time working for pay, watching TV, and socializing, but increasing amounts of time studying.[5]

Our choices about whether to contract out for the services that we might otherwise perform as home production depend upon how valuable we think that our time is and how expensive are the services that we might contract for. If we can use the time to earn a lot more money, we might value our time more highly and it might make sense to forgo a bit of the enjoyment from cooking, walking the dog, or cleaning the house, and instead outsource the activity. This is especially likely to be true if chefs, dog walkers, or maids are available cheaply.[6]

People certainly do consider the value of their own time and the cost of alternatives in deciding whether to outsource these services. One study that looked at France and the United Kingdom showed that men and women whose wages are higher—who can earn more than other people when working for pay—cut back on time spent in housework.[7] They also do less housework when and where maid services are available more cheaply, and they even reduce their time spent cleaning up and cooking where and when household appliances are cheaper. The effects are not huge, but in decisions about contracting out, people respond to the value of their time and the cost of alternatives to doing things themselves.

Time spent in home production is not distributed evenly across the week: Americans do about thirty minutes more of this work on weekend days, not surprisingly, since most of them do less work for pay on Saturdays and Sundays. Most of this difference does not stem from extra time preparing food or cleaning up; that only increases, on average, by two minutes on Saturdays and Sundays. Part of the change across the week is in shopping habits: people tend to concentrate shopping more heavily on weekends, spending on average fifteen minutes more shopping per weekend day than on weekdays. The rest of the difference arises from more time spent caring for kids and, especially, from extra time taking care of residences: gardening, for example, is usually a weekend activity.

A comparison to Germany, Italy, and the United Kingdom in the early 2000s shows that Americans spend slightly less time in home production than adults in these other rich countries, about thirty-five minutes less per day than Germans, and nearly one-half hour less per day than Italians. One reason for this difference might be cultural and institutional: Americans might somehow enjoy going out to restaurants to eat and get more pleasure than Europeans from taking their clothing to laundries and cleaners. These explanations are not likely to be very important. Instead, the amount of services that we wish to contract out depends on their prices, and these services are usually performed by people who do not earn a lot. With incomes being less equal in the US than in these other countries, it is relatively cheaper to outsource them in the US than it is in other rich countries. Compared to what average Americans can earn, the low-wage substitutes for their time are relatively less expensive than they are elsewhere, leading Americans to buy more services—to outsource more.[8]

While the US is different from other rich countries—Americans do outsource more activities—it is not that much different. That's not surprising, since the other countries are also rich Western democracies. And the high incomes in these countries give most of their citizens the option to outsource those activities that they don't enjoy or are just not very good at doing.

The differences are greater if we compare rich countries to those whose citizens are much worse off financially. Figure 2.2 shows the relationship between the average time spent in home production in each of twenty-five countries and real GDP (gross domestic product) per capita—the standard

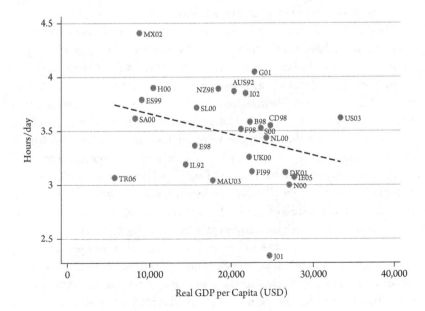

Figure 2.2 Home Production Time, Twenty-five Countries, Early 2000s

of living. Incomes in these economies in the early 2000s ranged from nearly $35,000 in the US to a low of barely $5,000 in Turkey. Each dot in the figure represents one country and indicates its name and the year when its time diaries were collected. As income per capita increases by $10,000, home production time falls by about ten minutes per day on average. Going from the poorest to the richest country along the dashed line (------), which describes the relationship between home production time and living standards generally for these twenty-five countries, produces a decline of around thirty minutes per day. Less time is spent in home production in richer countries.

The reasons are very simple. First, people in richer countries can afford to buy household appliances that can save them time: clothes washers and dryers, dishwashers, microwave ovens, and so on. The second reason is subtler. In richer countries, the markets for providing substitutes for home production are more extensive and better developed. With services like Craigslist and many others available on the Internet, it has become easier for people in rich countries to avoid some of the fixed costs associated with outsourcing some activities that previously might have been included in home production.

We know that in the US between 1985 and the early 2000s, the time spent in food preparation and cleanup dropped by about 20 percent per household partner. But for the longer term we need to think about the forces that have changed the incentives to do home production and bring in the few available statistics. Between 1900 and 1970, the number of domestic workers per household—such as live-in maids, nannies, cooks, laundresses—dropped by nearly two-thirds.

You would think that the tremendous decline in the number of domestic servants would have raised the amount of home production people engage in. But that is not the case at all. The drop was a result of the burgeoning of household appliances that substituted for the time of live-in workers. In 1920 there were no dishwashers, clothes-dryers, or microwave ovens; fewer than half of households had vacuum cleaners or clothes-washers. Even the machines that did exist were far less time-saving than today's models: anyone age seventy or over probably saw as a youth the semi-automatic washing machine with a hand-operated wringer instead of today's automatic spin cycle. By 1990, all the newer machines were pervasive, and most households had all of them. Those that didn't have them had easy access to substitutes, such as laundromats, in the neighborhood.

Any suburbanite age seventy or over probably also mowed lawns as a child using a reel hand mower. Today, most people mow their lawns using devices with electric or two-stroke gasoline engines, saving time and effort. Except in childcare, technology has liberated us from many of the more arduous and probably less enjoyable aspects of home production. The data show that time spent in such specific home production activities as cooking, cleaning up, and doing laundry has dropped a lot over the last century, perhaps as much as two-thirds.[9]

PERSONAL CARE

By far the most important personal-care activity is sleep, and this is why in many of the comparisons of people's use of time it is separated out from other personal-care activities. But even for this universal activity—the single thing that nearly everyone who completes a time diary reports doing each day—there are many dimensions along which the timing of people's sleeping behavior varies. We may sleep more on some days of the week than on others. We may sleep more in some months, perhaps, a little bit like bears, "hibernating" at least in part during the winter months.

Not surprisingly, the big sleep day in Americans' lives is Sunday. On average they sleep over an hour more than on weekdays—they "sleep in" on Sunday mornings. Even on Saturdays people get more z's than on weekdays, over thirty minutes more sleep time. In France, Germany, and the UK, for example, people also sleep much more on Sundays; the same is true in many other countries. Perhaps we should begin calling the second Western weekend day "Sleepday" instead of "Sunday." That would be a good description of its apparent function in our lives.

Neither are all weekdays the same—the average American sleeps nearly fifteen minutes less on Fridays than on the four previous weekdays, a pattern that is mirrored in other Western countries. Average sleep time drops off sharply on Monday, tapers off further over the week, and then rises sharply as the weekend begins. The average American does not sleep eight hours each night, and her average sleep changes drastically over the week.

We are not hibernating mammals, but Americans do tend to sleep more in December and January, the darkest months in the North American year, than in other months. Even ignoring holidays, which are more prevalent in the US in those months than in the average other month, Americans sleep about seven minutes more per night—one hour more per week—in those darkest months. Perhaps the reduced daylight keeps us inside more, and inside is a good place to sleep. Perhaps it and the cold weather in much of the US mean that there are fewer outdoor alternatives to sleeping. The possibility of reinvigorating oneself with extra sleep in winter does not seem likely, so that the additional sleep almost certainly arises because the alternatives to sleeping are less attractive in the winter.

It's really hard to believe that 10 percent of adults sleep fewer than six hours per night, but maybe some of them sleep very little one night, then a lot the next. The American surveys do not permit examining whether people generally average out their sleep over the week, or whether some folks sleep very little on each night, while others log many hours in bed every night. Because Dutch time diaries cover a full week of a person's activities, and because the average amounts of time spent in personal activities in the Netherlands don't differ much from the US, we can find out whether the same person varies sleep patterns across the week. As in the US, a few of the Dutch report not sleeping at all on some nights, but all report some sleep during the week, with even the lightest sleeper averaging 3 1/3 hours per night over the week. Moreover, nearly half the differences in sleep across the population on a given day disappear when we examine average sleep time over the week. Nearly half of the explanations of differences in sleep time on, for example, Mondays are that the people who get little sleep on Mondays make up for it by sleeping a lot on some other days of the week.

No doubt biology is a major determinant of how much people sleep on average. Regardless of their family and economic circumstances, some people need less or more sleep than others. But there are things that we do to ourselves or that we face in life that lead our sleep time to differ from that of other people. Having kids, especially little ones and pre-teens, leads us to sleep less, but only five minutes less on a typical night.

One might think that those who are married or partnered would sleep more than others. After all, a single might desire to have more of a life outside the home—might be dating, socializing, or entertaining himself away from home more often than a married person. The truth is exactly the opposite. People who are married or cohabiting state that they sleep fourteen minutes less per night than singles of the same age. This difference is the same on weekdays and weekends. Over an entire week, singles sleep one and a half hours more than others of the same age.

Kids matter, marital status matters, and age matters. But while these demographic determinants of sleep time are important, and except for age, are results of choices that we have made, we also choose to sleep based on our opportunities—on what else we could do instead of sleeping. Sleep is costly—we might be making money working. Even if we are not earning money, we might be spending what money we have, along with our time, out at a restaurant or bar drinking and eating, on a date, shopping, or anything else that we can do while we are awake that we might enjoy.[10] That we choose to sleep in the face of all these other enjoyable things that we might do instead says either that we enjoy sleep per se, or that it is an investment in our well-being that increases our productivity and enjoyment during the times when we are awake.

Ever since I was a teenager I've been bothered by tossing and turning in bed—by sleeplessness. Gilbert and Sullivan's "Lord Chancellor's Nightmare Song" from *Iolanthe*,

> When you're lying awake with a dismal headache and
> Repose is taboo'd by anxiety,

resounds in my head occasionally at such times, which doesn't help the problem. Fewer than 2 percent of Americans report losing sleep on a typical night—its incidence is very low. This doesn't mean that 98 percent fall asleep instantly, just that for only a small fraction of people is the tossing and turning memorable enough to be recorded in their time diaries the next morning. Its intensity, though, is high among those who do report sleeplessness, on average, over one and a half hours of tossing and turning—which, as anyone who has lain awake knows, seems like an eternity. There is little relationship between age and sleeplessness, but men are more likely to report being sleepless and, if they do, they report a greater intensity than women. But we shouldn't worry too much: for every ninety minutes that people report being sleepless, they report thirty minutes of extra sleep. Time spent tossing and turning is not fully made up, but one-third of it is.

Doing research on the economics of sleep in the late 1980s was not my original intention. I really wanted to study the economics of sex—to examine how people's labor market opportunities, the value of their time, affected the incidence and intensity of their sexual activities. After all, I thought, every economist knows that the value of our time affects how much we wish to work for pay, so why shouldn't it also affect the time we devote to sex—the trade-offs between paid work, sex, and other activities? Regrettably, the small 1975–1976 US time-diary survey had no reliable information that might have allowed me to conduct this research project. Wanting to examine how incentives alter behavior in an unusual area, I switched to studying sleep.

Those data did show that the daily intensity of time spent in "personal/private activities" was about 23 minutes, roughly consistent with the intensity of sexual activities reported in interview surveys. But the reported incidence of sexual activity on any day was only 3 percent, far below what interview surveys report for a typical day among married couples. Either the data disproportionately cover people who have undertaken vows of abstinence or, much more likely, people are willing to report correctly in interviews but are unwilling or unable to report in their time diaries that they spent time engaging in sex.

The most detailed interview study ever done in the US about sexual behavior analyzed the practices of nearly three thousand Americans ages eighteen to fifty-nine in the early 1990s.[11] Among men, 10 percent stated they had no sexual activity in the past year; 18 percent said a few times per year, 35 percent said a few times per month, 29 percent two or three times a week, and 8 percent four or more times a week. Women report slightly less frequent sex. A good estimate is that on a typical day the incidence of sexual activity among these non-senior adults is no greater than 20 percent, perhaps somewhat less. Among those who do engage in sexual activity, the entire event probably averages around thirty minutes. According to this, the best available study, Americans are not monks and nuns, but they are closer to celibacy than one might glean from impressions in popular culture.

We saw that sleep takes up the most time in our days. All other personal activities consume only two hours of the day, and among these others, the only two that account for more than a very few minutes are grooming and eating. The overwhelming majority of us spend some time each day grooming—washing up, combing our hair, showering, using the toilet. All these activities account for about forty minutes of the average American's day. There is almost no variation over the week—we spend about forty minutes doing this whether it is a weekday or a weekend day. Perhaps people groom themselves more on Friday and Saturday evenings in preparation for social events; but they spend the same amount of time on weekdays preparing to look good for their jobs.

Even if we don't work for pay, our economic circumstances affect the time we spend grooming. One of the wealthiest women in Austin, Texas, commented to a friend that she was having permanent eyeliner "tattooed." This woman did not work for pay, but she had several children and, more important, so many things to spend her substantial wealth on each day, things that took time, that it made economic sense to avoid spending time applying mascara each morning. A few men depilate their facial hair to avoid spending time shaving regularly; my beard serves the similar function of removing the need for me to shave daily.

Eating is a funny thing. It is clearly a personal activity—we need to eat to live—but it is also a social activity, perhaps the most important activity when we can interact with partners, children, friends, or co-workers. Despite the opportunities eating provides for socializing, the average American spends only seventy-three minutes per day on eating, when reported as the primary activity that she is engaged in.

Seventy-three minutes per day seems low, and it is. Most of us are spending much more time than that eating. We are engaged in secondary eating and drinking, what we call grazing, foraging, noshing, and other sobriquets. Of all the things that we do, eating is most likely to be occurring but not reported when we account for our time. I eat popcorn while watching *Law and Order SVU*; my wife drinks tea at her desk while doing legal work; a college student drinks a latte while socializing with friends in front of the university library. I am sure that in these cases I would list TV watching as my main activity, my wife would list working, and the student would list socializing. Yet all three of us are also eating or drinking.

The US Bureau of Labor Statistics has occasionally asked people to guess while filling out their daily time diaries how much time they spent drinking or eating on the previous day while doing something else that they considered primary. Nearly all of us acknowledge that we spend some time grazing, and most of us do this more than once a day. Not surprisingly, a majority of our grazing takes place at home, as anyone who notices his or her weight increase on days when working at home should know. And the average time Americans spend grazing is not small; it is almost identical to that spent in eating as the main activity.[12]

We are devoting at least 2 1/4 hours per day to eating and/or drinking once we add in time spent grazing. And the data on time spent grazing are likely to understate the fraction of the day that we are eating. I might not remember that I spent ten minutes today walking to the nearby coffee shop to buy a dark roast and chocolate chip cookie when I complete my time diary tomorrow morning. A shorter interlude is even more likely to be forgotten.

LEISURE—THINGS WE DON'T HAVE TO DO

We may need to work, either for pay or doing things around the house, and we do need to sleep and eat, but we do not need to engage in any leisure activities. One can imagine a hermit (perhaps even a very well-groomed one) who spends all his time working (perhaps hunting/gathering), cleaning his cave, cooking, and sleeping.[13] This would not be a very happy hermit. Leisure activities are the ones we enjoy the most. Along with sex, which is a personal activity, playing, relaxing, taking a walk, watching TV, and exercising are all viewed as more desirable by most people than any activities that we classify as home production, other personal activities, or work for pay.[14] We engage in leisure activities because we enjoy them more than we enjoy most other activities.

We indulge ourselves a lot in our attempts to get pleasure from leisure activities. The average American adult spends nearly 360 minutes—nearly six hours a day—in leisure activities. With leisure activities being among our most enjoyable, an important question is whether we are enjoying more leisure time than our parents and grandparents. The best estimates suggest that time spent in leisure activities did rise in the US between 1965 and the 2010s, perhaps by as much as five hours per week for the average American adult.[15] This increase shouldn't be surprising: if we like leisure time more than anything else, as our ability to earn incomes rises—as our living standards increase—we will substitute toward enjoying more leisure. As time spent in home production has decreased in increasingly wealthy industrialized countries, time spent in leisure activities has risen.

TV watching is by far the largest component of leisure. For the average adult American, TV watching (or the very unlikely occurrence nowadays of listening to the radio) is the main activity for 2 3/4 hours per day. This varies from only 2 1/2 hours on weekdays to 3 hours and 10 minutes on weekends. This may seem like a lot, but monitoring reports by the Nielsen media ratings company would lead you to think people's time diaries understate our TV watching, that 2 3/4 hours is very little.[16] The Nielsen reports suggest that we watch five hours per day on average. The discrepancy arises because the Nielsen ratings cannot demonstrate that anyone is watching the tube—they merely measure whether your TV is on. If, as in my household, the TV news is on as background during dinner, Nielsen would include the half-hour as TV watching, but in our time diaries we would list our main activity as eating. Which measure is correct depends on our purpose: if we are interested in whether people are getting messages about the world, about products or other things, perhaps the Nielsen information may be more appropriate. If we want to find out how people think that they are spending their time, the average from time diaries is more useful.

The availability of television and the events that are on TV affect our lives. The vagaries of television shows offer us incentives that alter when and even how much TV we watch, and thus how much leisure time we choose to have and how it varies across the week, month, and year. In the early 1950s my father used to take one of his vacation weeks in September, so that he could watch the World Series games (which in those days were only played during daytime) and, not often enough, his beloved Brooklyn Dodgers. He did not take vacation time in September before 1950—the year we bought our first television set. Moving from anecdote to data, Americans cut back their worktime in the spring and summer of those quadrennial years when the FIFA World Cup takes place, presumably to watch the matches on television (and increase their leisure time).[17] While there are no studies of this,

Europeans probably also cut back on paid work, and other activities, when World Cup or even less important football matches are being played.

By international standards, Americans watch a lot of television. The average German watches only 1 3/4 hours per day and the average Dutch citizen only 1 1/2 hours per day; even the average Briton watches fifteen fewer minutes per day than Americans. It is interesting to speculate why this might be. It is difficult to argue that the enjoyment that Americans derive from an hour of television and the opportunity cost of their time are very different from those of people in other rich countries. But the breadth of choices about what to watch (hundreds of channels accessible at low prices) and the relatively high quality/originality of US television (perhaps evidenced by the large volume of exports of American TV programs) give Americans a greater incentive to enjoy this form of leisure. Americans may be couch potatoes because the ground for growing this kind of potato is more fertile in the US than elsewhere.

Going beyond television watching, other leisure activities are a tremendously diverse group. Take time spent in religious activities—praying, religious devotions, and similar uses of time. The average American spends less than ten minutes per day in religious activities, and even only twenty minutes on weekends. Perhaps we fail to report very brief religious interludes, such as Jews lighting candles on Friday evening or a family saying grace before dinner. But the incidence of such activities is still quite low. Among the small fraction of people who do report religious activities, those doing so on weekdays report 1 1/4 hours, and on weekends they report spending two hours per day. Although most of us don't engage in religious activities on most days, they take up a substantial chunk of the time of those who do. In terms of religious behavior, American society is quite heterogeneous—a few do a lot, and most do none or very little.

The US is reputed to be a quite religious country, and despite the clearly small amount of time we devote to religion on average, that reputation is not wrong, at least compared to other wealthy countries. Germans spend on average four minutes per day on religious activities, the Dutch five minutes, and the British also five minutes. Many people in Western democracies may see themselves as being religious, but very few devote much time to religion. The incidence of time spent in religious activities on any given day is low in all Western democracies, but it is a shade higher in the US than elsewhere.

Only one in five adult Americans reports engaging in sport or exercise on a given day, but those who do spend 1 3/4 hours in their sporting activity, enough to go for a ten-mile training run or engage in a quick softball game or a tennis match. Volunteering is something Americans do proudly. Yet on a typical day, only 7 percent of Americans engage in volunteer activities—defined to include time provided through social, religious, or other organizations—so that on average nine minutes a day are volunteered. If we add time devoted to caring for people outside our own households, we get up to twenty-two minutes per day, still low. And should we count it as volunteering if I help a sick aged parent with some daily activity? Probably not—that should be considered home production, just as childcare is. Volunteering is important in the US but it is optional—after all, it is volunteering—and it doesn't take up much of Americans' time.

A GRAND ACCOUNTING OF TIME

We use our time in four major categories of activities: personal time, leisure, home production, and paid work. Among people ages twenty to seventy-four, the first two account for the overwhelming majority of the day, over sixteen of the day's twenty-four hours, as Figure 2.3 demonstrates. Home production accounts for another 3 1/3 hours, leaving about four hours per day for paid work. And although the US differs from other rich countries in many ways, its time use is typical in these broad details. Take information

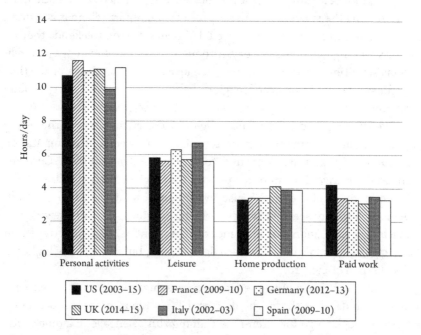

Figure 2.3 Daily Hours in Major Time Use Categories, Six Countries, Ages 20–74

for Italy, which we think of as having a somewhat different culture from the US. Despite the cultural differences, Italians spend nearly the same amount of their day in personal care and leisure as Americans, 16.6 compared to 16.5 hours. Although the categorization of time use differs across the surveys in each country, the time spent in personal care and leisure together shows a narrow variation, only between 16.5 and 17.3 hours per day.

People care deeply about their nonwork time, but they give its determinants relatively little thought compared to the tremendous attention that they pay to the determinants and vagaries of work time. This is not surprising. Economists and others in wealthy economies are focused on the amount that we produce—on GDP; with a given technology, what we produce is generated in great part by how much and how hard we work. But the mix of things that we do outside of work—the choices among personal time, leisure, and home production—is affected by the incentives that we face, both those generated by our family structure, location, and education, and by the incentives that the broader society, including government, provides us.

I have dealt here with around twenty hours of the average person's day, yet I have ignored the most-studied variety of time use: work for pay. That is also the area that, among the four main categories of time use, has attracted the greatest interest of governments—the greatest efforts to influence outcomes that the free market might produce. Given its importance, it's time to get to work.

CHAPTER 3

✧

How Much Do We Work?

Unless they are totally or mostly retired, or have inherited a lot of money, most people rely on paid work to finance most of the purchases they use during their leisure, personal, or home production time. Leisure activities require purchases—football tickets, a television, books to read. Personal activities require buying things—a bed and bedding for sleep, grooming products to apply each day, soap for showering and washing up, and—most important—the dwelling that shelters people while they engage in these activities. Home production activities such as meal preparation and cooking combine time with purchases, such as food and dishes. Whether or not work is enjoyable, people do it because the purchases that it finances make more pleasant, nonwork activities possible.

We work to be able to buy things to use outside work. But discussing the amount we work, how work varies during our lives, how Americans' work compares to that of people in other wealthy countries, and how work time has changed over time requires defining what we mean by "work." Work is what one is paid to do, either as an employee or as a self-employed worker generating income through a business, professional practice, or similar activity. Work can, in a few cases, be unpaid, for example, in the case of teenagers working more than a few hours a week in family businesses that generate income (which in turn provides financial support that the teens can use together with time spent in leisure or personal care).

We need to measure how much time we spend working. As with any use of time, the issue is how many of us are engaged in the activity—its incidence—and how much of it those of us who are engaged do—its intensity. We call the incidence, the percentage of people age sixteen or over who are working or actively seeking work, the labor force participation rate. Because much of the monthly information on work time in the US and other countries is based on asking people what they were doing over a short period of time, we measure the intensity of work as hours worked in one week by those in the labor force who were working during that week.

Here, as in discussions of home production, religion, and other nonwork activities, the distinction between incidence and intensity is important. If all adults worked, but each worked twenty-five hours per week, our lives would be a lot different from what they would be if half of the adult population worked fifty hours each week and the other half didn't work at all. (Spoiler alert: the actuality is somewhere between these two scenarios.)

HOW MANY OF US WORK?

In the late 2010s, a bit less than two-thirds of all Americans age sixteen or older were working or actively looking for work in any particular week of the year. They were participating in the labor force. The labor force participation rate includes some small percentage—in 2017, roughly 3 percent of the US adult population—who are looking for work but not employed. They are the unemployed. This participation rate seems low, but that's because it is a snapshot based on what people were doing during the one week before the survey.[1]

Over an entire year, a higher percentage of the population is working or looking for work for at least some weeks. Take a typical eighteen-year-old—me in 1961. Like many teenagers then and now, I had a job from June through August, but was not working for pay during the school year. I was in the labor force in those three summer months but not during the rest of the year. Other teens might work for pay, and thus be in the labor force, only over the Christmas holidays. Even people in their prime—ages twenty-five to fifty-four—might take seasonal jobs, quit in May for a well-deserved four-month break, and return in September to a different job.

The impression that most of us do work for pay at some point is reinforced by data on labor force participation by age. Between the ages of thirty and fifty, over 80 percent of Americans are working or looking for work in any particular week. But if we examine behavior over an entire calendar year, more than 90 percent of Americans in their thirties and forties are working at some point. We do earn our bread "by the sweat of our brow"—and nearly all of us are sweating at some point in our lives. Even many of the "idle rich" are not currently idle and are doing paid work, and most have not been idle during their entire adult lives.

The US has been keeping excellent statistics on labor force participation since 1948, mainly because these statistics underlie the calculations of the crucial economic indicator: the monthly unemployment rate. The US was the pioneer in obtaining data on labor force participation and unemployment. Labor force participation in the US shows remarkable changes over the past seventy years. The labor force participation rate rose between 1950 and 2000 by nearly eight percentage points, from 59 to 67 percent of all people age sixteen and older. In an adult population of 212 million in 2000, the growth in participation over the previous half century meant that over 16 million more people were working or seeking work in 2000 than would have been expected based on the labor force participation rate in 1950. The immediate cause of this growth was the huge increase in the percentage of women working, offset only slightly by a decline in the percentage of men working. This labor market revolution totally altered the US economy and has been hailed by most people as evidence of the liberation of women and an increase in gender equality.

Since 2000 something totally unexpected has happened—the labor force participation rate has dropped to 63 percent, shedding half of the increase that occurred between 1950 and 2000. This decline was not, or at least not directly, the result of the Great Recession of 2008–2010. The rate of decrease has been no less rapid since 2010 than it was between 2000 and 2010, and there was no sign in 2018 that the decline had been reversed. Of the roughly 250 million Americans ages sixteen or over in 2016, we might have expected nearly 11 million additional people to be working than if the labor force participation rate had not declined. Eleven million American workers can be viewed as missing from the labor force, a remarkable partial turnaround in the revolution that had occurred in the second half of the twentieth century.

The recent reverse-revolution has not been limited to one gender. While men's participation rate continued to drop after 2000, women's participation also began to fall (although not so sharply as men's). The drop has not been isolated by age: teens and young and prime-age adults of both genders have cut back a lot on their working or seeking work. Whether this has occurred because they freely chose not to work so much or because they believed there were no jobs available is not clear. The latter explanation seems less likely given the continuing decline through 2018, long after the Great Recession had ended and a time when the US could reasonably have been viewed as being at full employment.

It is difficult to construct satisfactory explanations that point to changes in government policy as the cause of the turnaround, as these changes have been minimal at most. Remember that the labor force participation rate is a snapshot measuring the percentage of the adult population working or seeking work in one week of a month. One explanation for the decline that seems appealing is that the same percentage of Americans are doing at least some work during the year, but many are choosing not to work in as many months of the year as before. Perhaps today's working-age population is satisfied with the incomes they can earn without working quite so much as their parents' generation.

HOW MUCH WORK PER WEEK?

While the average American adult works roughly 28 hours per week, in 2016 the average American who did any work reported 38.6 hours in the typical week. Over half reported a forty-hour workweek. Even this average varies substantially by age: for someone in the labor force, average work hours rise to about forty hours weekly between ages thirty and sixty, and then drop off. These averages mask tremendous differences across the working population in the intensity of work. Nearly 14 percent of American employees ages thirty to seventy work forty-eight hours or more per week. And nearly 6 percent of workers put in even longer hours, at least fifty-five per week. But a lot of American workers are very part time: 5 percent work twenty or fewer hours per week. The archetypal forty-hour week hides outcomes that arise from people's varying preferences and differences in the opportunities they face.

Weekly hours of work in 2016 were not the same as in earlier years. Just as labor force participation rose between 1950 and the early 2000s, during much of this period so too did average weekly hours worked by US labor force participants, with the increases also starting in the 1970s. In 1979, the average worker put in only 38.2 hours per week. This had risen by over 1 hour per week—to 39.4 hours—by 2000. This increase seems small, but it implies more than 60 additional hours of paid work per year. With weekly hours down to 38.6 in 2016, we can conclude that, just as did labor force participation, weekly hours of workers have fallen about halfway back from their post–World War II peak that occurred around the turn of the twenty-first century.

Going back much further than 1979, the story about hours per week is much different. Between 1900 and 1940, the average American workweek fell sharply, from nearly sixty hours per week in 1900 to just over forty in 1940.[2] A bit of this drop may have been due to federal legislation—the Fair Labor Standards Act (FLSA) of 1938, which defined a standard workweek as forty hours—but most of the decrease occurred before 1938. Some of it may have been due to higher incomes, which enabled people to live decently without working so much, an explanation that might also describe the drop in average weekly hours between 1940 and the early 1970s. It fails to explain the slow rise in hours per week from the 1970s to 2000.

The same partial reversion of average annual hours after the peak around the year 2000 has taken place in the extremes of the workweek. The percentage of workers putting in forty-eight or more hours per week fell to 14 percent by 2016 from nearly 16 percent in 2000, after having risen from only 13 percent in 1979. The percentage of workers putting in twenty or fewer hours rose between 2000 and 2016 from 5 to 6 percent, after having fallen from 7 percent in 1979.[3] The pattern of average hours and even the patterns of long or short workweeks over the past forty years mirror that of labor force participation—first rising, then since 2000 falling partway back to where they were in the late 1970s. Fewer Americans are seeking to work than was true twenty years ago, and those who are working are putting in fewer hours per week than before. People are increasingly satisfied with the incomes they can earn and are willing to trade off some extra earnings in favor of a bit more nonwork—more leisure, more personal time, and perhaps even more time in home production.

HOW DOES THE US STACK UP AGAINST OTHER RICH COUNTRIES?

Americans are hardly unique. Comparing labor force participation in the US to that in seven other wealthy countries reveals that American adults in 2015 were about equally likely to be working or seeking work as the average adult in other rich countries. A much higher fraction of adult Australians and Swedes than Americans were working or seeking work, while a much lower fraction of adult French were in the labor force. The stereotype of the hard-driven Japanese—of an unusually high labor force participation rate—is incorrect. The participation rate in Japan is now substantially lower than in the US. This is evident in Figure 3.1, which tracks changes since 1979 (the dotted bars), 2000 (the striped bars), and 2015 (the solid bars). These are all years in which the economies in most of these countries (except France) were doing well—with low unemployment.

Looking at the historical perspective doesn't change the perception that the percentage of Americans who are in the labor force is typical among wealthy countries. Americans have been about average in the percentage of the adult population participating in the labor market. Comparing 1979 and 2015, the only substantial changes in the forty-year period were the

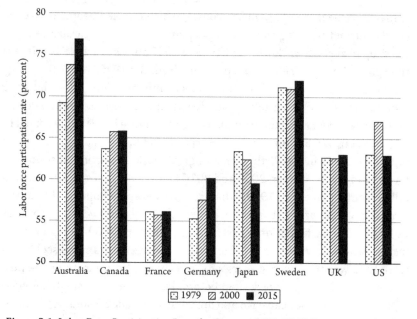

Figure 3.1 Labor Force Participation Rates by Country, 1979–2015. Data extracted on May 19, 2017, from http://stats.oecd.org/viewhtml.aspx?datasetcode=LFS_D&lang=en#

drops in the willingness of Japanese adults to be working and the increases in participation in Australia and Germany. These sharp changes may have resulted from the continuing economic stagnation in Japan and from changes in the currently booming Australian and German economies. But the fact that these changes were underway between 1979 and 2000 suggests they were produced by longer-term choices that people made in response to longer-term changes in the incentives to work, including the changing availability of household appliances, rising hourly wages, and changing household incomes.

The US is about average in labor force participation among rich countries, and the same was true forty years ago. That is not the case with the intensity of Americans' work time. In 2015, American workers were the champions of work effort, putting in more hours per year than workers in any of the other seven rich countries, as Figure 3.2 demonstrates. Holidays, vacations, and absence from work reduce annual work time well below fifty-two times usual weekly hours. As such, American workers are putting in over 34 hours on average in each of the fifty-two weeks, with an accumulated annual total of nearly 1,800 hours per year. In 2015 this was over 1 1/2 hours per week more than workers in any of the other countries shown in Figure 3.2, a remarkable eight hours more of additional weekly

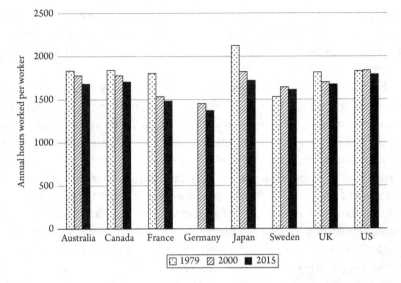

Figure 3.2 Annual Hours Actually Worked per Worker by Country, 1979–2015. Data extracted on May 18, 2017, from http://stats.oecd.org/viewhtml.aspx?datasetcode=LFS_D&lang=end#, and OECD, *Employment Outlook*, 2017

work time than German workers put in, and six hours more than French workers. Those Americans who are working put in exceptionally long hours per year compared to workers in other rich countries.

Americans have not always held their dubious championship in the hard-work league. In 1979 they were about average among rich countries in the amount of time that workers spent on the job. Between 1979 and 2000, other rich countries sharply reduced annual hours per worker. The US did not. The reputedly hard-working Japanese did work much longer in 1979 than Americans, a difference that had entirely disappeared by 2000. Between 2000 and 2015, most of the other countries continued to cut hours of work. The US did too, but the cuts were smaller than elsewhere, except in the UK.

WHAT'S SPECIAL ABOUT AMERICANS' WORK TIME?

The usual workweek in the US—less than forty hours per week—does not seem onerous. In Western Europe, the length of workweeks when people are working is also around forty hours. Yet somehow actual hours worked per year in the US exceed those in Western Europe, often by a lot. The explanation is quite simple: American workers have much shorter vacations and many fewer public holidays than other workers. Over the last forty years, people in other wealthy countries have made the political choice to accept slightly lower annual incomes in exchange for less time working. Americans have not.

First consider paid vacations. Although there is no legal mandate for paid vacations in the US, about 75 percent of US workers do receive some vacation time, ranging from two weeks per year for junior workers up to four weeks a year for more senior ones. Every other wealthy country mandates paid vacations, but the US does not.[4] In France, the mandate is twenty-five days per year (five workweeks); in Germany, twenty-four days, although in many Länder (states), additional paid vacation days are required. Even the UK mandates twenty-one days of annual leave. Switzerland, a country with living standards perhaps even higher than those in the US, mandates four weeks of annual leave; Norway, with higher living standards than the US, mandates five weeks of paid annual leave.

The champions of paid leave are in the Antipodes. Australia, for example, mandates only twenty days of paid leave, but in the three most populous Australian states, "long-service leave" requires employers to offer workers an additional two months of paid vacation after each ten years of service. Other Australian states offer even more. Combined with annual leave, this policy essentially enables most Australian workers to enjoy the equivalent of an academic sabbatical semester, perhaps not quite so frequently as the one-in-seven years that is customary in academe, but not much less.

Even the 75 percent of American workers who do receive paid vacations obtain less than the average of all workers in other wealthy nations. Taken together, the data suggest that a major reason for the difference in annual worktime between the US and other rich countries is the extreme chintziness of paid vacation time in the US.

The American shortfall in paid time off for holidays is less pronounced than that in paid vacations, but it is not insubstantial. The average American worker enjoys between eight and ten paid public holidays. Think of the list: New Year's Day, MLK Day, Presidents' Day, Memorial Day, Independence Day, Labor Day, Thanksgiving, and Christmas. Even with adding in the day after Thanksgiving and a day before or after Christmas, there are only ten days, and most Americans are not paid or don't even receive time off on several of these. But the typical French worker receives eleven paid holidays, and German workers receive nine to fourteen paid holidays, depending upon where they live. In addition to their generous mandated annual vacations, Swiss workers receive between seven and fifteen paid public holidays, depending on the canton where they work. Despite their generous mandated annual vacations, and the existence of long-service leave, Australians still enjoy more paid holidays than most Americans—between ten and thirteen holidays per worker.

The difference in annual work hours between the US and the rest of the rich world does not stem from differences in labor force participation, nor from differences in hours worked during a typical working week. It arises instead from a sociopolitical decision, the result of the complex political dynamic in the US, that Americans will take many fewer days and weeks off from their jobs than workers in other rich countries.

An increase in vacation and holiday time does not necessarily mean that there will be an equivalent reduction in total hours worked. But in practice this tends to occur. A comparison across European countries, where mandated days of paid vacation increased at various times from the 1960s through the 1980s, showed that each additional week of paid leave reduced annual hours by nearly thirty—a reduction of nearly three-quarters of a week of work time for each extra week of vacation.[5] A Canadian study using similar methods found an impact almost identical to that in the cross-country comparison. A study of American workers demonstrated even stronger negative effects of additional paid vacations on annual work hours—almost exactly one-for-one.[6] The best conclusion from existing research is that there may not quite be a one-for-one drop in work time when paid vacations are lengthened, but there is clearly a substantial reduction in annual work hours when people receive longer paid vacations.

A good conclusion from the sparse research on the impact of additional paid holidays on annual work time is that the effects on total work time are like those of paid vacations.[7] In most countries, both are, after all, government mandates requiring that people take time off from work. There is one difference, though: when you take a week of vacation in the US, your spouse may be at work, or your children may be at school. Americans do not have the French tradition of *les vacances*, a cultural equilibrium in which much market economic activity ceases during the month of August, allowing families to spend time together. Since public holidays, unlike paid vacations, mandate time off for everyone on the same day, they facilitate the coordination of people's leisure activities—they facilitate togetherness.

WHY DO AMERICANS WORK SO MUCH?

There are various explanations for Americans' "extra" time at work. Perhaps there is a special American work ethic that values time spent at work more than in other countries. Maybe, but Americans' work orientation was the same as that in Western Europe in the 1970s, as the comparisons in Figure

3.2 suggest, and it is hard to believe that the cultures changed so much and diverged so considerably over so short a period of time that it has caused Americans now to be working so much more than Europeans.

Another possibility might be that changes in American labor market institutions, particularly the protection offered by trade unions, which have nearly disappeared from the private sector in the US, have resulted in the relative absence of paid vacations and holidays. Unionized workers in the US do receive more paid vacation time than otherwise similar workers, but evidence from Germany suggests that trade unions increase only very slightly the amount of vacation and holiday time that workers receive.[8] The near absence of private-sector unions is not a good explanation for the very sparse paid vacation time offered in the US.

Another explanation is that American taxes on work—payroll and labor income taxes—are low compared to those in most rich countries, giving workers incentives to seek more work and providing employers incentives to offer it to them.[9] This argument is difficult to credit, since Americans' tax rates have been lower than those in Europe for over fifty years, yet until the late twentieth century, Americans' work time differed little from Europeans'. Japanese tax rates are also low, yet the Japanese too work increasingly less than Americans. Even taking some high estimates of the impact of taxes on labor force participation or weekly work hours, the US-European difference in tax rates cannot explain the differences in work time.

Another possibility is an argument made in the early 1990s that Americans work harder because the barrage of advertising that assaults us daily leads us to desire more goods—leads to consumerism—that must be financed by the additional work that we do.[10] The premise of the argument was correct—we are constantly deluged by advertisements, including now when we surf the Web, but so too are people in other rich countries. Unless one believes that Americans are more easily manipulated by advertisers than Europeans or others, why should they be more desirous of "things" than people elsewhere? Also, advertising has been big in the US at least since the end of World War II. Yet it is only since the late 1970s that Americans' work time has departed from that in Western Europe. The timing of the departure of the American from the European trend in annual working hours is inconsistent with the timing of any changes in advertising/consumerism that might have occurred.

Why should we care if people choose to work a lot? As a Chicago-style economist, I believe in freedom of choice, in letting people do what they want. If people want to work a lot, that should be their own free choice. But that belief must be tempered by the view that in many cases what we do affects others in ways that may be detrimental to them, generating costs that we don't account for when we decide to do something. These costs may involve long work hours that my behavior imposes on my fellow workers or employees, and in the short term they might include fewer job opportunities for others who seek to work.

Take working long hours. The issue is not that I work a lot—that's my own choice. Rather, it is that I may be addicted to work—I may be a workaholic, someone who cannot let go and who suffers withdrawal symptoms when not working. Workaholics rationalize their behavior by viewing work as something morally desirable. They cannot give it up even when they would rather do so. The evidence suggests that, like other addictions, workaholism stems from a combination of inherent preferences plus early exposure and reinforcement from the activity. We are not born workaholics; our predilections and experiences turn us into workaholics.

So what if I am a workaholic—isn't that my own business? No, no more than my being a drug addict, a three-pack-a-day cigarette smoker, or an alcoholic is my own business.[11] If I am a workaholic, and a high-paid, highly placed, powerful one, my workaholism will spill over onto the work time of my subordinates. Executives will work long hours and insist that their assistants do the same if they wish to keep their jobs. The assistants will put in those long hours and will remain in their jobs, since they are paid more than they would receive starting off anew elsewhere. But because they would value the leisure that they would enjoy with reduced work time more than they value the gains from their extra earnings, they are worse off than if they hadn't started on their jobs and their workaholic bosses hadn't imposed the long work hours on them.

Workaholics have similar impacts on their families. I may work long hours in my later years because I have become a workaholic, working longer and enjoying less leisure with my wife than she would want. Our family income is higher as a result, but my wife would happily give up some of the extra dollars to be able to spend more time enjoying leisure with me. She is better off than if she divorced me but not as well off as she would be if I worked less, earned less, and spent more time with her. The workaholic's behavior, like the behavior produced by any other addiction, has negative effects on people who spend time around the addict.

The impact of workaholic behavior on co-workers and family may be accentuated if people compete to demonstrate to the boss that they are hard workers, worthy of promotion and higher pay. Especially if the boss finds it difficult to discern which subordinate is more productive, all of them will work a bit more than they would if the boss could tell who is producing exactly how much—which worker is most deserving of promotion. Workaholism is an addiction that affects other people. It generates what economists call "externalities," negative impacts on others that we produce by our freely chosen activities.

SIMILAR, BUT DIFFERENT

The discussion of why Americans' work habits are now different from those in other rich countries has either been negative—describing what demonstrably does not explain Americans' long annual work hours—or theoretical or institutional—offering some descriptions of behavior that make sense but are difficult to prove. But these explanations are consistent with people's behavior. They explain why the US did not differ from other countries in the 1970s but does now, and they provide strong hints at how public policy might be changed to improve Americans' work lives.

CHAPTER 4

⌒∿⌒

When Do We Work?

How much we work matters—it obviously alters the amount of time that remains for home production, personal activities, and leisure. And we know that Americans now have less time to allocate to those activities than people in other rich countries. But when we work also matters. Let's say we work two thousand hours per year, assuming the common American two-week vacation and a forty-hour workweek. Is it better to work forty hours per week in each of the fifty nonvacation weeks or fifty hours per week in each of forty weeks, leaving an additional ten weeks for paid vacation on top of the two weeks? I would guess that most American workers, and workers in other wealthy countries too, would prefer the forty-week schedule. We are not indifferent to how we spread our work time across weeks of the year.

We're also not indifferent to the months when we work. Most people in the northern hemisphere would prefer to take their vacation in mid-July, and my Australian friends' behavior suggests that they prefer the opposite, taking their paid vacations in the Australian summer of January and February. We're also not indifferent to the days of the week when we work. Even putting in five eight-hour days each week, most of us would prefer that they be Monday through Friday in Western countries rather than Sunday through Thursday, as in Israel. We also care about how many days of the week we can avoid working, even with the same forty-hour week. It is not obvious what most people's preferred schedules would be, but there is substantial anecdotal evidence supporting the belief that more people would like a ten-hour day, four-day workweek instead of the current American schedule.[1]

Within the framework of eight daily hours of work we also care about the times of day when we are working. For most of us, 9:00 a.m. to 5:00 p.m. is probably preferable to 4:00 p.m. to midnight, and probably still more desirable than midnight to 8:00 a.m. The crucial point is that most of us have strong preferences, based on our biology, on our family and economic circumstances, and on what other members of society are doing, about the timing of our work—and implicitly about the timing of the home production, personal activities, and leisure that take up most of our day.

One question that I would love to answer, but on which sadly there is no convincing evidence, is, "Does the early bird get the worm?" It is the case that those with morning schedules earn more than other people, and there is some evidence that "early birds" wind up healthier than "night owls," which might make them more productive. But the excess earnings by morning people could just result from employers scheduling more productive work for morning times, not that those who choose morning schedules are more productive or that the same person would be more productive in the morning than at other times.[2] Preferences matter: for example, I prefer working early mornings, as I think that I do my best work—writing and trying to think about economic problems—well before noon. In high school and university, I never studied after 10:00 p.m. and have never done any work late in the evenings or at night. Judging from the behavior of fellow students and academic colleagues, my behavior is quite weird. But it works for me—I am more productive with this schedule, and because of that greater productivity I prefer it.

WORK BY THE MONTH AND THE DAY

There are seasonal variations in the amount of work that the average American performs on an average day, but they are not huge. On average, Americans work less in July and August, months that we typically think of as summer vacation time, and November and December, associated with time off during the Thanksgiving and Christmas holiday seasons. The differences between these and the other eight months are not large, though; they are less than twenty-five minutes on a typical day.

To understand the importance of culture and institutions in determining the timing of work across the year, compare the American experience to that in France. While the French work a lot less than Americans on average, the differences over their annual cycle of work are more pronounced. During the summer months the average French person is working nearly one hour less on a typical day than in the eight months of the year that do not coincide with vacations or end-of-year holidays. With little more than half of French adults working, that means that the average worker is doing two hours less work each summer day than on other days. There is over twice as much month-to-month variation in work time as in the US. The reason for this difference is simple—it stems from the extra holidays and substantially greater paid vacation time in France, time that is typically taken in July and especially in August. By choosing to have little paid vacation time and few public holidays, Americans have implicitly chosen a less variable pattern of work time over the year.

Work can also vary across days of the week. If it were equally distributed across all days, people would be spending 28 percent of their weekly work time on weekends. In fact, Americans do 14 percent of their weekly work on weekends, half of what would occur if work time were spread evenly across the days of the week. But in four other wealthy countries— France, Germany, the Netherlands, and the UK—the percentages of work performed on weekends are even lower, ranging from 12 percent in the UK down to 6 percent in the Netherlands. The US leads in the amount of work done outside of the five-day workweek that we now think of as being the "normal time" for people to be working. Americans' lead in weekend working matches their leadership in the total annual work-time league. Not only do they work more hours per year than people in other wealthy countries; they do more of their greater total amount of work at unusual times like Saturdays and Sundays.

All weekdays are not the same. Americans ease into the workweek, adding on average nearly a half-hour per adult to work time between Monday and Tuesday. Despite its nickname of "hump day," Wednesday involves slightly less work than Tuesday, on average, and the tapering continues into Thursday and Friday. Not surprisingly, the two weekend days are not the same either. Americans perform more work on Saturdays than on Sundays. In other countries, where people put in a smaller fraction of their work time on weekends than Americans, people concentrate most of what little weekend work they do on Saturday. Sunday work in other wealthy countries is quite rare. Americans' greater dispersion of work over the week, and the greater amount performed on weekends, may be cultural, but it could also result from the near absence of legal restrictions on work timing—so-called Blue Laws.

On average, Americans' work time over the week did not change much during the forty years between 1975 and 2015. Identical percentages of total work, a bit over 4 percent, were performed on Sundays in both years. The shares of work done on weekdays also did not differ greatly. The biggest difference is that a much greater fraction of work in 1975 was performed on Saturdays than in 2015. Since 1975, Americans have cut back on work on weekends, at least on Saturdays, even though they still do much more of it than people in other rich nations.

WORK ACROSS THE DAY

Even if we are working on a "normal" workday, when most places of business are open and most workers are on the job, the time of day when we work matters a lot to us. Most of us would prefer to work during daylight hours for a whole variety of reasons. Being alone or with very few others at one's workplace may be scary and, if nothing else, may generate feelings of loneliness and/or boredom. Synchronizing our work time with that of others, especially our partners, allows us to enjoy our leisure with them. Also, working during daylight hours is safer physically than working at night, since the latter can require travel to and from work in the dark, which the evidence suggests increases the chance of becoming a victim of violent crime.[3]

A lot of American workers do begin their labors at 6:00 a.m., and many others are still working at 6:00 p.m., but the percentage at work tapers off quite rapidly after 6:00 p.m., dropping to a low of less than 5 percent of all workers around 3:00 a.m. This is clear from Figure 4.1, which presents the pattern of daily work time in the US in the mid-2000s in more detail.[4] It shows the percentage of workers who are at work at each quarter-hour of the day compared to the peak daily work time—around 11:00 a.m.— which in the figure is set equal to 100.

Figure 4.1 has a little "pucker" around noon that stands out. The pucker—the temporary drop in the percentage of work performed in the US at that time—represents people taking time off from work to eat lunch, at the workplace or elsewhere. This pattern is typical of work time in other countries. But fewer Americans report switching from working to eating in the middle of the day compared to people in other wealthy countries, and those in the US who do switch to eating report less time away from work during those midday hours than their counterparts elsewhere.

Large surveys that asked people whether they were usually working at each hour of the day were collected roughly every five years in the US from 1973 through the early 2000s and provide information that substitutes for the absence of large-scale time diaries for that period. They show that in 1973, 8 percent of male workers and 6 percent of female workers reported being at work at 3:00 a.m. These percentages exceed those shown in Figure 4.1.[5] They also exceed those implied by the most recent comparable

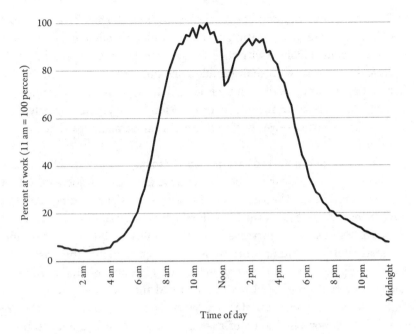

Figure 4.1 Percentage of Workers on the Job at Each Quarter-Hour of a Typical Day, US 2006–2007

non-diary data from a 2004 survey conducted by the federal government. The information in that survey implies that only 6 percent of male workers and 4 percent of female workers were on the job at 3:00 a.m. More recent evidence suggests the same conclusion—night work is quite rare in the US, rarer than it used to be, but still more common than in other rich countries.

We enjoy talking about the idea of the twenty-four-hour economy, a concept that the media love to publicize. Because of the globalization of finance and commerce, we picture many Americans being on the job at unusual hours to mesh their work schedules with those of colleagues around the globe. The twenty-four-hour economy is a myth: most Americans are not at work in the evening, at night, or early in the morning (say, between the hours of 7:00 p.m. and 6:00 a.m.). During those eleven hours—nearly half the day— we perform only a small percentage of our total work: just 15 percent.

The American economy is much more closely integrated with other economies than in the past. Today our exports and imports approach 30 percent of our GDP; in 1960, they accounted for little more than 10 percent. Despite this trend toward globalization—despite the greater integration of economies worldwide and the much greater ease of international communications and transportation—Americans are working less at night than they were forty or fifty years ago.

This development may seem surprising, but it shouldn't be. Most people do not like to work at night. Night work typically reduces people's chances of being involved with their fellow workers, makes them less likely to have quality time with their families, and puts them on a schedule that may not synchronize well with their circadian rhythms. As economies get richer—and per-capita income after inflation has increased greatly over the last half century—we "buy" ourselves away from things that we find unpleasant.

That we use our increased earnings ability to buy more desirable working conditions is made clear by the tremendous increases in job safety that have occurred in the US over the last forty years as our earnings abilities have increased: deaths on the job fell by more than half during this time.[6] We have also used our increased earnings ability to buy more desirable work schedules, including working less during the night. This seemingly surprising phenomenon is the natural result of people giving up some of the income that they could have earned had they worked at unpleasant times to obtain more satisfactory work lives, including better work schedules. Workers use some of their increased earnings ability to insist that employers pay them so much more for night than for day work that employers cut back on night work to save labor costs. By buying these more desirable work schedules, we are also able to schedule our nonwork activities, including our leisure, at more desirable times.

That people on average want to avoid work at nights and other unusual times is made clear by the existence of wage differences that compensate for this kind of undesirable work. If people didn't mind working at nights, the pay of nighttime workers who have the same education, age, race, gender, and ethnicity as daytime workers would be the same. It is not: nighttime workers receive higher wages per hour of work than other workers with the same characteristics—perhaps 10 percent extra.[7] That extra pay is needed to induce them to take jobs that require being at work at unpleasant times of the day. The extra pay compensates them for this unpleasantness.

This average effect doesn't mean that all jobs performed at night pay more than does the same work performed during daytime. Businesses are sensitive to supply and demand and will pay more, or less, depending on the availability of workers and on customers' demands at various times of the day. The Pinkberry yogurt outlet in the shopping mall near my home pays higher wages to workers during the afternoon than in late evening. The reason for this unusual daily pattern of pay is that its workers are mostly college students who are otherwise busy in classes during daytime and need an extra incentive to show up for work in the afternoon—a time when there are many mall customers seeking frozen refreshments. But this counter-example is unusual—most jobs do pay more for evening and night work.

Americans are working less at night than they previously were, but many more of them report being at work at some point during the night than do workers in continental European countries. The incidence of night work in the US is higher than elsewhere. Even British workers, whose work patterns are much more like Americans' than those of workers in continental European countries, are less likely to perform any of their work at night than Americans. This is apparent in Figure 4.2, which presents comparisons from time-diary surveys in the US and other countries from the first decade of the twenty-first century. It shows measures of both the incidence and intensity of night work—work between 10:00 p.m. and 6:00 a.m.[8]

While many more Americans than Europeans are likely to be doing at least some work at night, those who do so are rarely working all the time between 10:00 p.m. and 6:00 a.m. As the striped bars in Figure 4.2 show, the average American who does any work during nighttime hours is only working for about two hours, little different from night workers in European countries. The intensity of Americans' night work is about the same as in other rich countries. Almost the entire difference in work timing across the day between the US and other countries results from differences in the incidence of night work. The reasons for the similarity in intensity but sharp difference in incidence have not yet been studied, so any explanation is pure speculation.

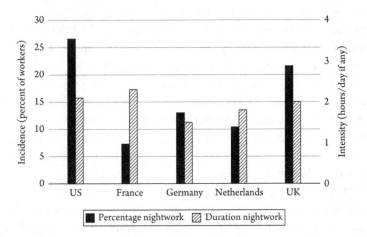

Figure 4.2 Incidence of Paid Work between 10 p.m. and 6 a.m., and Intensity of Those Working, Five Countries, Early 2000s

Most workers know before their workday begins what time of day they will be working. Most manufacturing workers report to the plant where they work at specific times of the day, workday in and workday out. Some retail workers do the same, as do many professionals. But not all do. Academics involved at least partly in research are free to schedule their working time at their convenience, except for the fixed times of lectures/classes and office hours to consult with students. They are flexible workers, working on schedules that they presumably enjoy, since that flexibility is something they have chosen. Their work timing varies across the days, but it is only loosely determined by their employers' demands for their services.

Some workers' timing during the day does vary from day to day or weekly and is set by their employers, depending in most cases on employers' predictions of demand for the products or services that they sell. Information from 2004 on Americans' weekly work schedules shows that 8 percent of male employees and 7 percent of female employees worked on varying schedules. The percentages differ very little if we exclude managers and professionals, such as academics. The percentage of Americans whose schedules vary over the workweek is quite low. Moreover, this percentage was decreasing over the three decades before the early 2000s.

The average extent of day-to-day variability in work scheduling masks some important differences. We think of the work schedules of retail workers as being required to be more flexible than those of other workers, due to day-to-day and within-day variations in customer flows. That is exactly what we observe: in 2004, 9 percent of male and 11 percent of female retail workers had variable schedules across the week.

In Germany, workers who report unusual varying hours across the days of the week represent a small percentage of all workers. As with work at night, German workers who must endure varying schedules receive a pay premium compared to the pay received by workers with the same skills but who work on fixed schedules.[9] Although there is no evidence on this for the US, one would expect that the American who is willing to work at variable times of the week will receive higher pay than an identical worker who does not wish to be burdened with a variable work schedule.

The so-called gig economy is a growing example of flexible work timing. But the gig economy is just a new form of flexible work timing for people who, although employed, work on schedules where they can choose their work hours, within limits: occupations like stadium vendors, taxi drivers, and others. Uber, Lyft, and their fellows are just recent examples. Whether workers find the flexibility of work timing desirable undoubtedly varies from person to person. And the evidence shows that those participating in these work formats do more work when they can make more money per hour. For many of them the flexibility enhances their total work experience—time spent plus money earned—suggesting that it is desirable to the majority of those who choose to do it.[10]

One of the most-discussed worldwide phenomena is climate change and the likelihood of global warming. A change this major will affect when people work—and when they engage in other activities. Across different areas of the US, people typically work less when it is hotter and spend more of their leisure indoors.[11] That suggests that global warming will be accompanied by a reduction in total work and a reduction in work time in the middle of the day (and shifts in the location and timing of leisure in response to the changing location and timing of paid work).

THE US LABOR MARKET IS WEIRD

Work timing in America is strange. It differs substantially from that in other rich countries, just as does the amount that Americans work. The unusual propensity to work evenings, nights, and weekends is not due to the industrial structure of the US economy nor to the demographics of its workforce.[12] Instead, like the very short paid vacations that Americans receive, it probably reflects the conjunction of political decisions not to undertake policies that might reduce the substantial spread of work time over the day and across the week, and the general state of workaholism in the US compared to other nations.

CHAPTER 5

ᴄᴠᴐ

Women and Men

Gender is a defining characteristic of human existence. I have shown lots of interesting differences between the US and other countries in how time is used and have illustrated how the US stands out from other countries in the important dimension of work for pay. But every fact shown, and every argument, has either been for the entire country or for the average person in a very wide age group.

Ignoring gender is useful for summarizing broad differences across countries and for demonstrating how the *average* person uses time, but it neglects what might be differences between men and women that can reflect but also alter our views of their roles in society and in the economy. These differences stem partly from discrimination that limits women's opportunities, but they may also be generated by differences in preferences. Given the importance of possibly different outcomes and behavior by gender, it is useful to focus on how and why men's and women's time spent in major activities—work for pay; home production; personal care, including sleeping; and leisure, including TV watching—differ, and how these differences in the US compare to those in other wealthy countries. With people's different sexual preferences, it is also useful to examine how time use differs between heterosexuals and gays/lesbians.

The stereotype is of women at home cooking, cleaning, and taking care of kids, with men being the "breadwinners." This stereotype was never perfectly accurate. How inaccurate it is and its importance in determining gender differences in time use are informative about gender roles today. Earning money provides spouses with power within a marriage, leading the higher-earning spouse to assert more control over what the partners do with their time and their income. The role of earnings in determining each partner's power is made clear from direct evidence on spending on items that might be viewed as "gendered," such as pocket money, or women's and men's clothing, and on more indirect statistical evidence on couples' behavior.[1]

Gender differences in time use matter because they are central in helping to determine how men and women view and treat each other. But whether the difference is the result of fundamental biological differences or instead is traditional, rooted in culture, and thus perhaps amenable to change as technology and incentives change, is important for predicting how men's and women's roles will develop over the next century.

The term "chore wars" connotes that people perceive "chores"— presumably activities that comprise much of home production—as unpleasant.[2] With "chores" historically performed mostly by women, this view of them as undesirable activities implicitly defines women's activities as somehow less desirable than men's. Knowing who performs chores today is therefore important for understanding the current outcome of the "wars."

The fundamental and totally obvious fact underlying any comparison of how women and men use time is that every woman, and every man, has only twenty-four hours in a day. The person who spends more time working for pay has less time available to engage in home production, to spend on personal time (sleeping, as the major example), or to enjoy leisure (TV watching, for example). More time spent in one area must produce an equal and opposite deficit of time in at least some of the other areas. The opportunity cost of working for pay for one more hour is the one hour of home production, personal time, or leisure that the man or woman must give up.

MEN AT WORK—AND WOMEN TOO

Both time diaries and recalled estimates of usual work time show that male workers spend more time per week working than do female workers. A neat perspective on this is provided by the fact that only 14 percent of male workers are part-timers, usually working fewer than thirty-five hours per week, while 29 percent of male workers usually put in long work hours— fifty or more. The percentages are almost completely reversed among female workers: 30 percent are part-timers, while "only" 13 percent work long hours for pay.

No matter how we measure paid work time, its intensity per week is greater among male than female workers in the US. In time-diary data, the difference is about seven hours. The incidence of work for pay is also greater

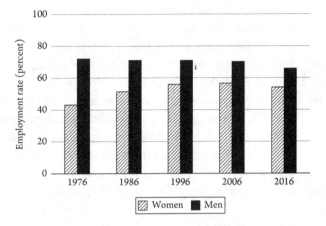

Figure 5.1 Employment Rate (Percent of US Population Age 16+ at Work) by Gender and Year

among men. In Figure 5.1, the striped bar for women in 2016 rises only to about twelve percentage points below the solid bar for men. Compared to the adult female population, more adult males are working for pay. This is a substantial difference, but it is only half of what it was just forty years ago, although the majority of the change occurred by 1996. The American labor market is not yet unisex, but it is much closer to being unisex, in terms of men's and women's labor force participation and work time, than it was less than two generations ago. This development is remarkable—it represents a true revolution in the nature of work in America.

The increasingly unisex labor market in the US does not stand out compared to those in other rich countries. The slightly higher employment rate of men, and their somewhat longer hours of paid work per week, are typical among rich European countries too, and the recent history of these differences is similar to that of the US. Indeed, some Northern European countries have achieved near equality, at least in terms of incidence: in Sweden, men's employment rate is only four percentage points above women's. But the difference in the US is much less typical of middle-income countries. Brazil, Chile, Mexico, and Turkey, for example, show much greater disparities between the incidence of men's and women's paid work.[3] It is also not just a country's income that determines this difference; culture and history matter too. As an illustration, the difference between men and women is greater in Japan than in Europe, even though incomes in Japan and Western Europe are roughly equal.

The reasons for this striking approach to equality in the US and Western Europe are many. One is the nature of the work required in most jobs in a modern economy that contains predominantly tertiary industries—retail, communications, finance, and services. With only tiny primary (agriculture and mining) sectors and increasingly less important secondary (manufacturing and transportation) sectors, physical strength is a less important job requirement than it used to be. While biological differences may make men relatively more suited for work in primary and secondary industries, it is difficult to argue that gender differences give men an advantage as workers in tertiary industries. One could easily argue that it is women who have an advantage as workers in such industries, and in the white-collar positions that abound in them, due to such factors as gender differences in personality, organizational ability, or the ability to avoid conflict.

I was fortunate enough to serve as the sole male with twelve women on a committee concerned with the role of women in the economics profession. I've been on many committees, usually mixed gender but with men in the majority. This was the only one where I was a unique minority. It functioned differently from any other in my experience. There was more listening, less argumentation, less confrontation, less "in-your-face" behavior. While standard psychological inventories of attitudes and personality show stark differences by gender, contrasting this committee's functioning with the others that I had experienced brought the differences home in a way that looking at these inventories could not and suggested a reason for the growing importance of noncognitive skills in modern labor markets.

With most tasks in today's economy requiring little physical strength, and with men biologically as well suited to market work as women, biology does not seem to be a good explanation for the increased gender equality in time spent working for pay. Another explanation for the converging patterns of work by gender is a change in the culture of what are socially acceptable roles for women. Attitudes in rich countries toward what women "should" be doing have obviously changed toward greater acceptance—by both men and women—of women in the workplace. I am reminded of a comment made by a seventy-year-old German professor who was leading a meeting I attended in Berlin shortly after the fall of the Berlin Wall in 1990. Commenting on the potential integration of East Germany into the enlarged Germany, he expressed the hope that East German women, who performed much more paid work than West German women, would soon return to "their appropriate roles at home." Nervous, embarrassed laughter was the common reaction of other attendees, and surely no seventy-year-old academic would dare to make that kind of statement in public today. That professor would not have been very pleased with subsequent developments: female labor force participation in the former East Germany did fall somewhat over the following decade, but it remained far above that in the rest of Germany.[4]

Culture has changed, and it is easy to attribute the increasingly unisex labor market to that change. But perhaps cultural change does not just happen, and instead results from underlying changes in the technology of work that provide incentives that equalize opportunities across genders. Those greater opportunities, and the liberating incentives that they have provided, might be the ultimate cause of what are obvious changes in how we view gender roles in the workplace. We can't disentangle whether the cultural change "chicken" came before or after the technology change "egg," but regardless, both have altered incentives to work for pay and done so in ways that have contributed to growing gender equality in paid work time.

WOMEN AT HOME—AND MEN TOO

Home production consists of time spent caring for household members (for example, reading to kids, driving teenagers to soccer practice, ministering to a sick household member), home activities (buying food, cooking, cleaning the dishes, or doing laundry), and purchasing (grocery shopping, doctor's visits). These are all activities that anyone can do. It is hard to imagine anything inherent in any of them that makes women or men more suited to doing them either biologically or in terms of personality.

Among all American adults less than seventy, the substantial difference between men and women in paid work time is stark, over ten hours per week. The difference in home production time is just as stark, but in the opposite direction. Despite the apparent absence of any other than cultural and historical reasons for gender differences in time spent in home production, as most people know, women perform more of it than men. The difference in weekly time spent in home production between adult women and men is over eleven hours (on a yearly basis, nearly four extra weeks per year). Women perform about 67 percent again as much home production as men.

Men and women in the US are little different from their counterparts in rich northern countries. For example, in a recent year, time-diary data show that Dutch and German women also spent more time in home production than men in those countries, 79 and 85 percent more, respectively. Women doing more home production than men is a universal phenomenon, but the difference by gender varies a lot even across rich countries: in a recent year in Italy, for example, adult women spent over three times as many hours per week in home production as did men![5]

My coauthors and I noticed this huge female-male difference in Italy and included it in our lectures on the subject. Many attendees asked questions like, "I suppose the difference is because Italian women spend a large amount of their time cooking as compared to other women, correct?" This is not the case, despite any American stereotype about Italy. Italian women spend so much more time in home production than women in other rich countries because they spend a huge share of their days cleaning their abodes (although the time diaries don't show exactly what actual cleaning activities they spend so much time on). This big difference between men and women is about the same in the much wealthier northern part of the country as in southern Italy, and it is nearly the same among younger and older Italians.

With available time spent per week fixed at 168 hours, the increased equality in time spent working for pay between men and women makes it nearly certain that the difference in time spent in home production by gender has also narrowed. The time-diary data suggest that since 1975, men's time in home production in the US has increased by a bit less than three hours per week, while women's time in this kind of activity has decreased by nearly six hours. With women doing more work for pay, they are performing fewer of what some might view as the chores of home production. Men, who are working for pay less than they used to, are performing more home production tasks. There is nowhere near complete gender equality in home production activities, no more so than there is equality in time spent in paid work, but America is much closer to equality in this area than it was even two generations ago.

These comparisons are averages—and within the averages there is a huge degree of variation. In Germany, for example, even though partnered men spend much less time in home production on average than women, 25 percent of them are spending more time than their partners. A similar fraction of French male partners spends more time in home production than their female partners. American husbands on average are spending much less time in home production than their wives, but 30 percent of American husbands do more than does the average American wife.

One reason for the gender difference in time spent in home production is that in some couples more than others it pays for the wife to do more home production, and to work less for pay or even not work for pay, than her partner. Women whose partners can earn more per hour do more home production than other partnered women and are less likely to work for pay—incentives to perform more paid work, and less home production, matter.[6] In couples where the wife can earn more than the husband, the incentives that both partners face to work for pay or do home production matter too, but the incentives for a husband to spend more time in home production have a much smaller effect on his time use. Husbands of higher-earning wives do only slightly more work at home than husbands whose wives can earn less than they do. Women respond more to incentives to do home production than men, and with women still earning less than men, the lesser pay that women receive on their jobs gives them a greater incentive than their partners to specialize in work at home.[7]

Another reason for the gender difference in time spent in home production is that women who marry tend to be those who did more home production than other women even when they were single. These women might either enjoy the activities of home production more than other women, or for other purely personal reasons feel the need to do this, whether they are married or not. This reason, based purely on differences in preferences, can explain as much as half the discrepancy between men's and women's time spent doing tasks around the house.[8]

These explanations treat each hour of each spouse's time in home production as having the same opportunity cost—as requiring one to forgo the same amount of pay. That is obviously wrong—most of us are not equally productive at all times of day. For most of us there is little demand for our services on the job at many times of the day, week, or year, and many of us have paid jobs that prevent us from doing any home production during much of the day, especially on weekdays.

The importance of daily variations in the value of our time is illustrated by the way my wife and I divided up cooking chores when we were both working full time. We agreed that she is a much better cook than I am. She also enjoys cooking much more than I do, and she never earned more than two-thirds as much per hour as I did. Yet for about twenty years, I cooked dinners on several weekdays each week, while she remained at her office doing her legal work. The reason is that my job as a university professor gave me near-total time flexibility, while hers required her presence in the office from around 9:00 a.m. to 6:00 p.m. I prepared dinner (with my repertoire limited to grilling fish or chicken, or boiling water for spaghetti), so that the meal was ready for us upon her return from the office. This mutual decision made sense to us, given the limits—or lack of limits, in my case—imposed by our jobs.

EVERYONE WORKING

Only 6 percent of men who completed time diaries in the US surveys reported that they did no work for pay, nor any home production, on the day of the diary; most of these days with no time spent in either activity were on weekends. Only 3 percent of women reported neither paid work nor time in home production on the single day when they completed their time diary. Some people were sick in bed for days at a time, but most engaged in one or both activities on other days of the week. Nearly all of us do some work, be it for pay or as home production.

But what is work? One person's work is another person's fun. My first paid job was as the "basket boy" at the local swimming pool, which most people would rightly view as a menial job. My job was to give (male) swimmers a basket to put their street clothes in, take the filled basket back from them (without the identifying safety pin), put the basket on a numbered position on a shelf, and return it when the swimmer presented the pin. From a perspective of sixty years later, the work sounds boring and unpleasant. It wasn't—I got a chance to socialize with people, and after a week I had memorized the locations of all the baskets, so my mind could wander. I could daydream most of the "work" time. After one summer I was promoted—to janitor. That was also menial paid work, but it got me used to doing cleaning around our house, to developing a skill that has paid off in home production (although, according to my wife, only very slightly). This home cleaning is home production, but it is enjoyable, just as being the basket boy was at age fifteen.

Thinking about home production and work for pay in this way should lead you to ask whether the home production you do is more enjoyable than your market work. This question might include all your paid work and home production tasks, and then the part of each activity that you might not do if you had to cut back one hour. As my work experience indicates, the answer isn't clear. It might be sensible, rather than comparing men's and women's time working for pay, or time engaging in home production, to compare total work time—the total of the time spent working for pay and the time spent in home production—between men and women.

Ask yourself: Who do you think works more in total—men or women? If you pick women, then ask yourself: How much more do women work in total than men? We asked this question in surveys of various groups of people, including economists specializing in issues of work time, experts on macroeconomics, eighteen-year-old students in my introductory economics course, and sociology faculty and graduate students. In every group a majority responded that women work at least 5 percent more than men in total. Among foreign economists specializing in labor issues, over 50 percent said that women work at least 10 percent more, and sociologists had the strongest opinions, with 60 percent stating that in total women work at least 10 percent more than men.

The average person in every one of these groups was wrong (although some were less wrong than others, with American labor experts being closest to the mark). Over the past decade in the US, the average adult American male worked somewhat more than fifty-three hours per week in total, while the average adult American woman worked somewhat more than fifty-four hours in total. There is near equality in the US in the total amount of work performed by men and women. Men specialize more in work for pay, although much less compared to women than they used to; women specialize in home production more, although also relatively less than they used to. "Iso-work"—equal total work time—is a pretty good approximation to the gender division of all work time in the US in the second decade of the twenty-first century.[9]

Iso-work is not just an American phenomenon; it exists in many rich countries. In Germany, women today do a little more total work than men, about one hour per week; in the Netherlands men even do a bit more work in total, perhaps one hour, than women. Figure 5.2 depicts total work by

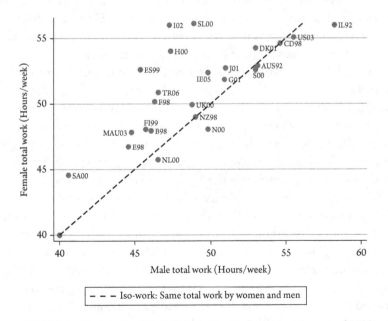

Figure 5.2 Male and Female Total Work Time in Twenty-four Countries around 2000

gender in twenty-four countries, with each comparison based on data from the 1990s or the early 2000s.[10] Each dot represents one country, with its label denoting the country's one- to three-letter abbreviation and the year its time-diary survey was completed. The diagonal dashed line indicates complete equality in total work time. A point on this line shows that men and women in the country are spending the exact same amount of time working for pay or performing home production tasks. This is the "iso-work line."

Most of the points in Figure 5.2 are concentrated very close to the iso-work line, with some of them even being well below the line: Israel (IL92), Norway (N00), and the Netherlands (NL00). But others are well above the line; in those countries, women work more in total each week than do men, with a difference of over four hours per week in a few countries: Italy (I02), Estonia (ES99), Slovenia (SL00), Hungary (H00), Turkey (TR06), South Africa (SA00), and France (F98). While iso-work does characterize the US and many other wealthy countries quite closely, it is by no means universal even in the industrialized world.

The characteristics that lead to iso-work in some countries but a substantial excess of female over male total work in others are implicit in the lists of countries above. First, the richer the country, the closer men's total work time approximates women's. We cannot chart the development of iso-work over long periods of time, but the fact that women's and men's work time is nearly equal in the richer countries in Figure 5.2, but not in the poorer ones, suggests that, whatever the underlying cause, iso-work is a phenomenon that accompanies economic development.

The other factor in common among those countries where iso-work describes behavior and those where it does not is culture. Despite the wealth of predominantly Catholic countries such as Italy, France, and Spain, women in those countries do substantially more total work than men. Taking this general difference together with the difference by level of economic development suggests, perhaps not surprisingly, that both economics and culture determine the gender division of total work.

It is easy to measure economic differences—we have information on GDP per capita in every country, and many years of data on wages for men and women, measures of employment, and other metrics. Measuring "culture" is tougher—we are thrown back on things like religious or racial/ethnic background or answers to questions about attitudes that might be viewed as proxies describing culture. As manifested in people's attitudes toward women's and men's roles, culture helps determine differences in the total amount of work. When people in various countries were asked about the statement, "When jobs are scarce men should have priority," there was a strong positive correlation between their likelihood of agreeing with this statement and the amount by which women's total work exceeds men's in that country.

An important question is what will happen to the gender difference in total work time over the next several decades. Prediction is always a risky business, but the growth of a worldwide (or at least rich-worldwide) culture, in which international differences are partly smoothed out by increased travel, internationalization of available media, and other homogenizing factors, should contribute to increasing gender equality in total work time. Also, as living standards in the less-wealthy countries depicted in Figure 5.2 and in other, even poorer countries increase, we should see a closer approximation of men's and women's total work time worldwide. A reasonable prediction is that the expression of gender roles worldwide will change in a way that leads to greater equality in total work time.[11] But it will be a long time before gender differences in the division of total work into paid work and home production disappear. Long-lasting cultural attitudes will prevent change from occurring very rapidly. Even in the US in the 2010s, women were less happy when their partners were doing less paid work than they are, while men were happier when they were doing more paid work than their female partners.[12]

One might be tempted to infer from the existence of iso-work that, with men and women doing about the same amount of total work, in rich non-Catholic countries we are about at a position of gender equality. One argument against this inference might be that the household tasks that women do more than men are less pleasant—less enjoyable—than the paid work that men do more of than women. Perhaps this is true in some cases but not in many others. On average, people report that paid work, disproportionately a "man's activity," is less enjoyable for them than what are disproportionately "women's activities" such as childcare, doing housework, or shopping.[13]

With paid work being less enjoyable than home production, one might conclude that, with men doing more of it and commensurately less home production than women, it is men whose spending time disadvantages them. That conclusion may be wrong: there are economic and cultural reasons why it is reasonable to conclude that, even though men and women may do the same amount of total work, women's specialization in home production disadvantages them in their households. Most important, because providing income for the household gives a spouse power in making decisions about how the couple spends its money and time, when the man brings in a greater share of the family's income, he has a greater say in determining what the couple does in its leisure time, how much the couple donates to charities, and the kinds of charities it chooses. The reverse is true where the woman brings in a larger share of the couple's income.[14]

To some extent, governments ratify this de facto grant of power to men. A country's production (GDP) measures and values only paid work, treating time spent in home production as having zero monetary value. This is, of course, logically incorrect, as anyone who has spent time babysitting for his children or fixing her toilet instead of working for pay knows. GDP only measures production in markets, not well-being; yet because people confuse the two, we implicitly think of work for pay as being more valuable than (unpaid) home production.

Many economists have argued for adding the value of home production to a nation's GDP accounts, to measure correctly what people are producing, and much thought has gone into doing this. The difficulty is how to do it—how to value the time that we spend in home production. Should it be what the person could earn working for pay? Should it be the cost of hiring someone to do the task? For example, if Bill Gates chooses to fix his clogged toilet, should we value his time at his astronomical hourly wage, or simply as what it would cost to hire a plumber to do the task? Even more difficult, what tasks should be valued?

Creating national income accounts that supplement our calculations of GDP, in order to value time spent in home production, would recognize that time spent in home production has economic worth, even though determining its value per hour is difficult. Without altering our calculations of GDP, doing so—creating supplemental national accounts—would officially recognize the importance of activities in which women have specialized, although to a decreasing extent over time, by putting a monetary value on them. That recognition might to some extent change our views of what women and men do and give women more say-so in decisions about how a couple allocates its time and its income. It might reduce the market-oriented bias that men's predominance in work for pay produces in marital decisions.[15]

That there will be increasing equality in total work worldwide seems like a secure prediction. Implicitly underlying it are predictions about trends in gender differences in work for pay and home production. With an approach to a unisex labor market in rich countries such as the United States, the same forces that will lead to increasing male–female equality in total work will also lead to greater equality in work for pay (and, by definition, to greater equality in time spent in home production). Homogenization across genders in both components of total work time—work for pay and work on home activities—may not occur, but we have been moving toward it. Women are unlikely to achieve total "victory"—total equality—in the chore wars any time soon, but the advances that they have made in the past fifty years and are likely to continue making will, by reducing the degree of gender specialization, also equalize men's and women's roles in determining what the couple decides to do together.

PERSONAL TIME—SLEEPING AND OTHER ACTIVITIES

Because men and women have the same 168 hours per week at their disposal, iso-work in many rich countries means that there is also iso-leisure/personal time: the total of personal time and leisure of men and women is about equal. But near equality in the total time spent in non-work activities does not mean that men and women spend the same amounts of time on the individual activities that constitute personal time and leisure. Time spent sleeping, by far the largest component of personal time, differs by gender: the average American woman between age eighteen and seventy spends about one hour more in a typical week sleeping than does the average American man in that age range. This difference does not arise because men spend more time working for pay.

While women do sleep a bit more on average than men, that is not true for women with young children at home. Having preschool children, and especially infants, reduces the time that women spend sleeping compared to their partners. The presence of a young child reduces men's sleep time only very slightly. A now-deceased distinguished educator and scholar told me that he was pleased when his first child woke up at night to be breastfed, since he could then spend some of the time that his wife was awake working on his first book or sleeping. He was typical (at least in terms of sleep time, clearly not in terms of his unusual work behavior): While everyone sleeps more on weekends than on weekday nights, differences in sleep time between men and women are more pronounced on weekdays, when most work for pay is done. Men vary their sleep time over the week more than women do, using their weekends to "sleep in" more than women. Because time spent in home production varies less over the week than time spent in paid work, women's sleep time varies less over the week.

Sleep time constitutes an overwhelming majority of the personal time of adult Americans—over 80 percent—but there are also gender differences in the remaining 20 percent of time devoted to personal activities. Men spend a bit more time eating than do women—one half hour per week. But the main gender difference in the use of personal time, aside from sleep, is in time spent grooming. While Henry Higgins in *My Fair Lady* was not correct singing, "Straightening up their hair is all they ever do," it is true that American women spend 1 1/2 hours more each week than men on this personal activity—devoting over five hours per week to washing up and showering, dressing, and hair preparation.[16] Together with their additional sleep time, this means that women spend about 2 1/2 hours more per week in personal activities than men.

Even adjusting for age differences, unmarried women spend about one half hour more per week grooming, 5.8 versus 5.3 hours per week, than married women. Unmarried men also spend more time grooming themselves than married men, but compared to women the difference is tiny, just a few minutes more per week. The economic theory of marriage explains this difference perfectly. In looking for a partner, men are more concerned with the potential female partner's looks than with her ability to generate income for the family. Women prioritize earning ability over looks, since they typically earn less than men, although this gender disparity is changing as women's labor market opportunities approach men's more closely. That being the case, it pays unmarried women to spend relatively more time on their looks, compared to women who are already married, since it might help them attract higher-earning spouses. The evidence on the role of grooming in affecting women's perceived looks is weak, but women do spend more money to go with the additional time they spend grooming.[17]

The peculiarities of markets for spouses in rich countries explain the gender difference in grooming time by marital status, but why do married women spend more time grooming than married men? Perhaps it is habit—they spent more time than men grooming before marriage, and this has carried over into married life. Another possibility is that grooming is a more enjoyable activity for women than for men, although there is no evidence on this argument. Yet another possibility is suggested by evidence that being viewed as good-looking, with looks perhaps enhanced by additional time spent taking care of oneself, increases a woman's happiness more than a man's.[18]

LEISURE—TV AND OTHER ACTIVITIES

With adult American women working, both for pay and at home production, about one hour per week more than men, and with women spending 2 1/2 hours more per week on personal activities, women must be enjoying about 3 1/2 hours less leisure per week than men. The entire difference is accounted for by differences in time spent on one activity: television watching. Adult American men spend 19.6 hours per week watching TV; adult American women spend "only" 16.2 hours a week in front of the tube. While most vegetables are not gendered, the American couch potato is male.

Men in other countries also watch television more than women. But in France and Germany the gender difference in viewing time is less than two hours per week. In the UK, where time use approximates the US pattern more closely along many dimensions, men's additional TV watching is about as much as in the US, although both men and women in the UK watch less TV than their American counterparts. TV watching is a "guy thing" in every country where we can measure how people spend time.

Much of the excess time that men sit in front of the tube is spent watching sports. In the UK, about one hour of men's weekly "extra" (compared to women) TV watching is spent watching sports. The importance of watching sports on television in the US is demonstrated by the big increase in the time men spend in front of the tube on weekends, when more major sporting events are broadcast—one more hour watching TV than on weekdays. Among women, TV watching increases by only twenty-five minutes from Friday to the weekend.

Married American men and women watch less TV than their single counterparts, even accounting for differences in the ages of singles and marrieds and in the amounts of time that they spend in work and personal care. A reasonable explanation might be that television functions as a companion to a single person who is home alone. But the difference between men and women in time spent watching TV is about the same, roughly 3 1/2 hours per week, for both marrieds and singles.

With TV watching accounting for almost the entire excess of male leisure time over female leisure, the remaining nearly twenty-two hours of weekly leisure that are available to both American men and women are spent on a variety of different activities, with no sharp differences by gender in how this time is allocated. Adult men spend a half hour less each week than adult women engaged in social activities, including religious and civic activities, but they spend roughly one hour more per week engaged in active sporting or recreation.

SEXUAL ORIENTATION AND TIME

Neither the American time-diary data nor any other country's similar data identify survey respondents by their sexual orientation, since people are not asked to indicate their sexual preferences or past sexual behavior.

This matters a lot, as alternative definitions of sexual orientation tremendously affect the size of the population that might be classified as gay or lesbian. One study in which people were asked to identify their orientation (without any information on how they spent time) showed that between 1 and 3 percent of men and women identified themselves as gay or lesbian in response to a direct question.[19] This rises to nearly 8 percent if all those who state that they are at least somewhat attracted sexually to members of the same sex or would find sex with a same-sex partner at least somewhat appealing are classified as gay/lesbian.

In the US time-diary data we can count as gay or lesbian those people who state that they are married to or partnered with a person of the same sex. This produces a much lower estimate of the percentage of lesbians or gays in the US data, a bit less than 1 percent of all married or partnered American women or men. With the increasingly widespread legality of same-sex marriage over these years, the percentage identified using this criterion rose in the US from 2003 to 2015, but it remains tiny.

Gay men and lesbian women have far different demographic characteristics than their heterosexual counterparts. For example, 36 percent of lesbians identified as married or partnered have masters' or doctorate degrees, while only half as many straight women do; the difference between heterosexual and gay men is smaller, but still substantial. In the US the average lesbian or gay adult is about four years younger than other American adult men and women. These demographic differences all affect time use. For that reason, any comparisons by sexual orientation must account for the effects of differences in age and education.

To compare heterosexuals to gays and lesbians, I measure the additional or lesser time spent in the major categories of time use. Figure 5.3 presents the differences between straight and lesbian women, and between straight and gay men, in time spent on each activity, statistically adjusted for differences in age, education, and many other demographic characteristics. A bar extending above the zero line shows that heterosexuals devote more time to the activity than gays/lesbians; a bar going below it shows that they spend less time in the activity than gays/lesbians. The striped bars show the differences among women, the solid bars those among men.

By far most striking are the differences between heterosexual and lesbian women in the two components of total work: work for pay and home production. It is well known that lesbians spend much more time in the labor market than do heterosexual women. Much less well known is that lesbians make up for their additional time working for pay by doing much less home production. Part of this difference arises from their being less likely to have children in the household. Even adjusting for differences in

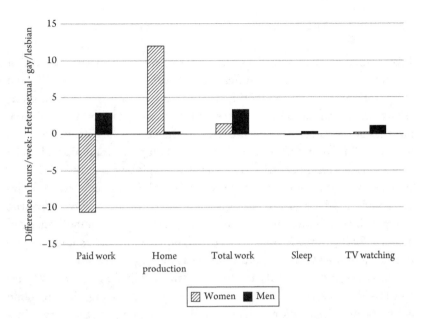

Figure 5.3 Difference in Hours per Week between Married Heterosexuals and Married Lesbians/Gays, US, 2003–2015

the presence of children of various ages, lesbians still spend more time—over eight hours per week—working for pay than do heterosexual women, and they spend nearly six hours less per week in home production. Taking these differences together, we see that heterosexual women perform two fewer hours of total work each week compared to lesbians of the same age, education, number of kids, and other characteristics.

Among men, the differences by sexual orientation in the amount of time spent in paid work and home production are less but still substantial. Heterosexual men spend more time in paid work per week than gay men, and they do not compensate for this difference by spending less time in home production: they perform a bit more of this too. This means that gay men do substantially less total work than heterosexual men, leaving gay men more than three additional hours per week for personal care and leisure.[20]

Neither among gays nor among lesbians does the lesser total work time produce much extra time devoted to the two major nonwork activities: sleeping or TV watching. For both, their time spent in these activities differs little from that spent by heterosexuals. Instead, their additional nonwork time is spread around a variety of different activities, with some of the bigger differences being that lesbian women spend about one hour more per week on exercise and sport than other women, and gay men spend about a half hour more per week on grooming than heterosexual men.[21]

ARE WOMEN AND MEN DIFFERENT?

This is an obviously silly question, but to answer it in the context of spending time, yes, there is a difference between men and women. Men do more work for pay, spend less time in home production, and—most interesting, at least in the US—do very slightly less work in total than women. But these differences have been narrowing in wealthy countries. They will narrow still further. Cultural attitudes based on past economic and social conditions will disappear with the demise of people who reached adulthood sixty years ago, and with the entrance into adulthood of people who are accustomed to today's social and technological conditions and who face the changing incentives for engaging in paid work. Only 14 percent of American men age forty or under agreed with the statement that men should be preferred if jobs are scarce; 25 percent of those over age forty did.[22]

The near gender equality in the total time available for personal care and leisure does not mean that men and women engage in the same nonwork activities. Women sleep more than men, spend more time grooming than men, and spend much less time watching television. Even these differences are likely to decrease over time. With greater equality in the labor market will come greater equality, and fewer differences, in how people behave in the market for dates and spouses. Men now spend more money on toiletries—powders, deodorants, perfumes—than they do on shaving accessories, suggesting increasing gender equality in the time spent grooming that uses these products.[23] With the growth of women's sports, perhaps stimulated in the US by the mandates of Title IX, which requires universities to provide men and women with the same opportunities to engage in athletic activities, there will be increasing gender equality in the time that the adult population spends on exercise and sports.

We will see a continued narrowing of gender differences in most aspects of how we spend time. Partly this will result from increased equality in the labor market, which has already narrowed the difference between men and women in the opportunity cost of their time; partly it will stem from continuing changes in technology in the workplace and at home. Is this a good thing? Probably yes. The benefits that iso-work and more equal division of tasks within iso-work will create in terms of equalizing power within households seem substantial. But it imposes costs, especially on old fogies like me, forcing us to get used to a different world from the one we grew up in.

CHAPTER 6

༄

Togetherness

People partner for a variety of reasons, whether for the broader rationales of legitimizing offspring and ensuring clear lines of inheritance or for narrow economic goals like saving on housing costs. These are well known. But there is another crucial economic reason—the potential saving of time—for forming marital and other household partnerships. These savings can be just as important but are not always thought about as being based in economic behavior. There are benefits to partnering in terms of home production—more satisfaction produced per hour of each partner's time, because the partner who is more efficient in a task can be the one who performs it. This enables people to expand their opportunities by economizing on items purchased and on the time that they spend using those items. The person who enjoys doing the task more, or finds it less painful, can make the other partner better off by specializing in it. Laundry and meal preparation are obvious examples, but so are such less common activities as car repair, which my daughter-in-law did early in her marriage because she was more efficient at it than my son.

PARTNERING—MORE EFFICIENT HOME PRODUCTION, OR SHARED LEISURE?

This titular question is in some ways phony—one can have more efficient home production *and* more shared time. After the kids left home, my wife and I were both working fifty to sixty hours per week, fifty weeks per year, on our jobs. We did the weekly grocery shopping (a home production activity) together, not because that saved any time for us in total. On the contrary, my wife claimed that my shopping with her increased the amount of time that it took her to complete the task, because I dawdled moving down the store's aisles. But shopping together gave us the chance to be with each other for an extended period of time. Cooking together is another home production activity that can be shared and can enhance togetherness. When we have dinner parties I help my wife out in the kitchen, peeling carrots or doing other low-skilled tasks, to the point that she occasionally refers to me as her *sous-chef*.

The economic theory of marriage suggests that each partner benefits from specialization—from their *comparative advantage* in doing various tasks—just as nations benefit from exporting the products that they can produce relatively efficiently and importing those that they are relatively inefficient at producing. Partners get together because one is relatively more efficient in some activities, perhaps time spent in home production, while the other devotes her or his time to paid work. Since earnings from paid work increase with education levels, economists expect that the more educated partner will specialize in paid work and will partner with someone who is less educated but at least as efficient in home production.[1] Given labor-market discrimination against women, and with men historically being more likely to work for pay, these considerations gave rise to negative assortative mating, with highly educated men seen as partnering with less educated women as a way of increasing the total well-being of the couple.

Comparative advantage means that if men and women are equally efficient in performing home production activities but men are paid more per hour for market work, men are likely to do more paid work. Historically, given that women's fecundity peaks quite early and a major function of marriage has been to ensure that reproduction occurs in a system of well-defined rights to inheritance, the theory of partners' matching implies that the male partner will be substantially older than the female. Like the low fraction of home production performed by men, and the low female participation in market work, this theory did a good job historically of explaining the large age differences between spouses in wealthy countries: in 1900 the age difference between American men and their wives was 4.0 years. And that difference is still more or less what exists in low-income countries. Even as recently as 1979, the age difference between American spouses averaged 2.7 years.

But this large age difference no longer prevails in wealthy countries. By 2016, partners in the average American couple differed in age by 2.1 years, an even more rapid narrowing than had occurred between 1900 and

1979. In twenty years the difference will be even less: the age difference in American couples where the man was under age fifty was only 1.1 years in 2016. This decline in husband-wife age differences has been paralleled in other wealthy countries. For example, in France the difference is 2.4 years, but among couples where the man is under fifty the difference is only 1.7 years. By historical standards this convergence of partners' ages is remarkable. It has occurred because women have increasingly entered the workforce and generated their own earnings, so that they are no longer as dependent on older men for financial support.

The result of these changes is that positive assortative mating, with the partners being more alike along the dimension, has increased: age differences between partners have decreased. The same is true for mating along the dimension of education. In 1979, only 40 percent of American men with at least a college degree had wives who also had at least graduated from college. By 2016 the comparable percentage was 70 percent. A similar increase in positive assortative mating has occurred in the level of education as has occurred with age.

Along the dimensions of age and, more important, in terms of the split between the time spent in home production and in paid work, marriage today brings together people who are more similar than was true only forty years ago. Because of increasing gender equality in labor markets, and because of the approach, although a slow one, to gender equality in home production, people now choose partners based less on their relative productivity in home production and paid work, and more on shared backgrounds and presumably shared preferences for different leisure activities. They pick partners with whom they can enjoy time—with whom they can be happy together.

WHAT DOES TOGETHERNESS MEAN, AND HOW MUCH IS THERE?

Togetherness can mean a variety of different things, but at a minimum it should refer to a time when neither partner is working for pay, so that both could at least conceivably be doing something together at the same time. If the partners' work schedules overlap, they have more chance to be together. To describe the possibilities facing the partners, Figure 6.1 divides the day into twenty-four hours—100 percent of daily time, with section A being that part of the day when one or both spouses are at work and are assumed to have no chance to be together. During the rest of the day, depicted by the remaining sections of the "pie" that is Figure 6.1, the

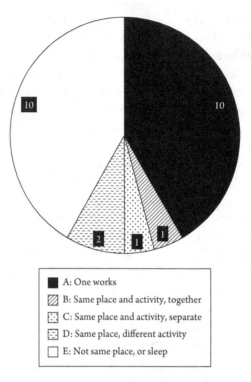

Figure 6.1 Classifying Time Spent Together

partners do have the opportunity to be together, but are they? And what does it mean to be together?

A narrow definition might delineate togetherness as time spent in the same location, doing the same thing, and interacting with each other. That might be represented by section B of Figure 6.1. As examples, the partners might be in the kitchen, cleaning up the dinner dishes together (home production); they might be in bed together, enjoying sex with each other (personal care); or in the living room, reading a play aloud (leisure). A somewhat broader definition would have them together, but each reading a book to themselves, as described by sections B and C together. The partners are engaged in the same activity, but they are not interacting. They are doing what their preschool teachers were concerned about my kids doing: engaging in "parallel play." This doesn't mean that they aren't together, or even probably enjoying each other's presence, but they are not really interacting. Behavior like this is depicted in a cartoon by William Haefeli showing a mother, father, and two kids in a room with a television, a computer, and several e-readers. Each person is watching a different screen, and the mom is saying, "We're all together watching television, but we're not all watching television together."[2]

A still looser definition of togetherness would include all three sections B, C, and D in Figure 6.1. By this broader definition, the partners state that they are together in the same location, but they need not be interacting or even doing the same thing. My wife might be in her home office doing her volunteer legal work, while I am in the living room watching *Game of Thrones*. I might be at the computer in my home office looking at Facebook, while she is cooking dinner in the kitchen. In both cases we are together at the same location, but we are neither interacting nor even engaged in the same activity. This still leaves a substantial part of the day, section E, when neither spouse is doing market work and they are available to interact with each other, but they are not together by any definition. One might be out shopping, the other donating blood at a nearby hospital. One or both might be sleeping.

These distinctions are the finest that the available data allow. But even they are not hard and fast. If my wife and I are cleaning up the dishes after dinner, we are both engaged in the same activity at the same place and time, but are we interacting or not? As the cartoon suggested, it is difficult to gauge the extent of spousal togetherness without directly observing the couple's interactions. Those observations are not available in data that we might use to measure togetherness. Even if direct observations were available, we probably shouldn't believe that they correctly represent the reality that occurs normally. After all, the very fact of being observed would in most cases probably alter the nature and length of the couple's interaction.

As a first step, consider information on the sum of B + C + D + E— the amount of time on a typical workday that spouses could possibly be spending together. Take a married couple, compare them to a randomly chosen man and a randomly chosen woman. The evidence is clear—and totally unsurprising—that the couple's time is planned so that they at least have opportunities to be together more than a randomly paired man and woman. In American couples with both spouses working nearly full time (thirty plus hours weekly), the average couple has the possibility of about fourteen hours each day when neither spouse is working. In terms of Figure 6.1, B + C + D + E comprise about fourteen hours of the typical day in these couples, with section A accounting for ten hours.

The amount of time available to be together depends on the spouses' abilities to schedule their work times. Those spouses with more education— and higher earnings ability—typically have more freedom to set their work hours than do spouses with less education. This means that, for two couples in which the men spend the same time in paid work and the women spend the same time in paid work, the couple in which the spouses earn more per hour will have more potential time together. Since time together is desirable, this finding for the US implies that couples that are better off financially are also more able to enhance their happiness because they have a greater opportunity to schedule more time together. Also, evidence for the US shows that B + C + D + E is larger if the pair's total time spent working for pay is spread more equally between them.

Of this possible fourteen hours of time that the partners could be together, much will be devoted to sleep. While sleeping together involves being in the same place at the same time, and being engaged in the same personal activity, being unconscious/asleep leaves little room for personal interaction. Sleep should be counted as part of section E, the part of the day when the partners are not truly together. So too should time when the spouses are doing home production—shopping or driving kids to music lessons; engaging in other personal care; or enjoying leisure, but not in the same location. He might be watching TV at home while she is jogging by the lake; she might be gardening while he is shopping at a clothing store. The remaining time, sections B + C + D, totaling four hours, is that part of the day when the partners are together in the same location and are awake.

You would think that spouses would view the time spent together the same way—whether they are in the same location seems like a question of fact. They should, but they don't. In several countries where this has been studied, the US, France, and Spain, women report slightly less time together than their partners do on the same day.[3] Not much less, perhaps just twenty minutes per week, but it is a remarkable regularity that presents an interesting mystery.

In the US in the first decade of the 2000s, spouses spent about four hours per day together awake and in the same location, which doesn't seem like much time. But remember, this figure does not include sleeping, and the computation that produced it also excluded time spent together on other personal activities, such as showering or sex. That it is less than such time in several other countries where this has been measured (Spain and France) is the natural result of the longer American work year.

The American time-diary surveys do not collect diaries from both partners in a household. They do not allow removing the time in section D, both partners in the same place but doing different things, from the total of B + C + D to isolate time when the partners might be interacting. To do so we need to rely on data from another wealthy country where diaries of both partners were collected for the same day. French data from 2009 to 2010 satisfy this criterion. While French and American cultures differ, both are wealthy industrialized countries with most workers employed in tertiary industries.

What is clear from the French experience is that there is a tremendous difference between the time that people say they are together and the time they are doing the same (nonsleep) thing together. On an average day, French couples are together for about six hours, which is somewhat more than American couples and would be expected given the shorter work years in France. But of this weekly average of six hours per day, couples spend fewer than two hours together and doing the same thing. Applying this result to the US suggests that barely one-third of the American average of four hours per day that members of American couples are together in the same location is actually spent together and doing the same thing.

Time together, and time together and engaged in the same activity, are both about one-third greater on weekends than on weekdays. This is because in most cases one or both partners spend many fewer hours in paid work on weekends. The greater equalization of work time across the seven days of the week in the US than in France or elsewhere suggests that in America there is more equalization across the week in the amount of time that couples are together doing the same thing.

Comparisons across months of the year demonstrate the same limits that time spent working for pay imposes on partners' time together and possibly interacting. In summer, and in the frequent holiday months of November and December, French partners are more likely to be in each other's presence, and they accordingly spend more time doing the same thing together. This results partly too because children are on school holidays, the timing of which even affects the amount of togetherness and leisure time enjoyed in households where no kids are present. Since it pays childless workers—operators of vacation retreats, for example—to adjust their schedules when couples with kids change the ways that they spend time, partners in those couples also enjoy enhanced togetherness during school holidays.[4]

As partners age, their preferences for spending time together may change, especially due to changing circumstances, including their earnings, the presence of children, and other family responsibilities. Even adjusting for all these factors, though, shared time—sections B + C + D and sections B + C alone—varies in the French data as the couple ages. Both calculations of shared time decrease from the couple's early twenties to their mid-forties, then begin rising again. And by their early fifties, shared time equals what it was among newly partnered couples.

Even if we observe partners spending a greater fraction of possible nonwork, nonsleep time together once they move through middle age, it might be because they are both older; it might arise from their getting more enjoyment doing things together than before; or it might just happen because those couples that stay together are the ones whose partnerships have survived precisely because they do enjoy being together more than most couples. I rarely attended religious services as an adult before I was married, but my wife had gone more often. Over our marriage my religious attendance has increased steadily and now nearly matches hers. Has this change resulted just because I am older, since religious activity generally rises with age? Or is it a result of the "contagion" of my wife's preferences and our desire to be together leading us to undertake this activity jointly? I don't know.

Any parent will tell you that having children at home reduces the time that a couple can spend together. Part of the reason is that while preschool kids are in the house, parents have a greater need to arrange their work schedules to facilitate one of them being home with the kids. American parents in the early twenty-first century who had a child under age five at home spent about 1 1/2 fewer hours per week together than parents of the same age and education, with the same amount of time spent on paid work, but no preschool child at home. On average, an extra child age over five at home reduces time together by an additional forty minutes per week. Kids cost money, and they cost time; they also cut into parents' opportunity to spend more time together. Children, especially preschool children, also reduce the time that parents spend together doing the same thing: in France a young child reduces parents' time spent interacting by over a half-hour per day.

American parents today are spending more time together than American parents in the 1960s, a clear result of having fewer small children at home than their grandparents.[5] But compared to the 1970s, by which time many fewer American families had small children in the household than even a decade earlier, there has not been much change in parents' time together. Nonparents too are spending more time together than in the 1960s, but this hasn't changed much either since the 1970s. With no decrease in the US in the amount of paid work per year, and with no decrease in time spent sleeping, couples have chosen to take the same fraction of the (unchanging) remaining time to do things together, or at least be together. This lack of change might reflect the interaction between the average couple's underlying preferences for being together with the increasing opportunities to do different things, either together or separately, that increased incomes and easier transportation have provided.

Togetherness—sharing—keeps couples together. Among couples that are identical in age, location, education, and time spent working for pay, those that manage their household finances together are less likely to get divorced. The likelihood of divorce is especially low if the couple manages all its finances jointly. It is also lower among partners who spend time eating together with their children. Doing things together indicates a happier and less divorce-prone pair of partners and may itself help reduce the likelihood of divorce.[6]

That a man and woman are domiciled together in the US no longer means that they are married, if it ever did. Most are married, but some are cohabiting. This distinction makes a difference in terms of the partners' togetherness. Taking a man and woman who are identical in education, age, race, income, number of children, and numerous other characteristics, those who have chosen to cohabit rather than marry spend about twenty fewer minutes together per day (compared to the average time together among all couples of about four hours). This doesn't mean that the same couple would spend more time together if they were suddenly to marry. Instead, those who choose to cohabit are different from those who choose to marry, perhaps because their relationship has been of shorter duration, perhaps because the partners desire more independence from each other—because they are less interested in "committing."

This discussion leads to the issue of how much time partners would spend together if they did no paid work and thus had about sixteen hours per day of nonsleep time to be together? In France, even on weekends when very little paid work is performed, partners choose to spend only seven of their roughly sixteen hours of nonsleep time in each other's presence. Evidence for the US suggests the same thing. Partners apparently choose to spend less than half of their nonwork, nonsleep time together, even though they could devote their entire waking time to togetherness.

This is a bit disturbing, since we think love is at least partly about being together. That economists are not known for their sense of humor is revealed in Figure 6.2, a supposedly humorous "Valentine's Day greeting card" for economists to send to their lovers/partners. It states, "The Marginal Returns of Spending Time with You Will Never Diminish." The humor, such as it is, lies in the contrast between the dotted and solid lines: the dotted line represents the "principle of diminishing returns," the idea that extra time devoted to an activity generally yields less and less extra happiness. The straight line is the utility—the happiness—of the card's sender, and it violates the principle by failing to rise more slowly as more time is spent with the partner.

This is a very sweet sentiment, but evidently very far from describing reality. Couples, even those deeply in love, do not always wish to do the same thing at the same time or even be around each other all day. Several women who are facing the impending full retirement of their husbands have told

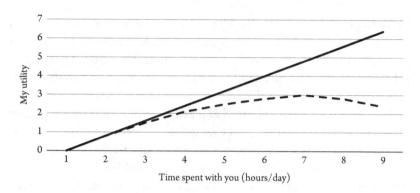

Figure 6.2 The Benefits of Togetherness.
Source: Adapted from http://www.businessinsider.com/14-economics-valentines-2013-2/#love-transcends-the-principle-of-diminishing-returns-1

me that they really don't want the old geezer hanging around the house with them all the time. Partly this sentiment reflects love and altruism— they want the guy to "have a life of his own"—but partly it reflects a desire for independence. In actuality, the extra happiness does rise more slowly with more time together, as shown by the flattening of the dotted line as the time spent together increases. It may even be that, after some time together over a day, "My utility [satisfaction]" might even decline, as shown by the dotted line in Figure 6.2 falling after seven hours together.

WHAT DOES TOGETHERNESS TELL US ABOUT MEASURING WELL-BEING?

The old line, "Two can live as cheaply as one," implies that the well-being of a couple is the same as that of a single person with the same household income. That is obvious nonsense. But a large line of research has compared well-being across households with the same income—to measure "equivalence scales"— indicators of the income that is required to make households of different sizes and structures equally well-off.[7] It has examined what extra income a couple would need to be as well-off as the single person, and how much extra income a couple would require to keep well-being unchanged after a child's birth.

The notion of equivalence scales may seem esoteric, but it affects our lives directly and indirectly every day. Many government programs in the US and other countries subsidize purchases or give aid to people based on their incomes, usually if their incomes are below some cutoff level that depends on the household's size and composition. This is true for Medicaid eligibility; the Supplemental Nutrition Assistance Program (SNAP), formerly called Food Stamps; and many others. In some cases, the provision of this money is based on a comparison of the household's income to the poverty level, a dollar figure the federal government determines, for a household of its size and structure. These scales are also important in setting the amount of child support payments, which depend on the number of children to be supported, that noncustodial parents must pay to their ex-spouses.

To see how this works, we can use the equivalence scales implied by the 2016 US poverty line and those produced by the Organization for Economic Cooperation and Development (OECD) to examine how much extra income is required to maintain a household's well-being as more adults or kids are added. Going from one to two adults doesn't double the income needed to maintain the household's well-being, but an increase of about 50 percent is required. Two can't live as cheaply as one, but they can live more cheaply than they could separately. Similarly, going from two adults to two adults and one child requires more income, but less of an increase than going from one to two adults and much less than a 50-percent increase.[8]

Just as equivalence scales show that couples economize on spending money, time spent together allows economizing on spending time. If individuals who live together take advantage of their ability to specialize in different activities and accomplish household production tasks more efficiently, they will not need as much income to maintain their well-being. One study estimated that a couple can reach the same level of satisfaction while saving about 10 percent of each partner's time compared to what each would achieve alone.[9]

The calculation of equivalence scales and official poverty levels based solely on incomes misses the point that being together can also create time savings. Less time per task might be spent by two adults together than by two separately. During our marriage my wife and I have saved time in doing laundry, with her doing the skilled labor of separating the clothing into loads to be washed together, and me doing the unskilled work of putting the loads into the washer then transferring them to the dryer. In addition to giving us more time together, this also saved us time as we each got good at accomplishing our specialized tasks. The phrase "got good" is a loose one, as my putting her silk blouse into the clothes dryer once demonstrated.

Not all couples take advantage of these economies. A young couple I knew in the early 1970s proudly proclaimed that they each did their laundry separately—loads in the washer and dryer, and ironing. They failed to take advantage of the gains that being partners might have allowed them along this dimension of home production. That struck me as being weird, especially as both spouses were economists. Perhaps unsurprisingly, their marriage dissolved after five years.

There are economies of scale in spending money that come with additional children. You can take advantage of these economies by giving the younger kid hand-me-down clothing or using the same stroller. There are also economies of scale in time use, especially on home production, as the number of children increases. Food preparation is the best example. It takes a parent little extra time to prepare scrambled eggs for twins than it does for a single child.

The same gains can exist with older children. My two youngest grandsons are cellists. Their cello lessons are scheduled back-to-back with the same teacher. This saves my daughter-in-law some money, because she employs the same instructor. Her savings illustrate why equivalence scales rise more from zero to one child than from one to two children. Even more important to her, she saves a lot of time—one round trip per week—by transporting the "cello boys" to their back-to-back lessons. Equivalence scales need to account for these savings of time, since time is money. Measures of poverty should do the same.[10]

Evidence, rather than anecdote, about the impact of having another child on time spent in home production arises from comparisons of how time is spent in households with one infant compared to households where twins were born. A large set of information on time use in Mexican households permits this comparison. Compared to parents with no children, mothers spent five additional daily hours on home production if they had a single birth, but eight additional hours if they had twins. The time spent doesn't double with the number of infants—adding a child allows some economies of scale in time use in the household.

GAY TOGETHERNESS AND GAY MARRIAGE

Gay men do less paid work than heterosexual men with the exact same demographic characteristics—age, education, location, etc.—other than sexual preference. This might give a partnered gay man the ability to spend more time with his partner than a man in a heterosexual partnership with similar demographic characteristics and total time in paid work. Section A in Figure 6.1 might be smaller for gay than for heterosexual male partners. Despite this opportunity, whether they are married or cohabiting, gay men spend no more time with their partners than do heterosexual men with theirs.[11]

This is not true for lesbian partners: they report nearly an hour more per day together than do straight women with their partners. The comparison to gay male partners is a bit surprising, since paid work by lesbian women exceeds that by women in heterosexual relationships with the same number of children. Partners in lesbian couples might perhaps be able to schedule the timing of their work to coincide better than seemingly identical partners in heterosexual couples, or perhaps they simply choose to spend more of sections B + C + D together than heterosexual women and their partners. Apparently, these opportunities, or preferences, are greater for them than for partnered gay men.

Time together represents an investment, and marriage provides a framework that allows partners to be together and to "invest" in the development of interests in leisure activities that will enhance each partner's well-being and thus the value of the marriage. Similarly, being together allows both to enhance their specialized skills in home production, as the example of my wife's and my laundry arrangement illustrates. This is possible because, even with divorce not too difficult in the US and most other wealthy countries today, marriage implies a commitment to a long-term relationship that provides partners the opportunity and incentive to invest through togetherness. The investment of time in the marriage, made possible through the legal commitment of a marriage contract, allows a couple to develop ways of saving time and money that increasingly benefit both partners as time passes.

The importance of the ability to create these gains was made clear to me in 2009 when I became involved in a legal case, *Perry et al. v. Schwarzenegger et al.* This was one of the cases that was referenced by the US Supreme Court when it delivered its landmark 2013 decision in *United States v. Windsor*, which struck down the limitation of marriage to heterosexual partners. I was asked by the plaintiffs' attorneys to consider how restricting gays/lesbians to domestic partnerships, as was voted in California's Proposition 8 in 2008, might reduce their well-being compared to allowing them the same right to marry as heterosexual partners.

The response to the request from the attorneys in this case was easy. Even though domestic partnerships generate the monetary savings that result from cohabitation, they do not produce gains for the partners that are as large as those created by marriage. Because domestic partners lack the same contractual permanence of their relationship, they have a reduced incentive to invest in the relationship—to spend time together and to create the specialized skills in home production activities and the development of additional leisure activities together that enhance the value of the relationship. My response noted that, by limiting gays/lesbians to domestic

partnerships, Proposition 8 limited the potential value of their relationship. It imposed possible economic losses on them. I doubt that this argument was central in judicial decisions in the case, but it surely was an
economic argument for the legal notion that domestic partnership does
not provide equal treatment of partners compared to the institution of
marriage.

HAPPY TOGETHER?

That partners choose to be together for perhaps four to six hours of their
waking nonworking days is an expression of and a way to develop their
commitment to each other. Couples living together typically even spend
one to two hours per day together engaged in the exact same activity
at the same time while awake. Does this mean that they are happy together? Yes, it does: on average, even after adjusting for large numbers
of the partners' demographic characteristics, the time spent with one's
spouse/partner is happier than the time spent apart.[12] But the fact that
people spend less than half of their nonwork time awake and together,
and far below half of their time together doing the same thing—and
presumably interacting—should tell us that there are limits to the happiness that togetherness can produce. Perhaps the spousal motto should
paraphrase St. Augustine: Lord, give us togetherness, but not too much.

CHAPTER 7

൰

"The Last of Life, for Which the First Was Made"

Every stage of life is interesting and important—especially to those experiencing it. We are learning—preparing ourselves for the rest of life—when we are young. We are earning from our twenties through our sixties or longer, and we are using those earnings to finance more leisure in our later years. The teenage years are especially important in forming the habits of time use that persist throughout adult life. School, the main activity that we associate nearly uniquely with youth, is an investment in the development of marketable skills, both cognitive and noncognitive. It can be regarded for teens as the equivalent of paid work by adults. Like much of paid work, it raises future productivity, provides a venue for interacting with others of the same age, and consumes a substantial fraction of the (week) day. Like paid work, spending time in school or on schoolwork also requires forgoing other activities that may be more pleasurable. The main difference, other than the age at which school is experienced, is that it yields no income directly.

One's so-called twilight years ("partial eclipse years" might be a more appropriate term) differ from one's earlier years. Whether all at once—going from full-time work to complete retirement—or gradually, almost all who survive past age seventy have more nonwork time available to them than they possessed earlier. This time gift can be spent on the other three main uses of time: home production; personal care, including sleep; and leisure, including TV watching. But even if we are no longer working for pay, an hour spent watching TV is costly—we could be using it to sleep, to cook a gourmet dinner, or to go jogging. Retired people still have to make economic choices about how to spend their twenty-four hours per day outside of paid work: time has an opportunity cost for older people whether they are working or not.

Our opportunities change as we move from youth, through young and middle adulthood, and into old age. When we are young, we worry about having enough money, but we don't think of time as being particularly scarce. As we age we get more money, both what we can earn from working and what we receive in income from the wealth that we have accumulated. But we feel that we have less time left to enjoy all the additional income. Even if our preferences don't change as we age, we still behave differently as we get older because of the altered incentives that arise from the changing relative scarcity of money and time in our lives. We have more opportunities as we age—more money. But we have the same twenty-four hours each day in which to spend this additional income. We know in planning our lives that our days are quite literally numbered.

TEENS' TIME USE: SUGAR AND SPICE, SNAILS AND PUPPY-DOGS' TAILS

When my older granddaughter was sixteen years old, her parents had a problem with her cell-phone bill: she had greatly exceeded her monthly data limits by spending too much time browsing social media. Socializing was a large part of her existence, but she was a good student, and her schoolwork was important and time consuming too. I'm not sure my granddaughter was typical, but school work and socializing are the stereotypical activities of teens.

The American time-diary data only include people at least age fifteen. Over six thousand diaries were kept by teens ages fifteen through seventeen who stated that they were full-time high school students, representing the roughly 80 percent of all American teens in that age range who are in school. The limited length of the school year makes seasonal variation in life, and time use, greater for teens than for adults. December, January, and June through August are months when most American teens are not in school full time, when they can relax or perhaps spend time working for pay. The other seven months are school months and include what we might expect to reflect the majority of the life of high school students.

How full-time high school students ages fifteen to seventeen use time during the seven months when they are most likely to be in school is shown in Figure 7.1, which focuses on differences by gender. These activities, which

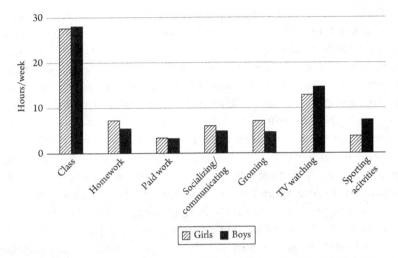

Figure 7.1 Time Use by Full-Time High School Students Ages 15–17 during School Months, US, 2003–2015 (Hours per week)

do not include time spent sleeping, account for about one-half of teens' time during those months. During the typical week in a school month, boys and girls both spend about twenty-eight hours in class. With school in session five days per week, this means that high school students report being in class for about 5 1/2 hours on school days. There is very little difference in class time between boys and girls, because in high schools they are generally taking the same courses.

Teenagers who are full-time high school students average nearly seven hours per week doing homework during school months. Including time spent in class, this means that the average fifteen- to seventeen-year-old student is spending about thirty-five hours per week on schoolwork. Defining thirty-five weekly hours of paid work as full-time employment, one might think of attending high school as working at a full-time job during the school year. It is equivalent to paid work, and although it doesn't yield income immediately, the skills developed and the knowledge learned make school equivalent to a full-time job investing in one's future earnings ability.

Few countries have sufficient numbers of time diaries of teenagers to allow comparisons to the homework time reported in American teens' diaries. But a standardized international survey of fifteen-year-old students suggests that American students differ little from those in other countries in the time they spend doing homework. In some countries, secondary school students report more homework time; in others, less. The US is roughly in the middle.[1]

While boys and girls spend the same amount of time in high school classrooms, there is a large difference between them in the amount of time that they devote to homework—girls spend nearly two more hours during each week of the school year than boys. Over the seven full-time school months, this amounts to an extra 60 hours; over the four years of secondary school it adds up to 240 hours of additional time spent studying.

Girls in the US graduate high school with higher grades than boys, are more likely to earn top grades, and take more Advanced Placement classes. The only reversal of this difference is in scores on the SAT math test, where girls consistently average thirty to forty points below boys.[2] While not explaining the reversal on the math SAT, perhaps the inferior achievements of boys in high school result from their spending less time on task—from their failure to devote as much effort to homework as girls.

The shortfall in boys' homework time does not stem from their spending more time working for pay than high school girls. Only one-third of high school girls, and one-third of high school boys, are doing paid work during school months. Of those who are working, both boys and girls average about twenty-four hours per week—about 3 1/2 hours per day—with half of that performed on weekends. Perhaps the boy-girl difference in high school performance in the US stems from basic gender differences in rates of mental or emotional maturation, as boys do mature mentally less rapidly than girls.[3] But it is not the result of boys doing more paid work.

As a comparison, on days when they are in school, German boys ages fifteen to seventeen spend more time than German girls in class, but the extra class time is exactly offset by the reduced time that they spend doing homework. In the UK the same thing is true for fifteen- to seventeen-year-olds on school days—boys are in class more but study less, so total school time is the same for boys and girls. Unlike in the US, in Germany and the UK the two sexes invest the same amount of their time in education—boys are not disadvantaging themselves (or being disadvantaged) by spending less time on their education. Something is special about boy-girl differences in the US, and it can't be a difference in the rate of mental/emotional maturation, since it's hard to believe that American boys and girls mature at relatively different rates than their European counterparts.

As with adults, high school kids' biggest expenditure of time is sleep, with full-time students ages fifteen to seventeen averaging a little more than 9 hours per night, leaving them asleep for 64 of the 168 hours per week available to them. Like adults, they sleep less on their workday equivalents—weekdays during school months—than they do on weekends in those same months. On weekends during the school year the average high school student sleeps slightly over ten hours per night, an amount that will surprise everyone except a parent who has tried to roust a teenager out of bed on a Saturday or Sunday morning (or early afternoon!). Unlike adults, teenage boys sleep more than teenage girls, but only very slightly more. Moving to adulthood reverses this gender difference in sleep time.

Sleep is something that we enjoy, but it is also an investment that "recharges our batteries" and lets us function better during daytime.[4] Anyone who has taught high school or even university classes at 8:00 a.m., or who has hustled a bleary-eyed teen off to school at 7:00 a.m., might wonder whether, even with over 8 1/2 hours of sleep on school nights, the child is getting enough sleep to perform adequately in school. This concern has led to movements to push secondary school starting times back a half-hour or even more each day, with the notion being that a delayed schedule will fit teens' circadian rhythms better and allow them to perform better in school.

A large amount of research has demonstrated that delaying school starting times does improve teens' success in school. This occurs because the timing of sleep affects teens' performance, and later school starting times and later bed and awakening times are better suited to their bodies' sleep needs. In a very clear example, some Korean provinces delayed school starting times for teenagers, while others did not.[5] In the delayed schools, performance on exams improved compared to the other schools, but kids also slept more—an extra half-hour per school night. This half-hour came entirely from time spent doing homework. Essentially the kids were investing more time in sleep, less time in studying. And the increase in school performance suggests that this trade-off between studying and sleep, both of which could improve their performance in school, was beneficial. Being able to start the school day later allowed them to substitute an extra half-hour of sleep for the relatively unproductive additional half-hour of homework beyond the substantial amount of homework that they were already doing.

My granddaughter's engagement in social media may have been excessive (her parents quickly learned to ration her phone account), but as Figure 7.1 shows, high school girls do spend more time communicating, presumably much of it with each other, than do high school boys. The difference is only one hour per week, but this additional time spent by girls amounts to an extra 20 percent compared to teenage boys.

As a teenager, my younger son would often spend twenty-five minutes in the shower, exiting it only when he had totally depleted the house's supply of hot water. My experience led me to believe that this excessive dousing was a typically teenage boys' activity. That may be—the American data do not allow distinguishing among very detailed grooming activities. But contrary to anecdotes inspired by my parental dealings, teenage boys spend less total time grooming than teenage girls, 2 1/2 fewer hours per week, or twenty minutes a day. This gender difference is even larger than that among unmarried adults in their late twenties.

All of these activities—work and school, grooming, sleeping and socializing—total 4.1 hours more among girls than boys, leaving boys with extra time to spend on other things. As Figure 7.1 shows, teenage boys spend 3.6 hours of this 4.1-hour weekly difference engaged in sporting activities. The additional time that boys spend in sports may even fulfill some of the same function of building social relationships that girls' more explicit socializing does for them. Boys also spend an extra 1.7 hours per week watching TV, a gender difference that is in the same direction but somewhat smaller than that among American adults. The extra time that boys spend playing sports and watching TV more than compensates for the lesser time they spend grooming, socializing, and studying.

This discussion of teens' time use referred only to the seven months when full-time high school students are attending school. In July and August, when high schools are not in regular session, if you're fifteen years old in the US it is difficult to get a job. In those months, the average fifteen-year-old is spending more time in class than working for pay. But even sixteen- and seventeen-year-olds spend more time in class and doing homework in summer than they do working for pay: during those months, high school students are devoting nearly half as much time to schooling as they do during the regular months of school.

Time-diary data give a less bleak picture of American high school students' activities than might have been expected. Most teens ages fifteen to seventeen view themselves as full-time high school students, and for most of them, school is the equivalent of a full-time job—at least during the months when it is in session. American high school students do devote time to their studies—or at least report that they do—and they spend less time socializing than one might infer from portrayals in the mass media. The difficulty is with the 20 percent who are not full-time high school students. Some are part-time students, but many are not. As a group they make up for the time that they are not spending in class or on homework doing two things: sleeping more and watching a lot more television.

YOUNG ADULTS IN THE MAKING—AGES EIGHTEEN TO TWENTY-ONE, AND A BIT OLDER

In 2016, over half of all Americans ages twenty-five to twenty-nine reported having spent some time in college, and 36 percent had obtained at least a four-year college degree. At any time, though, only 37 percent of Americans ages eighteen to twenty-one reported being enrolled in a college or university, with only 28 percent saying that they were full-time students.[6] The biggest groups of young adults are full-time college students and those who are not even enrolled part time in a college.

Between 1968 and 2017, I lectured in introductory economics to over twenty thousand eighteen-year-olds, usually at the start of the school year. I was always struck by how much more mature—socially and in terms of their ability to buckle down to studying—the young women seemed compared to the young men. I was also impressed by the disproportionate number of women among the top students in the class. I always wanted to begin my first lecture to these new freshmen with the line, "Welcome to the university, ladies and boys." I never had the guts to do this, but I viewed it as a good description of gender differences among eighteen-year-olds. Yet one student advisor opined to me that, while she too felt that freshman women are more mature than their male counterparts, something happens during the four years of college that leaves men at least equally mature by the time they graduate.

Perhaps the change in the apparent relative maturity of young women and men results from differences in the ways that young men and women use their time in college. Figure 7.2 provides the same information as

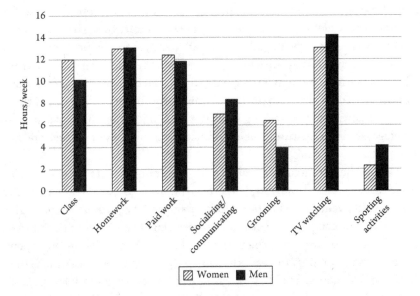

Figure 7.2 Time Use by Full-Time College Students Ages 18–21 during School Months, US 2003–2015 (Hours per Week)

Figure 7.1, but for full-time college students ages eighteen to twenty-one during school months. Female and male college students spend almost exactly the same amount of time doing homework, but women spend two hours more in class each week. Just as with high school students, female college students are devoting more time in total to their studies than males. It can't be differences in "time on task"—the amount of time devoted to the activity—that generate the apparent overtaking of college women by college men as they move toward graduation.

It also isn't that college men are obtaining "life skills" by spending more time in paid work—they aren't: male college students' paid work time is slightly less than women's during the semester. Sleep time is almost identical by gender too, not the extra sleep by boys that we see among teens, nor the additional sleep of adult women. As with high school students, the women spend more time grooming than the men. Even though male college students spend more time socializing than college women—a complete reversal from the differences in their behavior in high school—education, paid work, socializing, and grooming total three more hours each week among women. And as with high school boys, college men make up the entire difference by watching more television and spending more time in sports activities.

Totaling their time spent in class and studying, and their time spent working for pay, full-time college students are "working" over thirty-five hours per week during the semester. Being a university student is not a full-time job, but combined with paid work it is. It is more full time for women than men, about two hours per week more, over sixty hours per school year. It is difficult to believe that college men are more efficient in learning. Perhaps they are getting ahead faster because of gender discrimination. Perhaps men undergo greater biological changes that increasingly advantage them during their time at university. Either one or both of these explanations could be causing what is a striking gender difference in how college students mature. But differences in how they use time are not the cause.

While their contemporaries are in college, nonstudents are working for pay more than full-time students, but the average nonstudent was only putting in twenty-four hours of weekly paid work between 2003 and 2015. They are not using the nonstudy, nonwork time to socialize with others—they spend no more time than students in socializing. Nor do they spend more time grooming. Instead, they sleep three hours per week more than full-time students, and they watch nearly five hours more television per week. This deficit in time spent in activities that enhance young people's subsequent ability to earn incomes is another reason, beyond the benefits that the extra schooling itself contributes, for the earnings advantage of adult college grads over adult secondary school grads.

Nonstudents also spend much more time than college students in a large variety of miscellaneous leisure activities. Most striking among these is the time that nonstudent men spend in what might be called recreational computer activities, such as surfing the web or playing video games. Taking a slightly older group, men ages twenty-one to thirty, those who were employed or full-time students spent four hours per week on these activities. Those who were not employed spent nearly ten hours per week on them. Additional TV watching, computer playing, and sleeping are the main additional time sinks for younger men who are neither in school nor employed full time.[7]

SENIOR CITIZENS

Much of the earlier discussion focused on people ages eighteen to sixty-nine, ignoring the "last of life"—older people, of whom I am one. It's not easy to define what is "old," but it is easy to tell whether growing old is "a drag," as the Rolling Stones sang, in terms of how we spend time. Often the old are defined as anyone sixty-five or over, with the US Bureau of the Census breaking that age group into the categories "young old," sixty-five to seventy-four; "middle old," seventy-five to eighty-four; and "oldest old," those eighty-five or over. For purposes of analyzing time use, I focus here on people ages sixty and over, adding in those people ages sixty to sixty-four and dividing this "older" population into five-year age intervals, a categorization that allows the clearest view of how spending time changes as we age past our prime years.

The central issue as we move beyond age sixty is what we choose to do with our time as we cut back on paid work. We can spend it in leisure activities, including television-watching, or other leisure activities, for example, more sporting activities. We can sleep more or take more time to enjoy meals—enjoy more personal time. We can use the freed-up time to take care of our homes, automobiles, boats, or other possessions, or sharpen our culinary skills, all of which would represent additional home production.

The decline in the average amount of paid work we do as we move through our older years is gradual, but it can result both from a decline in labor force participation and/or a cut in hours of people who keep working for pay. In the US, the big declines in participating in paid work among older people occur between the early and late sixties, and the late sixties and early seventies. By our late sixties, the odds are very good that we will no longer be engaged in paid work. The process of withdrawal from paid work that begins in our late fifties accelerates well before the years that we are officially classified as old.

We know that having more education leads people to remain working longer, to some extent because additional education leads to higher earnings and thus a greater incentive to work more. With those incentives you would expect that the most highly educated people, with PhDs, MDs (physicians), or JDs (attorneys), who can earn far more than the average worker, would continue working much longer than others. And they do: in old age, over twice as many of them are working for pay as older Americans of average education. But even these highly educated people cut back on paid work. By age seventy, one-half of those people with this much education are no longer working for pay, and by age eighty, less than one-fourth are still in the labor force.

The people who choose to remain working do cut back on the amount of paid work that they undertake in order to spend more time enjoying leisure with their contemporaries, but only very slightly: the average older American who still works for pay reduces work time by less than ten hours per week. The same is true for the larger percentage of the most educated workers who remain in paid work.

This pattern of easing out of work leads to the question of why we work less when we're older than in our prime years. After all, except for the fact that you might be less healthy, or have less energy, it would seem to be better to spread your paid work time more evenly over the lifetime to be able to enjoy leisure when at your physical peak. Despite this reasonable proposition, concentrating paid work in the middle of life makes sense from a narrow monetary viewpoint. When we work we invest in our skills, and it pays off more to make this investment early, when it will yield higher earnings over a longer period of time, rather than late, when it is unlikely to pay off for very long. That is why we go to school early in life, and the same rationale applies for working and building up skills. As a teacher, friend, and coauthor of mine said, "It's not that you can't teach an old dog new tricks; it's just that it doesn't pay for him to learn to perform them."

Another reason for concentrating work in our youth and middle age is that we don't spend most of our leisure time just staring at the ceiling: we spend money and time together to enjoy leisure. And unless we have worked for a long time, we don't have the savings that allow us to enjoy leisure as much as otherwise. Working less in old age allows us to combine our accumulated savings with large enough chunks of time to make ourselves happier. We deny ourselves leisure in middle age, and we have a surfeit of nonwork time in old age.

Private pensions, and government-provided old-age pensions (Social Security in the US), create additional incentives to concentrate nonwork in old age. But private pensions are creatures that we have created, either ourselves, if we are self-employed, or jointly with our employers. In general, we choose them—we choose to create institutions that provide us with incentives to change our behavior in old age—they aren't forced upon us. Even Social Security arose from the collective expression of people's desires for protection from financial distress in old age—it too represents insurance against the risk of being unable to work. The best evidence suggests that, even if these programs didn't exist, we would still be withdrawing from paid work as we reach old age.[8]

A final reason why people cut back or even withdraw fully from paid work in old age is that their partners have retired. French evidence relying on differences in partners' ages suggests that the French pension system leads to women retiring in response to their typically older husbands leaving the workforce in order to claim pension benefits.[9] When they retire, the spouses are able to enjoy more leisure and home production time together. This evidence resonates with my personal experience. When my wife retired fully at age seventy, I felt pressured and greatly wanted to cut back on my paid work time so that we could do more things together.

The small drop in weekly paid hours of work performed by the decreasing percentage of older workers who are still working seems surprising. Yet there are very good explanations for this. Part of the reason is that those few working older people are such workaholics—having worked so much earlier in life—that they feel compelled to keep going at nearly the same pace as earlier. But as a workaholic who has cut back from sixty hours of weekly paid work to only thirty-five, I know that it is possible to slow down and reduce time spent in paid work without leaving the labor force entirely.

The reasons for the small decline in average working time among workers as they move into old age stem from the costs of working and the nature of the work itself. Getting up in the morning; incurring the costs of commuting to and from work; and, in some lines of work, buying the appropriate outfits to wear to work require spending money regardless of the number of hours worked per day or per week. Spreading these fixed costs of working at all over more hours per day and per week reduces the financial burden that they create. Very few people would take a job that requires a daily commute just to spend only one hour each day working for pay.

The other reason for the small decline in weekly work hours of older labor force participants is that, with the worker on the job only part time—and a short part time at that—the employer too is forced to incur additional costs. The employer must reconfigure workers' schedules, might be required to cover various types of insurance, and will have to do more supervising/managing. These extra costs cannot be justified with only a few daily hours of productive labor. Even if one is self-employed, as are 26 percent of those still working beyond age seventy-five compared to only 8 percent of workers under age sixty, one still must incur the fixed costs of getting to the office and of running an office. These costs are not worth bearing if the business is only operating for a few hours per day, or a few days per week. And only those few workers who are self-employed in certain professional occupations or some businesses can avoid these costs by working at home.

Cutting back on paid work as we age frees up a lot of time. Figure 7.3 shows the amount of time that the average American in each five-year age interval beyond age sixty spends each week on the five activities of paid work, home production, sleep and other personal care, TV watching, and other leisure activities. A move from one's early sixties to one's early seventies frees up fifteen hours per week for the average American. One-third of that freed-up time is spent on TV watching, another 40 percent on other leisure activities, and the rest scattered across the other three main nonwork activities. Surprisingly, relatively little time is devoted to additional home production—to cooking, cleaning, fixing up the house and car, or walking the dog.

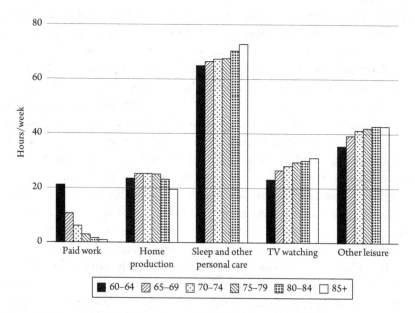

Figure 7.3 Time Use of Older Americans, 2003–2015 (Hours per Week)

Moving from one's early seventies to the eighties frees up only 4.5 additional hours of paid work per week. All of them, and then some, are redirected toward sleeping and other personal care, and TV watching. Home production decreases, perhaps because limitations on health lead us to purchase more services that substitute for our own time. Taking the final step that the underlying data allow, when one moves from the early eighties to being one of the "oldest old," there is very little paid work time left to be freed up. The major changes, which are much smaller than the earlier changes, are an additional cut in time devoted to home production and continuing increases in sleeping and TV watching.

Religious activity is strongly associated with age. Between their late teens and their fifties, Americans average only six minutes per day in these activities, but by their seventies they are up to fifteen minutes a day—still not much, but more than a doubling since youth. Time spent in religious activities is disproportionately an activity of the healthy elderly, as many authors have shown from interview data.[10] The time-diary data demonstrate that the increase with age arises entirely from the greater incidence of religious activities as people enter old age. Their incidence rises from 8 percent in the late teens to over 20 percent in people's seventies. If people do undertake a religious activity at all, its intensity is slightly lower when they are older than when they are in their teens.

The directions of the switches in time use as Americans move into old age cannot be entirely comparable to those in other rich countries, because even at ages sixty to sixty-four, people elsewhere are less likely to be in the workforce, and if they are, they put in fewer hours per year. But despite other countries' public pensions—the equivalent of American Social Security—providing incentives to retire earlier than in the US, things don't look that different elsewhere. In the UK, where working in one's early sixties is more common than in France or Germany but less common than in the US, a nine-hour drop in weekly work between one's early sixties and early seventies is split in remarkably similar proportions to the larger decline in the US. The average person ages seventy to seventy-four in the UK is only working three hours per week, which drops to almost zero hours by that person's early eighties. As in the US, home production drops a lot (nearly four hours), while time spent sleeping and in other personal care rises a lot. Overall, a picture for the UK would look very much like Figure 7.3.

Time use in old age in the two large continental economies, France and Germany, looks somewhat more different from that in the US. Despite the near absence of additional time freed up from paid work after age sixty-four, elderly French do alter the ways that they use time, just as elderly Americans do. Home production time in France decreases steadily from people's late sixties through their early eighties, while time spent sleeping and in other personal care increases a lot, as does TV watching, although hardly to American levels. The French oldest-old, like their American counterparts, are devoting much more time to sleeping, other personal care, and TV watching, and much less to home production. The patterns among older Germans are similar.

People in the US and in other rich countries move away sharply from paid work as they age past sixty, and they devote more time to leisure activities and sleeping and other personal care. Home production increases early in old age and then drops off. The main difference between the US and other rich countries is the greater importance of TV watching. The increase in free time—the greater amount of time outside the workplace, seems to belie the title of the Rolling Stones song. It's not surprising that senior citizens in the US and UK are happier than their middle-aged compatriots.[11]

HEALTH AND WIDOWHOOD

The reason for the decline in home production as we age past seventy, and for the increase in sleep, other personal activities, and the passive activity of TV watching, might be a change in how healthy we are, in our decreasing ability to engage in less passive activities. At issue is whether it is bad health or merely aging itself that alters how we use time. In some years the American time-diary surveys provide self-reported information on people's health, with them rating their health on a scale including "excellent," "very good," "good," "fair," or "poor." This measure is not as precise as some objective information on health obtained through a physical examination, but the evidence shows that it proxies objective measures of health, such as the presence of physical limitations, fairly well.[12] Before age sixty, only 16 percent of Americans say that their health is fair or poor; that number rises to 22 percent by the early sixties, and to 33 percent after age eight-four, with only a tiny difference between men and women who survive to at least sixty.

Being in poor or only fair health has substantial effects on how older people spend time. Compared to others of the same age and education, people sixty or over in fair or poor health spend five fewer hours per week working, four fewer hours engaged in home production, and three fewer hours in other leisure activities. They compensate for these declines by adding five hours of time sleeping and on other personal activities, and seven hours of TV watching.

Men are increasingly scarce after age sixty: they comprise 48 percent of Americans ages sixty to sixty-four, but this drops to 46 percent by ages seventy to seventy-four, 42 percent at ages eighty to eighty-four, and barely one-third after age eighty-four.[13] Moreover, even though only 10 percent of Americans in their late fifties have never been married, one-third of people ages seventy or over are widows or widowers, as are 60 percent of Americans age eighty-five or over. And these are predominantly women: from age sixty on, nearly 80 percent of those who have lost a spouse and not remarried are women, and among all women age seventy or over, nearly half are widows.

With widowhood being the lot of so many older American women (and women elsewhere too), examining how widows spend their time compared to women whose spouses are still alive provides an interesting insight into the impact of aging on women's lives. Widows work one hour more per week for pay than equally healthy married women age sixty or over; they spend an additional one hour sleeping or in other personal activities and an extra three hours watching TV. They compensate for their greater work, sleep, and TV time by cutting back four hours of home production and one hour of leisure activities other than TV watching. An elderly woman who is alone may feel that she needs to do more paid work to maintain her income, but she clearly feels less pressure to prepare meals or clean up than women who remain married. And, as with every change among the elderly, time is shifted away from home production toward sleeping or watching TV.

SNOOZE AND THE TUBE

In the US, sleeping and watching television are the main residual activities if you are not working for pay. Students in summers, widows in old age, the unhealthy, and young people who are not in school spend remarkable amounts of their week engaged in these two activities as compared to a healthy younger person who is a paid worker, a full-time student, or someone who is married. Not only do sleeping and TV watching rank first and third as Americans' activities, but they are the default for what we do when we're not doing anything else.

CHAPTER 8

⋄⋄⋄

The Perennial Issue and an
Old/New Concern

With time being an essential feature of human existence, it makes sense to consider how its use fits into the crucial American issue of race. An Irish long-term resident in the US remarked to me that he found astounding the extent to which Americans define themselves in terms of their racial or ethnic identity. Race underlay the most cataclysmic event in US history—the Civil War. It has continued to affect everyday lives and political life in America, as the "Black Lives Matter" movement so clearly demonstrates. Perhaps because of the issue's centrality in American life, the US has more information, statistical and other, that distinguishes people by race than does any other Western country. Race, especially the distinction between African Americans (blacks) and whites, is today perhaps the central unique demographic characteristic that differentiates the US from other rich Western countries.

Economists know that people's preferences are idiosyncratic, that there are "different strokes for different folks." But to analyze and predict their behavior, especially people's responses to the incentives generated by scarcity of money and time, economists assume there are no differences in preferences by race or ethnicity. Choices may differ, but on average if there is no discrimination against members of a group, there will be no differences in behavior that arise from race/ethnicity alone. That's a big if, and with people of the same age, education, and everything else facing the prospect of lower wages per hour of paid work and having to pay higher prices for the things they want to purchase because of discrimination—opportunities will differ across groups. Those differences in opportunities will lead people of different races and ethnicities to make different choices about how to spend their time and money.

US government statistics distinguish among three major racial groups: whites (which excludes Caucasian South Asians), African Americans, and Asian Americans (which includes all people of South and East Asian origin). But neither of the last two groups is today the largest minority group in America—that title belongs to Hispanics, who form an ethnic group not a separate racial group. One can belong to any of the major racial groups and can also view oneself and be viewed and counted in government statistics as Hispanic.

Given the overlap of race and Hispanic ethnicity, to make comparisons among demographic groups in the US, the population can be divided into four distinct, non-overlapping groups: African Americans, white or Asian-American Hispanics, Asian Americans, and non-Hispanic whites. These groups comprised 12.6, 14.7, 5.6, and 64.9 percent, respectively, of the American adult population between 2012 and 2016. The numbers of the remaining 2.2 percent of the population, consisting of Native Americans, Hawaiians and Pacific Islanders, Aleuts, and a few people who view themselves as being of at least three races, are too small in time-diary data to allow reliable comparisons to other groups' behavior.[1]

In my suburban Chicago high school class of 1961, there were two immigrants—both Western European—and only one Asian American among the nearly four hundred students.[2] There were no African Americans and no Hispanics. When I visited the school during my fiftieth high school reunion, the staff informed me that in the entire student body nearly fifty different languages were spoken in the students' homes and that there were Americans of all races. This striking change reflects the American experience generally and the demographics underlying the new concern about the old issue of immigration. From 1860 through 1920, immigrants accounted for around 15 percent of the population. With the restrictive immigration laws enacted in 1924 and not liberalized until the mid-1960s, immigrant representation in the US population had fallen to only 5 percent by 1960. Today, it is nearly back to 15 percent and, as the 2016 presidential election demonstrated, has again become the central political issue that it was in the first part of the twentieth century.

The US is truly a "nation of immigrants," but Americans often seem to forget that most of them have immigrants no further than two generations up their family trees. With immigration once again of political and social importance, examining how immigrants use time differently from natives and whether these choices change as they spend more years in the US can inform the discussion of immigrants' role in American society. The same is true in other rich countries: our stereotypes of racially/ethnically homogeneous populations in Western Europe have been rendered obsolete by the phenomenal increases in immigration into these countries that have occurred in the past fifty years.

RACE/ETHNICITY AND WORK TIME

The labor force participation rate includes those who are employed (or self-employed) and others who are unemployed, measuring the percentage of the population ages sixteen or over that is working or seeking work. During the five years 2012 through 2016 the differences in labor force participation rates by race/ethnic group were small, with participation ranging from 61 percent among African Americans to nearly 66 percent among white Hispanics. These differences are not large. But because Asian and African Americans, and especially white Hispanics, are underrepresented among older Americans compared to non-Hispanic whites, and because relatively few people in any race/ethnic group work after age sixty-four, even they overstate racial/ethnic differences in labor force participation. If we adjust for racial differences in demography—in differences in age, educational attainment, and location—the differences in participation become even less pronounced.

Labor force participation measures only the incidence of work or the desire to work. Average hours per week measure work intensity. Here too, racial/ethnic differences seem small, with average usual weekly hours among those who are working ranging from 37.9 among white Hispanics to 39.1 among Asian Americans. This difference too overstates racial/ethnic disparities along this dimension of work time. Once we account for age, education, and geographic location, we find that the three smaller racial/ethnic groups each spend about a half hour less per week in paid work than non-Hispanic whites. Among those who do work—who are employed or self-employed—the differences in average usual work time are tiny.

The calculations of weekly hours are based on reports by employed workers. They exclude the unemployed—those who are in the labor force and actively seeking work but who cannot find a job. In recent years the unemployment rate among African Americans has been twice that of non-Hispanic whites, with Hispanic unemployment being about halfway between those two, and Asian-American unemployment being even lower than among non-Hispanic whites.[3] These recent figures are typical of differences in unemployment over the last quarter-century. Together with information on labor force participation rates and workers' weekly hours, they suggest that non-Hispanic whites work very slightly more than otherwise similar African Americans and white Hispanics, and perhaps about the same as Asian Americans.

All this information is about whether people are doing paid work or not, and about how much time they spend at work. It says nothing about the actual amounts of time that they spend working—being productive—on the job. In the American time-diary surveys, workers record what they were doing at the workplace—whether they were engaged in what they viewed as work or instead were engaged in other activities. They allow examining differences in the amount of each workday that people are socializing, enjoying leisure, getting ready to work, eating, or some other nonwork activity on the job.

There are striking racial/ethnic differences in the fraction of the day at their workplaces that people report themselves as working.[4] Accounting for demographic differences such as age, education, location, sex, and many others, non-Hispanic whites spend about 1 percent more of their workday engaged in work activities than do members of the largest minority groups—African Americans, white Hispanics, and Asian Americans. This is a tiny fraction of the workday, but it is 20 percent less nonwork time at work than is spent by minority workers and amounts to over fifteen additional hours in a full-time work year.

It's not that minority workers feel safe from their employers' wrath because possible government-provided "protection" from being fired provides them incentives to reduce work effort: the majority-minority difference in the fraction of the workday actually spent working is independent of the extent of enforcement of regulations requiring equal treatment in the workplace. Nor does it result from differences in the kinds of jobs held by workers of different race/ethnicity.

The racial/ethnic differences in how time is spent at work represent a response to pure discrimination: if one knows his or her pay will be lower than majority workers' pay, and if one also knows that working as much or as hard as a majority worker will not generate the same chance for promotion, there is less incentive to work hard to get ahead. The evidence is consistent with this explanation. African Americans are as interested in working as whites: they are as likely to respond "Yes" to a question about how important work is in their lives and to their satisfaction with life.[5] In the end there is no totally satisfactory answer on this. But there is no doubt that the evidence on labor force participation, weekly hours, unemployment, and how time is spent at the workplace shows that whites spend more time working than do African Americans or Hispanics with the same age, education, location, gender, marital status, and other demographic characteristics, although these racial/ethnic differences are quite small.

RACE/ETHNICITY AND TIME OFF THE JOB—THE RACIAL DIVIDE

With African Americans and white Hispanics having a bit more nonwork time than non-Hispanic whites, the most useful comparison is of racial/ethnic differences in home production, personal care, and leisure by otherwise identical minority and majority group members. This means identical in terms of such demographic characteristics as gender, marital status, age, education, number of children, and geographic location. It means identical too in the amount of paid work—and so the time remaining to spread among these other three major categories of time use.

For each of the three minorities, and for each of the five major categories of time use outside paid work—home production, sleeping, other personal care, TV watching, and other leisure—we can see in Figure 8.1 how much more or less time the average person in the group spends in an activity compared to a non-Hispanic white of the same age, education, and so on,

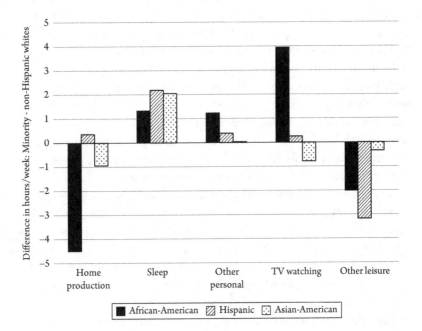

Figure 8.1 Differences in Time Spent by Minorities Compared to Non-Hispanic Whites Who Work the Same Hours, US, 2003–2015 (Hours per Week)

who does the same amount of paid work. A bar above the zero line indicates that members of the minority group spend more time in the activity than non-Hispanic whites; a bar below the zero line shows that minorities spend less time in it. For each race/ethnicity group the bars must sum to zero: since we are asking how these groups would differ from whites if they all did the same amount of paid work, the additional time that members of a minority group spend in one nonwork activity compared to non-Hispanic whites must be offset by less time spent in one or several other activities.

The average person in all three minority groups spends a greater fraction of nonwork time sleeping than does the average white, on the order of ten minutes more per day among African Americans, and nearly twenty minutes more per day among white Hispanics. Can this be true, especially in light of a study suggesting that in sleep laboratories African Americans slept less than whites?[6] The lab study involved very few people, whereas the time diaries were kept by over fifteen thousand African Americans and measured people's sleep in their normal settings, not the highly artificial environment of a lab.

One reason for the additional sleep by minorities is that sleep has a lower opportunity cost if one's wage is lower. Yet another, more subtle reason for the apparent additional sleep among minorities stems from the fact that sleep takes very little money per hour spent: only a bed that might last for ten years or more and the accompanying pillow and sheet set need to be purchased.[7] Numerous studies have shown that minorities, especially African Americans, pay more than whites for the exact same items, especially housing, cars, and other related goods.[8] That being so, even with the same income, it makes sense for minorities to spend more time in those activities that require fewer purchases of the goods that will cost them more than they would cost whites. Since sleep is such a relatively "time-intensive" activity—an hour of sleep time is accompanied by fewer purchases than any other use of time—sleeping more is a sensible economic response to discrimination in the prices of the things that we buy.

In addition to sleeping more than whites, members of each of the three minority groups also spend more time engaged in other personal care activities—mainly consisting of grooming and related activities. These activities, such as showering, washing up, and others, are also relatively time intensive. This additional time also seems explainable by racial/ethnic differences in incomes and the likelihood that these activities require relatively little spending of money, as opposed to time.

The other commonality among all three minorities is that they spend less time in other leisure activities compared to similar non-Hispanic whites. These differences are also consistent with the discrimination-based explanation for minorities' extra sleep time. Other leisure activities, such as attending sporting events, skiing, hunting, playing golf, or playing tennis, require a lot of purchases per hour spent on them. Even if there is no discrimination in the cost of attending a concert or going to a museum, the very fact of discrimination in other purchases—with minorities having to pay more for goods because of discrimination by sellers—leads to fewer minorities engaging in activities that require a lot of purchases. The lesser time spent in other leisure activities is the reverse side of the coin of the additional time that minorities spend sleeping and engaged in other personal activities.

The three largest minority groups differ from each other in the time that they spend on the other two main activities—home production and TV watching—as compared to demographically identical non-Hispanic whites. Most interesting is the huge amount of time that African Americans spend watching TV—3 1/4 hours, per day—compared to an average of around 2 3/4 hours per day among all Americans. Like sleep, TV watching takes relatively little money, so it may be the result of a racial difference in the opportunity cost of time and, like sleep, might also arise because of discrimination against minorities in purchasing goods for other activities. It may also stem from habits developed in childhood: among kids under age eight, minorities spend more time watching TV than do whites.[9]

While they spend more time watching TV than non-Hispanic whites, African Americans spend an equal lesser amount of time each day in home production (over 20 percent less than the average of over three hours per day among all Americans). While there is no obvious specific reason for this difference, with twenty-four hours in the day, incentives to spend more time on one activity (sleeping, TV watching) entail spending commensurately less on other activities, including home production.

White Hispanics and Asian Americans differ little from non-Hispanic whites in the time devoted to home production and TV watching. On average, the bars in Figure 8.1 are over twice as large among African Americans as among members of either of the other two minorities. In general, Figure 8.1 tells the same story that has pervaded American history and appears valid even in the second decade of the twenty-first century. The experience of African Americans remains different from that of all other minority groups, so that 150 years after the Civil War, race, and particularly the difference between blacks and others, remains the defining divide in how Americans behave, including how they spend time. Despite the election of an African American US president and expressions by whites of increased tolerance of African Americans in recent surveys of people's racial attitudes, differences in the crucial area of time use remain a striking reflection of the general racial gap.[10]

IMMIGRANTS AND THEIR DESCENDANTS IN THE US

With the role of immigrants again roiling and even determining the entire thrust of political discussion in much of the Western world, knowing how immigrants differ from natives, and whether they become more like natives sometime after immigration—whether they assimilate so that their patterns of time use begin to match natives' more closely—should be an important question both intellectually and as a factual basis for political debate. Because natives and immigrants differ in so many ways beyond simply the length of time since birth that they have been in the US, we can't simply compare differences in time use between them. American immigrants are concentrated disproportionately among the very young and the middle-aged: slightly fewer are between ages fifteen and thirty than are natives, and many fewer are older than fifty. More immigrants than natives lack a high school diploma, but the same percentage has a bachelor's degree or more. The comparisons vary in other wealthy countries, but in France and Germany, immigrants also differ from natives in terms of their age structure and the level of education that they have attained.[11] With these and other demographic differences in mind, it's important to compare immigrants' and natives' time use after accounting for as many ways other than immigrant status that the groups differ.

Immigrants to America work for pay slightly longer per week than do natives of the same age, education, and so on. The average immigrant comes to America and works. The stereotype of lazy immigrants is simply incorrect. Immigrants do sleep more than natives—a lot more, about an additional twenty minutes per day. They make up for the additional work and sleep time by spending nearly two hours less than natives each week watching TV and on other leisure activities. This is apparent in Figure 8.2. The solid bars in each of the six pairs show the additional (or lesser) time that immigrants spend in each of the six general categories of time use compared to natives. As was the style in Figure 8.1, a bar reaching above the zero line shows that immigrants spend more time in the activity than natives, while one going below shows that they spend less time. None of the differences depicted arises from such demographic differences as age, education, marital status, or number and ages of children—these have all been accounted for. They stem purely from whatever it is that might lead immigrants and natives to choose to spend time differently.

It might be that TV, the "default option" for how people spend time, is less accessible to immigrants because of language problems or a generally lesser involvement with the American culture that is usually depicted on the tube. It may be that those who migrate to the US have a greater work ethic than natives. It might be that immigrants arrive, as did my grandfathers, with the idea of working hard and leaving an economic and cultural legacy so that, even though they may do not do well economically, they make it possible for their children and grandchildren to rise into the middle or even upper-middle class. We can't tell what the underlying motivation is, but there is no doubt that immigrants work at least as much as natives.

A huge line of research has demonstrated that the age at which immigrants arrive in the US has a major effect on their economic success.[12] Those who arrived as children and obtained their education in the US earn more than others of the same age and from the same country who arrived as adults. That's true even if the adult immigrant spent the same number of years in school as the youthful immigrant but did so in the sending country. The additional work time of immigrants over natives shown in Figure 8.2 does not arise from differences in the age when the migrant arrived in the US, nor does the age at arrival affect most other uses of immigrants' time. One major difference between youthful migrants and others, though, is that those who came to the US as kids imbibed the American ethos of TV watching: youthful migrants do much more TV watching than other immigrants. The only other difference is that they sleep less than other immigrants, although more than natives.

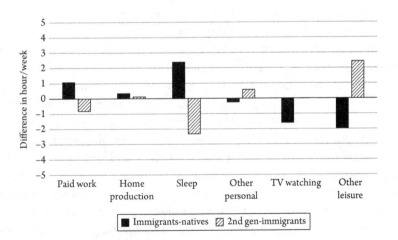

Figure 8.2 Differences in Time Use by Immigrant Status, Same Demographics, US, 2003–2015 (Hours per Week)

A central issue in political debates about immigration in all countries is its impacts on the native population. Concerns about the burdens of spending on social programs, such as income support, and even more about the impact on natives' job opportunities, have been paramount. A lot of Americans work at strange hours—nights and weekends—and Americans unsurprisingly find work at those times to be unpleasant. But work at these unusual, undesirable times is especially common among immigrant workers in the US: they are 15 percent more likely to be working at night (between 10:00 p.m. and 6:00 a.m.) than are native workers.

Immigrants work at times that natives find unpleasant; this relieves the pressure on natives. In US metropolitan areas where the share of immigrants among workers is greater, natives perform less work at night. The willingness of immigrants to take these unpleasant jobs reduces the need for natives to perform them. A similar result has been observed in Italy, both for evening/night work and for work on Sundays.[13] At least in the dimension of the timing of work, immigration benefits natives by reducing the burden of working at undesirable times.

Most immigrants remain in the United States, and the majority wind up producing children who count as natives and whom we can designate as second-generation Americans—born in the US, but with immigrants as parents. All four of my grandparents were immigrants, making my parents second-generation and me a third-generation American. About half of Americans with any immigrant parent come from families where both parents were immigrants. I use the narrow definition of "second-generation"—native-born Americans both of whose parents were immigrants—to compare the time use of today's second-generation Americans to that of today's immigrants.

The striped bar in each pair in Figure 8.2 indicates the additional or lesser amount of time that second-generation Americans spend in each of the six major activities compared to immigrants. For example, the bar for sleep shows that second-generation Americans spend less time sleeping than do immigrants. It and the other bars are remarkably different from the comparisons underlying the solid bars—the differences between immigrants and natives. Except for TV watching and home production, on which second-generation Americans spend about the same amount of time as immigrants, the differences between them and immigrants are almost exactly the reverse of those between immigrants and natives. Second-generation Americans spend about one hour less working for pay each week than immigrants, who spend one hour more than natives. They spend 2 1/3 hours less sleeping than immigrants, who sleep exactly that amount more than natives, and they spend just under 2 1/2 hours more in other leisure activities than immigrants.

If you add the solid and striped bars in Figure 8.2 together, you get bars indicating the difference between second-generation Americans and natives. Only one of these bars would reach more than one hour above or below the zero line. Except for TV watching, where they resemble immigrants much more than natives, second-generation Americans' use of time has mostly assimilated to that of natives. The comparisons in Figure 8.2 should reassure those who worry that today's immigrants will never "fit in." They may not, but at least their offspring will. As the song, "I'm easily assimilated," in the operetta *Candide* goes, the children of immigrants "do as the natives do."

This assimilation process into the US is not the same for all immigrants and their children. Those who come from countries where English is either the primary or at least a secondary language, such as India, behave differently from other immigrants and second-generation Americans.[14] Their patterns of time use approach those of natives more closely and more quickly after arrival in the US. But even among immigrants who come from countries where English is not widely spoken, with Mexico being by far the biggest example, patterns over time increasingly closely resemble those of natives.

IMMIGRANTS ELSEWHERE

Every country's immigrant experience is different. The timing of waves of immigration varies across countries—for example, immigration was extremely important in the US between 1880 and 1910, but much less so at that time in France or Germany. The countries from which immigrants have come vary across countries—for example, Mexican, Filipino, and Korean immigration has been very important in the US since the 1960s, but it is minuscule in France and Germany. For these reasons—plus others, no doubt—we can't expect that immigrant-native differences in time use will look the same elsewhere as in the US, nor can we expect to observe the same extent of assimilation that exists in the US.

The vertical bars in Figure 8.3 show the difference in hours spent per week between immigrants and natives in France and Germany for the same six major categories of time use as in Figure 8.2. The solid bars denote the differences in France, the striped bars those in Germany. As with the solid bars showing immigrant-native differences in the US in Figure 8.2, the bars in Figure 8.3 adjust for age, education, geography, gender, marital

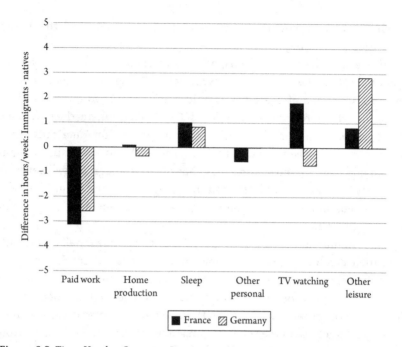

Figure 8.3 Time Use by Category, Immigrants-Natives, France and Germany (Hours per Week)

status, and other demographic characteristics. They show the gaps between immigrants and natives who differ only by their immigrant status.

The leftmost pair of bars in Figure 8.3 shows that immigrants perform less paid work than demographically identical natives in both France and Germany. They spend more time sleeping than natives and more time on other leisure activities too. They spend very slightly less time on other personal activities. The only major differences between the two countries are that immigrants in France watch more TV than natives, while immigrants in Germany watch less, almost exactly opposite the immigrant-native differences in time spent on other leisure activities.

The striking comparisons of the information in this figure are to the uses of time depicted by the lefthand bars in Figure 8.2.[15] That figure shows that immigrants to the US work more than natives with the same demographic characteristics, the opposite of immigrants in France or Germany. American immigrants spend less time in non-TV leisure activities than natives, while continental European immigrants spend more. The only similarity to the US is in time spent sleeping—more time by immigrants than by natives in all three countries. This might not be surprising: immigrants in France and Germany appear to face the same discrimination—lower earnings and incomes, even with the same demographic characteristics as natives, and higher prices for consumer goods—as American immigrants. This discrimination might be what leads them to spend time on time-intensive activities, those that require relatively little money and a lot of time to make engaging in the activity enjoyable.

Despite the tremendous contrasts between the experiences of immigrants in the US as compared to these other countries, there is one important similarity (at least for France, where the data are available). In both countries, immigrants who become citizens behave more like natives than immigrants generally. They do more paid work than other immigrants, although still less than natives with similar demographic characteristics. In general, their behavior along all but one of the other major dimensions of time use looks more like that of natives: they sleep even more than other immigrants. Overall, though, in France as in the US, immigrants' spending of time tends to assimilate toward that of natives.

THE UNIQUENESS OF RACE AND ETHNICITY IN TIME USE

Two of the three largest minority groups in the US—Hispanics and Asian Americans—do not differ greatly from non-Hispanic whites in how they spend their time. And the relatively minor differences between Hispanics and non-Hispanic whites are due partly to the recentness of many Hispanics' arrival in the US—more than one-half of American Hispanics ages fifteen or over are immigrants. The same point applies even more among Asian Americans ages fifteen or over—more than two-thirds of them are also immigrants. Since the children of immigrants to the US become like other Americans, even these racial/ethnic differences are likely to diminish over time.

In time use, as in so much of American life, the pervasive distinction is the black-white racial divide. Immigrant groups become like most other Americans. African Americans, of whom today only 10 percent are immigrants, do not spend time in the same ways as other non-immigrant, nonminority citizens. They do less work for pay and spend less time in home production; they sleep more and watch more television than native whites. Whether these differences directly reflect the impact of several centuries of racial discrimination or instead reflect "culture" (which itself may reflect discrimination) can't be determined. But the differences are striking and reflect America's greatest continuing anomaly and divide.

CHAPTER 9

✦

E Pluribus Unum?

All but the tiniest countries—Andorra, San Marino, and perhaps Liechtenstein alone in Europe—have identifiable regions within them. Most of us identify with a region, typically the one where we spent our teen years. Even though I have not lived in the Midwest since 1993, I think of myself as a midwesterner. Even though my wife has not lived in the Boston area since 1965, she thinks of herself as a Bostonian. The same is true elsewhere: somebody is Welsh or Scottish instead of British, Breton or Alsatian rather than French, Bavarian rather than German, Catalan rather than Spanish, Walloon or Flemish rather than Belgian.[1] Of course, we view ourselves as citizens of our countries, especially when interacting with people from other countries, but when dealing with our fellow citizens we often identify with our region.

Regional distinctions are important for many reasons. They spill over into politics, both indirectly during election seasons, and occasionally even disastrously, as the police-citizen clashes in Catalonia in 2017 so vividly demonstrated. Some exist even in the oldest polities and persist to the present day; they may be even more important the more recent are the events that created today's nation-state. These differences nurture stereotypes in the minds of citizens of one region about the behavior of groups of people in other regions within their country, and they reinforce our judgments and sometimes our prejudices about our fellow citizens from different regions.

In the US, these stereotypes include the laid-back Californian, the slow lazy southerner, the hurried and rude New Yorker, and the loud and large Texan. They reflect beliefs that people in another location have different preferences about how to spend their time, and they reinforce how we treat other Americans based on their regional identity instead of as individuals. Even if opportunities are the same across regions—even if there are no differences in age, education, race or ethnicity, wages or incomes, for example—people in different regions may spend time differently solely because their preferences differ.

Are these regional stereotypes correct—are they based on current behavior, or are they relics of a past that might never have existed? Being laid-back, lazy, or hurried relates to how we lead our lives, especially how we spend our time. A good way to study regional stereotypes is to examine how people use time in different regions of the US, in states or cities in the US, and even in different regions within other countries.

The artifice of time zones may reinforce regional differences in how Americans spend time. Since many other countries with broad longitudinal spreads have also created zones with different clock times, evidence on the impacts of this artifice in the US on interregional temporal relationships is useful in analyzing time use in both the US and elsewhere. In general, this issue and the geographical stereotypes that we hold can be informed by answering the question of the extent to which, in terms of time use, the US is more *unum* or more *pluribus*.

REGIONAL DIFFERENCES IN THE US

For statistical purposes, the US Census Bureau divides the country into four main regions: Northeast, Midwest, South, and West. These are broad divisions, with the South being perhaps the most diverse, including what are today viewed as northern states, such as Delaware and Maryland, Deep South states like Mississippi and Alabama, and even Oklahoma and Texas. The Northeast includes New England, New York, New Jersey, and Pennsylvania; the Midwest extends from Ohio to the Dakotas, Kansas, and Nebraska, while the West includes the Mountain states and all five Pacific Coast states (California, Oregon, Washington, Alaska, and Hawaii). With aggregates that are this broad we are asking whether there are major differences across geographic units that may be quite diverse internally.

We can't simply compare the differences in time use across regions. Many demographic characteristics generate regional differences in how time is spent. Only 5 percent of midwesterners are white Hispanics, but 26 percent of westerners are; only 5 percent of westerners are African American, but 19 percent of southerners are. Education level, which is a major determinant of earnings and income, also varies across regions: 31 percent of Americans in the Northeast have at least a university education, but only 26 percent of southerners and midwesterners (and 28 percent of westerners) do. Urbanization also varies, with larger fractions of the northeastern and western populations living in urban areas than in the Midwest and South.

It is remarkable how small the differences in time use are once we adjust for all the demographic characteristics that differ across US regions. This is clear from the regional differences in time use shown in Figure 9.1, which adjusts for inter-area differences in age and education, gender mix, marital status, and the numbers and ages of children. The figure shows the difference in time spent by activity in each of the Midwest, South, and West compared to the Northeast. A bar extending above the zero line means that more time is spent in the activity in the region than in the Northeast; a bar below signifies that less time is spent there. Comparisons of time use between, for example, the Midwest and the South can be made by subtracting the bars for the activity for those two regions.

Among all six categories of time use, there are only two cases where the difference in time use between any pair of regions exceeds one hour per week. One is in TV watching, where westerners watch 1 hour less of television per week than northeasterners, and 1.6 hours less than southerners. The other is in the enjoyment of other leisure activities, where westerners

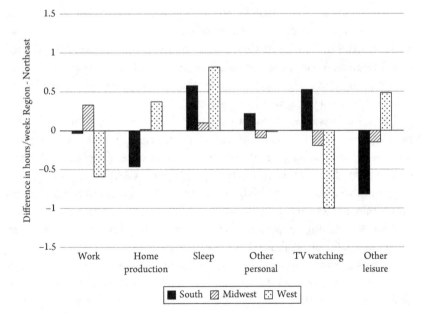

Figure 9.1 Difference in Time Use by Category Compared to the Northeast, US, 2003–2015 (Hours per Week)

spend 1.3 hours more per week than southerners. Total time spent in paid work and all leisure (TV watching plus other leisure) is similar across regions.

Regional stereotypes are not justified by differences in how Americans spend time. Paid work time varies little across regions: on an average of 28 hours of weekly paid work among all Americans ages fifteen or over, the largest difference by region (between the Midwest and the West) is only 0.9 weekly hours (3 percent). Comparing time use across the four broad regions of the US, they seem to be much more *unum* than *pluribus*.

With less than one hour variation in time spent on each activity by Americans according to region, perhaps there is more going on when we look at differences across smaller geographic units. Because there isn't enough information on time use in some of the less populous states, we can't consider differences across all fifty states and the District of Columbia. But California and Texas are the most populous states in the Union, with over 12 percent of Americans living in California and over 8 percent in Texas. Behavior in these two large economies is interesting too since they, perhaps more than other states, are the most heavily mythologized in song and cinema.

To examine whether Californians and Texans spend time differently from demographically identical Americans living in the other forty-eight states or the District of Columbia, we can make the same calculations that underlie Figure 9.1, adjusting for all the demographic and other differences that were used to calculate regional differences. For each activity the bar measures the difference in time spent in the state compared to the national average. A bar above the zero line shows that Californians or Texans are spending more time in the activity than other Americans; a bar below indicates that they are spending less time.

The solid bars in each pair in Figure 9.2 present the results of these calculations for California. Californians do appear to be "out there having fun," as the 1960 song goes, at least compared to other Americans with the same personal characteristics.[2] They spend nearly 1 1/2 fewer hours on average each week over their lifetimes doing paid work, about 5 percent less than other Americans. They do not spend the time that is freed up from paid work watching television: they also watch less television than other Americans, 0.7 hours (about 4 percent) less per week.

With less time working for pay and less TV watching, Californians have 2.1 hours per week to spread among the other activities that they might undertake. They do spend a half hour more per week sleeping than other Americans, but the biggest uses of this extra time are in home production, including such outdoor activities as lawn and garden work, and

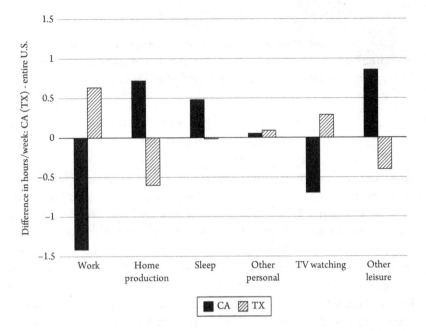

Figure 9.2 Difference in Time Use by Category Compared to Other Americans: Californians, or Texans, 2003–2015 (Hours per Week)

other leisure activities. Together these account for over three-quarters of the extra time. There is no single activity within these broad categories on which Californians spend hugely more time than others. But twenty extra minutes per week are spent on sports and exercise compared to other Americans, and almost twenty minutes more per week are also spent on childcare.

Are Californians "having fun"? It's hard to say, but since some of their additional leisure is outside the house, they may be "in the warm California sun." Moreover, since most people find paid work unpleasant compared to other activities, a reasonable conclusion from Californians' lesser work time is that, at least compared to other Americans, they are indeed having more fun.

Texans are different from other Americans, too. The most notable difference is ethnicity: over one-third of Texans are white Hispanics, compared to about one-seventh of all Americans. Once we adjust for demographic differences, though, Texans look remarkably like other Americans, as the striped bars in each pair in Figure 9.2 show. No difference in spending time across these six major categories amounts to anything near one hour per week. The biggest difference is that Texans work just over a half hour per week more over a lifetime than the average American. Texas is clearly less "special" than California, less different from the rest of the US in terms of spending time. The large and loud stereotype is not rooted in any major distinction in how Texans use time compared to other Americans.

"CITY SLICKERS," "COUNTRY COUSINS," AND LIFE IN THE "BURBS"[3]

American statistics divide the country into rural and metropolitan areas. When we compare the city slickers to their country cousins we need to remember that the latter are a small minority, only 15 percent of the population. America today is essentially an urban society. American minority groups are far less strongly represented in rural areas than elsewhere, and only 17 percent of rural residents have a college degree or more, while 31 percent of urban residents do. The calculations that produce the solid bars in Figure 9.3 account for these and other demographic differences such as race and age. The bars show how much more time, if above the zero line, or less time, if below, that people in rural areas spend in the activity compared to urban dwellers. These bars are tiny: the largest extend only about 0.3 hours above or below the zero line. These minute differences demonstrate that city slickers and country cousins behave the same, at least in terms of how they spend time. Our stereotypes based on rural or urban residence are either very out of date or arise from differences in demographic characteristics, not from how similar people in different locations use time.

Stereotypes about people who differ by where they live in a metropolitan area also abound.[4] The stereotypical suburbanite drives a truck or a minivan, spends time traveling among chain stores located in shopping centers or strip malls, and lives in a house that is identical to all the others in the neighborhood. Common stereotypes about center cities are that they are peopled by members of minority groups and by others who are generally downtrodden by poverty. Some studies suggest that people in cities move faster than others, even when only walking.

In terms of demographics the stereotypes are based on fact: center cities are 22 percent African American and 22 percent white Hispanic, compared to only 10 and 13 percent, respectively, in suburbia. The areas differ little in education level, with 30 percent of suburbanites having college degrees compared to 31 percent of city dwellers. Family incomes differ a lot, however, with an average over 2003–2015 of $77,000 in suburbia but "only" $63,000 in center cities.

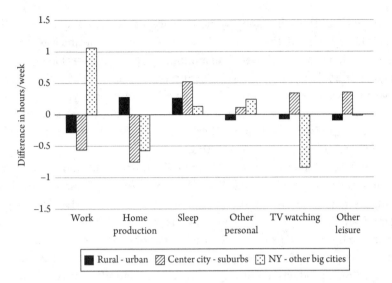

Figure 9.3 Difference in Time Use by Type of Area, US 2003–2015 (Hours per Week)

The striped bars in Figure 9.3 show the additional time spent in an activity in cities compared to suburbia after adjusting for demographic characteristics such as age, education, and race/ethnicity. The differences in time use are larger than those between rural and urban residents, but they are still small. Most interesting is that city residents do 1 1/4 hours less total work (paid work and home production) than suburbanites. This is not because they spend less time traveling to work or to stores—time spent in those subcategories is almost identical in the two groups. The difference is real, and city dwellers spread the freed-up time across the other major activities, doing more of each than do suburbanites. Despite these differences, a reasonable conclusion about city/suburb stereotypes is that they can't be based on big differences in how the same person would spend time living in one place or the other.

New York City is by far the largest US city, with a population of 8.5 million in 2016. Second through fifth in size are Los Angeles (4.0 million), Chicago (2.7 million), Houston (2.4 million), and Philadelphia (1.6 million). New Yorkers think of themselves as different from other Americans, as do even New York suburbanites. They see themselves as privileged to live in what is arguably the cultural capital of the United States. Their attitudes and perceived behavior have led to the term "New York minute"—a very short period of time.[5] As the now-deceased late-night show host Johnny Carson remarked, a New York minute is the interval between a Manhattan traffic light turning green and the guy in the car behind you honking his horn.

As with all the other geographic stereotypes, is there any truth in this one? Living part of the year in New York City, I sometimes feel that a "New York minute" is slower than a minute elsewhere, especially when the sign on the subway platform says "next train two minutes" for six consecutive minutes. Perceptions are fine, but whether this stereotype accords with the reality of how New Yorkers use time is a different issue. And the most useful comparison is not to people throughout the US, but to residents of the four other largest American cities.

The dotted bars in Figure 9.3 show the adjusted additional time spent in an activity by people in New York City compared to people who have the same demographic characteristics but live in one of the other four largest American cities. The most striking fact is that New Yorkers work for pay over one hour more per week than residents of other big American cities. They partly compensate for this additional time in paid work by engaging in less home production—less cleaning up, less laundry, less cooking, and less dishwashing. The lesser time spent on home production might result from the lack of space for washers/dryers and other machinery that complements that use of time, leading New Yorkers to outsource activities that people elsewhere are more likely to do themselves. The ubiquity of "take-out" might also explain the difference.

Taken together, New Yorkers' greater time spent in market work and lesser time spent in home production mean that their total work time is only slightly above total work time in other big cities. They more than compensate for even this small difference by watching nearly one hour less television weekly. Perhaps New Yorkers' extra work time leads them to hurry more than urbanites elsewhere and to the proverbial "New York minute." But even their additional time spent in paid work is not huge. The stereotype cannot arise mainly from any big differences in how New Yorkers spend their time compared to other big-city residents.

"A TALE OF TWO CITIES"

The United Kingdom and France are the two largest European countries where one metropolis dominates the nation—culturally, politically, and in terms of size. Greater London contains 13 percent of the UK population and is an entity that is different in many ways from the rest of the country—for example, in its strongly anti-Brexit vote in 2016. Similarly, the Paris *unité urbaine* contains 16 percent of the total French population, and as the 2017 presidential election demonstrated, is substantially different politically from the rest of the nation.

Despite differences in culture and behavior, the differences between metropolitan residents and others in the two countries are remarkably similar. Residents of the metropoles in both France and the UK do over one hour more paid work each week over their lives than their compatriots. They spend an hour more each week in other personal care, such as grooming, cleaning up, and so on. They more than make up for this additional time by doing two hours less home production each week than others and by watching one hour less television each week.

A comparison to Figure 9.3's dotted rightmost bars depicting the differences in behavior between New Yorkers and other big-city residents shows striking similarities. In all cases the residents of each country's largest city work more for pay, do less home production, and watch less television than other citizens. The comparisons of geographic areas within the US may reflect behavior that is uniquely American, but differences in time use between residents of the largest cities and other parts of these two European countries are remarkably like the comparisons between New York and other large US cities.

TIME ZONES AND TIME USE

The rural-urban distinction is based on differences in attitudes and behavior that might arise from location independent of artificial geographic distinctions. The city-suburb and megalopolis-other distinctions are somewhat artificial. It is possible for a metropolitan area to be substantially central city with relatively few suburbs. The city of Houston, for example, contains over one-third of the area's population. The opposite can also be true, as with Boston, where only one-seventh of the area's population resides in the city. Still more artificial are time zones, nearly longitudinal markings designed to create sunset/sunrise times that occur at the same clock time along each latitude line around the planet. While they relate to Coordinated Universal Time (UTC), choices about time zones and timing are left to the governments of the countries to which they apply and can and have been changed by governmental act. This artifice is also quite recent: for example, the idea of time zones in the US reached its centenary only in 2018.[6]

A remarkably large number of countries contain at least two zones, even ignoring distant island territories that might be viewed as integral parts of those countries. Australia, Canada, Brazil, Chile, Mexico, Kazakhstan, Mongolia, Russia, and the Democratic Republic of the Congo (formerly Zaire) are some of these. Sometimes even in our own countries we are unaware of the diversity of timekeeping. Most Americans are familiar with the Eastern, Central, Mountain, and Pacific Times, but this list ignores Alaskan time and Hawaiian/Aleutian time, respectively one and two hours behind Pacific Time.

The geographic delineation of time zones is not rigid and certainly not bound by the artificial distinctions of state boundaries. In the US, thirteen states lie in two different time zones. In all cases these apparent anomalies were created for economic reasons: parts of a state are linked to the time zone in a nearby state because they are more integrated economically with that adjacent state than with the bulk of their own state. The four counties in the Upper Peninsula of Michigan that border Wisconsin are in the Central zone, not in the Eastern zone like the rest of Michigan. The area around El Paso, Texas, is in the Mountain rather than the Central time zone, since economically it is linked more closely to parts of New Mexico than to the rest of Texas. Similar economic carve-outs exist in border areas of many other states.

If we were again a primarily agricultural economy, time zones would not be an issue of economic interest. People in each area would work, consume, and enjoy leisure at their own convenience, based largely on seasons and on the amount of daylight. They would not need to take account of when people elsewhere, perhaps three thousand miles away, were awake and working. But in an integrated economy with tertiary industry predominating, what I do in New York (Eastern Time Zone) must take at least some account of what people whom I deal with in the other American zones are doing. I shouldn't call my Denver-based coauthor (Mountain Time Zone) before 10:00 a.m. I even need to adjust my timing of leisure: if I need to telephone my sister in Northern California about a family matter, I know that I had better do that no earlier than 11:00 a.m. Eastern Time.

Many people's difficulties in coordinating their activities with those of other Americans are minor, since their work may not involve interacting with people outside their own time zone. But what if the clients of a stockbroker living in Los Angeles were concerned that she be able to trade for them when the New York Stock Exchange opened at 9:30 a.m. Eastern Time, 6:30 a.m. in Los Angeles? The national and even international focus of the finance industry means that some people involved in it will be keeping different hours on the clock from their peers located elsewhere.

The US financial industry contains only a small fraction of the total American workforce. But the need for coordination across time zones in that industry or others can spill over onto the activities of other workers. The coffee shop barista might be required to be on the job at 6:30 a.m. to satisfy the caffeine craving of the LA stockbroker; and while driving to her office, the broker may wish to drop off her dry-cleaning at a local shop that would open at 6:00 a.m. The effect of temporal coordination spreads through much more of the American workforce than just those workers who regularly deal with others across time-zone lines.[7]

The Eastern zone is the most populous and contains the center of the US financial industry as well as the headquarters of a large fraction of American corporations. Those facts suggest that people in other time zones have incentives to coordinate their activities with activity in the Eastern zone. And that is exactly what occurs: on average at 8:00 a.m. local time, 3 percent more people in the Western time zone are working than in the Eastern zone at 8:00 a.m. It is very difficult to work while asleep, so it's not surprising that people in the West are less likely to be asleep at 7:00 a.m. locally than people in the East will be at 7:00 a.m. their time. Americans synchronize their activities based on the need for some direct coordination of work time, whether through the requirements of their employers or their own desires to coordinate time. This need spills over into the timing of activities by people who do not interact directly with others elsewhere, and because of the twenty-four-hour daily limit on our life, the need for coordination of work activities spills over to the timing of nonwork activities.

Governments recognize the role of time zones and clock time in coordination. Through the first half of the twentieth century, China contained five zones, whose boundaries were based chiefly on differences in longitude. Presumably to unify the country, in 1949 the new government consolidated the five zones into one, Beijing (or China) Standard Time, which remains in effect today. The opposite can also occur: in 2007, the Venezuelan leader Hugo Chávez dis-coordinated the country by putting its time one-half hour back from the rest of its time zone, a change that was reversed in 2016.[8] There is no evidence on the economic impact of this dis-coordinating move, nor on the impacts of being one-half hour off the hours indicated by UTC in such places as India, Newfoundland, or South Australia. But especially in the less populous of these geographic entities, the strangeness of clock times might reduce economic activity by making coordination with other, larger parts of their economies more difficult.

If we sleep 8 1/2 hours beginning at 10:30 p.m. in Chicago instead of 11:30 p.m. in New York, that might not matter. But the contrast in sleep time near the edges of time zones can be stark and does have implications for how we live. In Marquette, Michigan, in late June it is not totally dark until 10:25 p.m. local (Eastern) time. Only 175 miles almost directly south, in Green Bay, Wisconsin, it is totally dark at 9:20 p.m. local (Central) time. The artifice of time zones creates anomalies with our bodily circadian rhythms that can alter the amount of time that we sleep.

Sleep time is reduced at the western edges of American time zones compared to the adjacent eastern edges of the next time zone. And this reduction affects how we live. Those on the western edges of time zones in the US are less healthy. In Russia, which has many more time zones than the US, the interaction of the artifice of zonal boundaries with circadian rhythms produces differences in alcohol consumption, health outcomes, and even homicide rates.[9] Again, the artifice of time zones affects people's behavior and well-being.

Anyone who has watched an evening of TV in the US is familiar with the mantra, "10:00 p.m. Eastern and Pacific, 9:00 p.m. Central and Mountain." For historical reasons stemming from the early days of network radio in the 1920s, when it was deemed desirable to broadcast live in both New York City and Chicago, national broadcasts appear at different clock times in different parts of the country. This is very American: in Australia, even though there are several distinct time zones, prime-time television shows and the nightly news shows appear at the same clock time throughout the country.

For the first twenty-seven years of my married life, my wife and I lived in the Eastern zone and typically went to bed on weekdays at around 11:40 p.m., since we wanted to watch the "Monologue" on NBC's *Tonight Show*. When we moved to the Central Time Zone, we began going to bed an hour earlier, with the Monologue remaining the anchor to our sleep time. While this changed behavior may be extreme, cues from the timing of television shows affect the timing of TV watching, independent of the effects of coordination across time zones. Six percent fewer people in the Central and Mountain zones are watching TV at 11:00 p.m. than in the Eastern and Pacific zones. This difference spills over to when we sleep and work. Because of the artifice of the timing of TV broadcasting, 3 percent fewer people in the Central and Mountain zones are sleeping at 7:00 a.m. than elsewhere, and 3 percent more are working at 8:00 a.m.[10]

HOW DAYLIGHT SAVING TIME AFFECTS OUR LIVES

Since the early twentieth century, the US and many other countries with land masses located outside the tropics have observed Summer Time, called Daylight Saving Time (DST) in the US, with nominal time "springing forward" in March or April, and "falling back" in October or November. The opposite switches occur in several countries, such as Australia, that are located far south of the Equator. Since 2007, DST in the US starts on the second Sunday in March and concludes on the first Sunday in November. Under US law, states have the right to opt out of DST, as Arizona and Hawaii currently do and as has occasionally been proposed in other states.[11]

DST is a misnomer—no daylight is saved. The amount of daylight in the twenty-four hours of a summer's day is not increased by having clocks read an hour later, nor is the smaller amount of daylight on a winter's day reduced by turning clocks back in the autumn. But these shifts may affect energy consumption or productivity, which was their original purpose and which in the US is enshrined in the Energy Policy Act of 2005 that created the current DST rules. They may affect interregional coordination by changing the time differences between areas that do or do not observe DST. They might affect behavior on the day of the time switch or even for several days before or after it.

During the energy crisis of the early 1970s, the US enacted the Emergency Daylight Saving Time Energy Conservation Act of 1973, which put the country on DST all year around effective January 1974. For us living during that year in Michigan, near the western edge of the Eastern time zone, this meant that it was totally dark at 8:40 a.m. when our kids were going to school in winter. Whether this Act reduced energy use is unclear, but it certainly increased parents' concerns about their kids' safety, which perhaps is why it was repealed later in 1974.

Whether DST reduces energy consumption has been debated for at least the last fifty years, with many studies of the issue but no firm conclusion either way. One survey of research published by the US Department of Transportation in 1975 suggested that DST has little positive or negative impact on energy use. A recent study took advantage of the fact that for many years some counties in Indiana observed DST while others did not. The authors found that, if anything, energy consumption was higher in counties where DST was observed.[12] At this point the safest conclusion is that, at the very least, Daylight Saving Time does not save much, if any, energy.

When the rest of the country goes on DST, residents of Arizona and Hawaii (and much of Indiana before 2007) become one hour more discoordinated from the Eastern zone than they were the week before. The same thing happens in the Australian state of Queensland compared to the two largest Australian population centers, New South Wales (Sydney) and Victoria (Melbourne). Their failure to change to DST and the need to coordinate with the rest of their countries' populations leads residents in those two American states and in Queensland to alter their schedules when their compatriots begin observing DST.

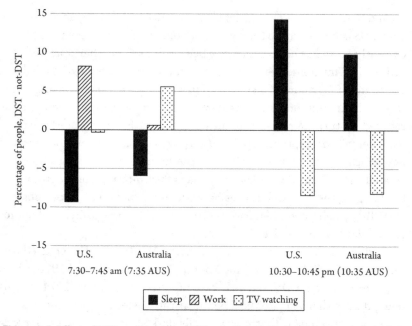

Figure 9.4 Effect of DST on Percentage of People Doing the Activity in an Area without DST.
Source: Calculated from Daniel Hamermesh, Caitlin Myers, and Mark Pocock, "Cues for Timing and Coordination: Latitude, Letterman, and Longitude," *Journal of Labor Economics*, April 2008, Tables 3, 5.

Figure 9.4 shows the difference in the percentage of people engaged in various activities in the early morning or late evening in Arizona and Hawaii, or in Queensland, when the rest of the nation is observing DST and they are not. It presents calculations for each of the three major activities: sleep, the solid bars; paid work, the striped bars; and TV watching, the dotted bars. People in these states are less likely than their compatriots to be sleeping in the early morning compared to other people and are more likely to be working (in the US) when the rest of the country is on DST. The opposite occurs in the late evening: they go to sleep earlier and watch less late-evening TV. The failure to "go along" with the majority alters how the small minority of citizens located in areas that don't observe DST spends their time. DST directly affects how we spend time, even in areas that don't use DST.

Some controversy was stirred by a 2000 study of the effects of shifts to and from DST on stock-market returns. It provided evidence that shares of stock on a variety of US stock exchanges yielded sharply lower returns on those weekends when clocks were set back or forward compared to other weekends. The authors attributed their finding to traders and investors having had their sleep disrupted. This seems like a reasonable proposition, but subsequent research covering a much broader set of exchanges world-wide found no such effect.[13] The difference between these studies might be because the initial study was incorrect. An alternative explanation is that investors and automatic trading programs reacted to the unusually low returns and made trades around DST-shift weekends in ways that eliminated the negative returns that had previously existed.

A Dutch time-diary survey was conducted in 1990 over the two weeks that surrounded the switch off Summer Time, allowing examination of what people did with the extra hour that they might have enjoyed on the twenty-five-hour day of the switch compared to the previous, twenty-four-hour Sunday. On average, women who completed time diaries reported using the extra hour almost entirely for additional sleep; that was also true among partnered men. Among single men, though, the biggest use of the extra hour was in sports and socializing.[14]

This extra sleep on the day of the shift back to winter time does not nec-essarily imply a gain in terms of safety or well-being. There is some evidence that children perform better on tests in the week before the shift than in the week after. Taking advantage of the move of the shift to DST from April to March that occurred in the US in 2007, recent evidence also suggests that the earlier shift to DST in the spring resulted in additional traffic fatalities.[15] Data from Germany, though, show that going off Summer Time in the autumn results in more sleep for a few days and in fewer hospital admissions.[16] The artifice of DST affects many outcomes around the time of switches on or off it. The average effects over the year are unclear.

Whether switches to and from DST affect people's happiness is a difficult issue, given how expected and temporary these changes are. Nonetheless, a study based on how attitudes toward life in Germany change around the shift to Summer Time suggests that happiness decreases after the shift, es-pecially among workers.[17] It's not clear that the same thing would happen in the fall or in other countries, but the results are a warning about the overall impact of changing clock times with the seasons.

TIME AND SPACE

Geographic divisions are natural, dictated in many cases by topographic features such as bodies of water or mountains. But often they are the non-natural results of political decisions and externally imposed changes. In both cases they can lead to differences in time use across regions, among cities, and even within metropolitan areas. Some of these differences are expected and form part of our urban mythos, while others may be more surprising. The most important unanswered question is whether these differences have diminished over the past fifty years. While one might expect that interregional differences in how time is spent have decreased with increasing regional interconnectedness, increasing social/income stratification may have caused widening inter-area differences in behavior.

While geographic differences are in some cases natural, time zones and the switching on or off DST are completely artificial—they are human constructs based partly on economic considerations, partly on political whim. Concerns about their effects, both the positive and negative ones, are partly based on economic analyses, but even more so on political beliefs stemming from one's views of the proper roles of government. The history of time zones, especially in the US, illustrates that they change often. With those changes come changes in economic outcomes, including time use, and governmentally imposed changes in clock time will continue to alter how we spend our time.

CHAPTER 10

᭡

The Rich Are Different from You and Me

In his short story "The Snows of Kilimanjaro," Ernest Hemingway commented mockingly on F. Scott Fitzgerald's line that the rich are different, noting, "Yes, they have more money." As Benjamin Franklin wrote, "Time is money."[1] So, one way the rich are different is that their opportunity costs are higher because their time is more valuable. We can't buy a much longer life, although we might use part of our incomes to pay for the medical care that might give us a few more years than others might get. We can't add minutes to the day. But with the same twenty-four hours each day, and possibly more years remaining at any age, the rich do have more opportunities and choices for how they spend their time. Even though the preferences of the rich may be the same as other people's, most people would agree that the rich are better off, having perhaps a bit more time, but much more money.

When we have more money, we can switch from doing things that require relatively little money per hour spent—time-intensive activities—to those that cost relatively more money per hour of time— "goods-intensive" activities. We might satisfy our need for food by switching from buying groceries, cooking a meal that we eat at home, and cleaning up afterward— which is relatively time intensive—to spending less time but more money eating in a restaurant—something that is relatively goods intensive. Both approaches satisfy our needs, but the first takes more time and less money than the second. How often we might switch between activities will depend on how much we enjoy them and on how easy it is to make the switch. But in all cases, we will use any increase in our incomes along with the fixed amount of time, twenty-four hours per day, to make ourselves better off.

The central economic question in time use is how monetary incentives affect the ways that we spend our time—when we can combine our fixed twenty-four hours per day with more purchases. What makes the rich "rich" is the amount of income they can get each year. Part of that income—by far the largest part for adults under age sixty-five—is the extra income that they receive by working more—their earnings. The other part is the income that they receive from other sources—their unearned income. For example, nonworking household members may be retired, receiving pension income; they may have chosen not to work and thus be out of the labor force; or they may be unemployed, looking for work but unable to find a job. All these people, though, have access to income from other sources. And for some of them the additional income may be so much as to make them rich even if they do no paid work.

This nonwork income includes money that represents payments on the wealth accumulated over a lifetime of paid work, such as interest on investments. It also includes pensions and public old-age benefits (Social Security payments in the US) that stem directly from one's lifetime of paid work. Also included are gifts from outside the household and other payments from government. People also have access to their working partner's earnings. Workers too may have access to incomes beyond their own earnings, possibly including income from all these other sources. For purposes of discussion and considering how incentives alter time use, we'll call this second motley group "unearned income," even though it may include one's partner's earnings.

As an example, I receive some earnings for my paid work time—I can sell my time for some wage per hour. I also have access to other parts of our household income, including my wife's and my pension and Social Security payments and some interest and dividends on the bonds and shares of stock that represent our wealth. When my wife was working for pay, I had access to her earnings, just as she had and still has access to mine. If we win the lottery jackpot this coming Wednesday, both my wife and I will have access to the unearned income that is the annual flow of payments from the lottery.

Income from both of these types of sources makes us better off—enhances our opportunities—but the two sources have profoundly different effects on how we choose to spend our time. An increase in the amount of money that I can earn each hour makes work more attractive—and makes nonworking costlier by raising its opportunity cost. Additional unearned income doesn't make work more attractive, but it does mean that I can now buy more things, and fancier things too. But the ability to buy more things creates a problem for me: buying and enjoying things takes time, and even with a rise in my unearned income, I have no more time in which to spend it. The only way to get more time with which to enjoy the extra unearned income and the purchases that it allows me to make is to cut back on the time that I spend at paid work or to outsource some things that I might otherwise have done myself.

The effect of the different incentives created by the ability to earn more per hour compared to having more unearned income was vividly illustrated for me by the behavior of a young colleague of mine. My first full-time teaching job, as a junior faculty member in 1969, paid $11,500 (per year, not per month!). One of the other two colleagues who was also hired in 1969 was the scion of one of the richest families in America. We all had doctorates and faced the same payoff to additional work—including the same rate of pay. And we had the same desire to teach well and publish to become promoted and granted lifetime tenure. The man from the very wealthy family did work hard, but not as hard as the other colleague and I. His huge unearned income was spent partly in buying things that he spent some time enjoying and that took him away from his academic work.

Additional earning power makes working more hours more attractive, leading us to work more. There is an opposite effect, though. When we have the opportunity to earn more per hour, the same time spent working will give us more money to spend, and to spend that money enjoyably will take time away from paid work. What predominates? The first effect, more work because work gives more earnings per hour? Or the second effect, less work because earnings from each hour of paid work are higher? The answer depends on earnings before the increase in earning power, how much paid work we were already doing, our family's other income, how much we might enjoy additional work time or additional nonwork time, and other factors. There is no single answer.

Even if we can't or don't want to work and earn any money, our time is still valuable because we need to choose how to spend and combine it with the other household income that we have access to. Studying the outcomes of those choices requires looking separately at the impacts of higher earning power and higher household incomes coming from other sources on how we spend time.

EARNINGS AND INCOMES IN THE US

To understand how incentives are changed when one's earnings ability or unearned income changes, we need to get a feel for what people's earnings look like, and how total income varies across households. There are lots of simple facts about people's earnings and incomes, readily available from published government-produced data, which are essential background to a discussion of how spending time is affected by monetary incentives. First take total household income, which includes earnings and unearned income. In 2016, households at the ninety-fifth percentile had incomes that were 3.8 times that of the median household—a household at the fiftieth percentile—and their incomes were 16.6 times that of a household at the tenth percentile. Those lowest 10 percent had incomes below $14,000, with the median being $59,000 and the top 5 percent at or above $225,000.

Accounting for inflation, incomes have risen for both lower- and upper-income households over the past forty years, but they have risen especially rapidly at the upper end. In 1979, the ratio of income at the ninety-fifth percentile to the median was only 2.8, and the ratio of income at the ninety-fifth percentile to the tenth percentile only 11.4. Clearly, there has been a substantial rise in income inequality in the US since the 1970s, a fact noted by many observers over the last quarter-century.

Perhaps $225,000 is not really Fitzgerald-level rich. Few people think of themselves as being rich, but the best estimate is that about $500,000 per year puts a household over the line into the top 1 percent of incomes in the US, which should count as being rich. This figure is fascinating gossip, but we can't use it in discussing how the rich might spend their time differently from others, because not enough time diaries in America or anywhere else focus on this narrow a group of households. We do, though, have sufficient information on people in the top 5 percent of households to consider how they spend time differently from other people.

The largest component of household income is earnings from paid work, and we saw that to understand what makes people choose how to spend time, and particularly how much paid work to do, we need to consider the separate effects of earnings compared to unearned income. Today a full-time American worker at the tenth percentile of earners makes a bit more than ten dollars per hour. The median—fiftieth percentile—full-time worker makes about twenty dollars per hour, while a worker at the ninety-fifth percentile of full-timers earns sixty-two dollars per hour, 6.2 times the tenth-percentile worker's earnings and 3.1 times the median worker's earnings. As with total household income, earnings too have become less equal in the US: in 1979, the respective ratios were 4.7 and 2.2.

How differences in earnings and unearned incomes and their variations over time alter the incentives to work more and how they change the mix of nonwork activities are the subjects of much of this chapter. But we can't simply look at how people with different earnings and incomes spend their time, because total earnings themselves depend upon how we spend time—on the number of hours put in. Even the hourly wage varies with the length of the workweek, definitionally for some workers since they receive time-and-a-half for overtime work (beyond forty hours in the US), but for many others too.

To describe how hourly pay affects the amount of paid work performed, we need to find something that has major impacts on the hourly wage—the gain from working one more hour—but that is not related to the number of hours one puts in. We need to find something that results in higher wages but is itself unaffected by work time. That something is education— the amount of schooling that one has obtained. That is true regardless of gender, race, ethnicity, age, and location: differences in education are the biggest single determinant of differences in hourly pay. Because our wage rates—the price of our time—depend on how much we work, using educational attainment to measure earning power is a substitute that avoids confounding hourly earnings and time spent in paid work.

The solid line in Figure 10.1 demonstrates how sharply wages rise with increases in education level. Letting the wage of a high school dropout equal 100, today a college graduate will earn 94 percent more than the high school dropout of the same race, gender, age, and location, and who works the same number of hours per week. Someone with an advanced degree—a

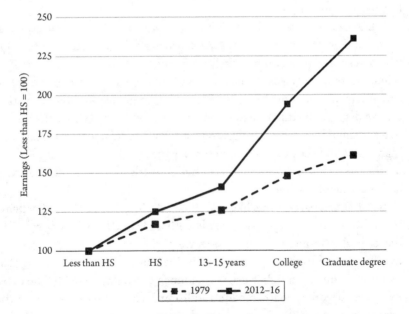

Figure 10.1 Earnings by Education Level, US, 1979 and 2012–2016 (Less than High School = 100)

master's or a doctorate, law degree or MD—earns 136 percent per hour more than an equally hard-working high school dropout of the same age, gender and race/ethnicity.

Similar comparisons for 1979, shown by the dashed line in Figure 10.1, repeat what we saw for incomes and earnings overall: wage dispersion was smaller at that time. Inequality in how well people with different education levels can do economically has risen sharply in the last forty years.[2] Along the dimension of education, America has become more unequal, not because of more inequality in the amount of education people have received, but because of increased inequality in the gains from obtaining more education.[3]

EDUCATION, WAGES, AND THE TWO DIMENSIONS OF PAID WORK

Because education alters earnings and is mostly acquired before people have obtained their full-time jobs and chosen how much to work, we can examine how education alters labor force participation and hours of paid work. The first dimension of paid work—its incidence—is strongly associated with a person's level of education, and since education is a major determinant of wages, it is also closely related the wage one can earn—with the value of one's time.

Whether someone works at all increases with the level of education. In the second decade of the twenty-first century a college graduate is twenty-two percentage points more likely to be working for pay than is a high school dropout of the same age. A person with an advanced degree is five percentage points more likely to be working than a contemporary with a college degree. The differences by education level in the choice of whether to work shouldn't be surprising: more education is strongly associated with higher pay, and the potential of higher pay that accompanies additional education provides an additional incentive to work for pay rather than stay out of the labor market.

In 1979, the pattern was like that of 2012–2016. The likelihood of being in paid work at each age rose steadily with additional education, but with one crucial difference: the increase in the rate of working for pay rose less rapidly with education in 1979 than it does now. Figure 10.1 shows that additional education didn't get you as much extra pay in 1979. The extra incentive to work that accompanies additional education has risen over the past forty years. With the more rapidly increasing incentive to work that accompanies additional education today compared to 1979, more-educated people have become more likely to choose to work for pay now than forty years ago.

The second dimension of paid work is its intensity—the hours (per day, per week, or per year) of employment if working. The question is whether the ability to earn more raises the amount of paid work that one performs, just as the ability to earn more raised the chances of working at all. Combined with the effects on labor force participation, this issue, referred to in economics jargon as the "elasticity of labor supply," is one of the most thoroughly researched topics in the field of economics.[4] Over one thousand academic studies have examined it, studying it at various times, in different economies, and considering many demographic groups. Various scholars have summarized this immense literature over the years. These summaries allow some general conclusions about how people's labor force participation and work hours respond to changes in wage rates—in the incentive to work:

1. If a person works at all, hours of paid work increase as the wage rate per hour increases.
2. This effect is small for adult men and larger but still quite small among adult women, with the difference between genders declining over the last forty years.
3. The effect is larger among teenagers and young adults than people in their prime years, perhaps ages twenty-five to fifty-four.
4. This effect is larger among unskilled people and those with less education than it is among people with more skills and those who have attained more education.

A good rule of thumb is that the paid work time of people who are high earners responds less to increases in the potential to earn more money than that of low earners. Among both men and women, weekly hours of paid work in 2012–2016 rose steadily with the level of education, consistent with the first general result on labor supply. But the difference in weekly hours between the most and least educated men was only 3.4 hours per week, while it was 4.4 hours among women. Incentives to work have bigger impacts among women than among men, consistent with the second general result.

Because the gains from paid work rose more sharply with additional education in the second decade of the twenty-first century than they did forty years ago, we should expect differences in hours of paid work among workers with different educational attainment to be greater in the 2010s. And that is exactly what we observe. Going from the least to the most educated men in 1979, weekly work time increased by only 2.6 hours compared to 3.4 in 2016; among women, the increase was only 3.6 hours, compared to 4.4. These changes over the years illustrate how the increased incentives to work as inequality in the US has risen have resulted in greater differences across groups in the amount of time that people spend in paid work.

Education is the single biggest determinant of wages and earnings, but even accounting for it and all the other personal characteristics that we can observe—age, gender, race/ethnicity, job experience—nearly half of differences in wage rates among workers arise from attributes that are not easily measurable. These include such characteristics as drive, ambition, social skills, and even—in the words of a distinguished economist—"early-birdness." Such fuzzier but important characteristics affect how much we can earn, but examining the direct impact of wages themselves on work time adds to an understanding of the relationship between the value of our time and the amount of paid work that we do.

Looking at the direct impact of wages, we see the same responses as when we examined the effects of the most important determinant of wages, a worker's level of education. Among male workers, going from the tenth to the ninetieth percentile of workers ranked by their hourly pay showed an increase of 7.9 hours per week in 2012–2016. Among women, the same move—from the tenth to the ninetieth percentile—led to an increase of 8.9 weekly hours. The same greater response to higher wages among women than among men existed in 1979. But both responses were smaller then than in 2016, again because the widening inequality of earnings has increased the dispersion of the incentives to work longer hours.

If one partner's earnings increase or if a household's other income rises, the other partner might be less interested in holding a job, both because spending the extra money takes time and because the desire for additional "things" may drop. Among women, who are less likely than men to be doing paid work, this is exactly what we see. Going from a household at the tenth percentile of household income to a household at the ninety-fifth percentile reduces the likelihood that a woman works for pay by about four percentage points. Not a huge decline, but it does show that whether people even do any paid work responds to their family's economic situation, not just their own earnings possibilities. Extra unearned income or additional earnings by one's partner makes one less likely to be working for pay.

Additional unearned income that reduces the likelihood of working also affects work intensity. Even if I could earn more per hour than someone else, if I also win the lottery jackpot or my partner receives a large inheritance I will cut back my work time. Taking only women, a move from the tenth to the ninetieth percentile of household incomes leads a working woman to cut her weekly paid work time by about three hours. Even if a woman has chosen to work, the amount of work that she performs is affected by how much her husband earns and how much unearned income the family receives. The same is true among men, although, as with men's responses along other dimensions of work time to economic incentives, the effect is much smaller than women's.

HOUSEHOLD INCOMES, WAGES, AND THE OTHER FIVE WAYS WE SPEND TIME

Those who do not work for pay—nonworking partners, retirees, nonworking students, the unemployed—face only the one choice: on what nonwork activities to spend their time. Because there are only twenty-four hours in their day—because their time is limited—their time is still valuable, even though they do not earn any money. Every extra minute spent grooming, for example, is one less minute available for watching television, cleaning the house, attending a religious service, or going to a museum. Spending time is always costly, even for people who have no interest in or ability to earn any money. And it is costlier for people with higher unearned incomes—who receive more dividends and interest, more pension income, more money from their governments, or whose spouses earn more. They need to chase around spending the extra money they have access to—they need to spend time spending money.

In the US the average person who performs no work spends twenty-nine hours per week on home production, sixty-five hours sleeping, six hours on other personal care, twenty-seven hours on TV watching, and forty-one hours on other leisure activities. Time spent on each of these activities exceeds that spent by workers: work takes time away from all the other things that people do.

When our household receives additional income, even if we ourselves don't do any paid work, there are clear patterns of how we alter our spending time. The solid bars in Figure 10.2 show how time use differs among American nonworkers with household incomes at the ninety-fifth percentile compared to nonworkers with household incomes at the tenth percentile. A bar above the zero line denotes that nonworkers in the very-high-income households spend more time in the activity; a bar below it shows they perform less of the activity. The impacts account for differences in the ages and education levels of people with low and high incomes, their race and ethnicity, their locations (state, city), their gender, and whether

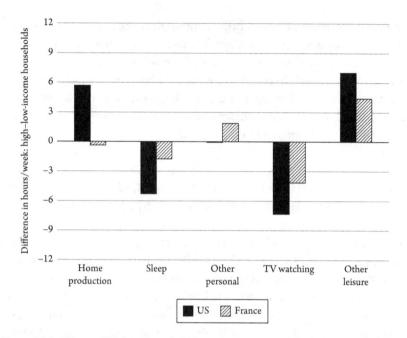

Figure 10.2 Effects of Higher Household Incomes on Nonworkers' Time Use, US 2003–2015, France 2009–2010, Hours per Week

they have young children in the home. The differences result solely from the fact that nonworkers in low-income households have lots of time and very little income, while those in high-income households have the same amount of time but access to lots of income to spread over their limited time.

In the US the very well-to-do who do not work for pay sleep less and watch much less television each week than their fellow nonworkers whose household incomes are very low. They spend much more time on other lei-sure activities and home production. Both groups spend the exact same amount of time on other personal care. The effects are not so pronounced in France, shown by the striped bars in Figure 10.2, but they are generally in the same direction. French nonworkers in high-income households sleep less and watch less TV than French nonworkers in low-income households, but they spend more time on other leisure activities. The differences be-tween the ways that French citizens in high- and low-income households spend their time are less than those in the United States. Those smaller impacts result from the smaller percentage differences in incomes between those households in France than in the US: with smaller income differences, the incentives to alter the ways that time is spent are lessened.

Sleep takes a lot of time but very little money. Even for a poor house-hold the total yearly expenditure related to sleep is a small fraction of its income, especially compared to the time spent sleeping, which amounts to more than one-third of each week. TV watching also doesn't cost much money per minute spent. With these two activities being the most time intensive and least goods intensive, it makes sense that people shift away from these uses of time when they have more money to spread over their 168-hour week.[5]

All of this is only about increases in household incomes that arise when other household members are earning more or when the nonworker receives more income from his or her wealth, such as stocks, bonds, and real estate, or payments from a government or rich relatives. But most adult Americans do work for pay, and it is likely that an increase in the opportunity cost of one's time—related to the wage rate one can earn—will affect how one spends time when not working.

That such affects occur was made abundantly clear to me by comparing how my wife and I spent our vacation in summer 1968, when I was just starting my economics career, and in 1988, when I was approaching the peak of my career and she was starting her legal career. In each case we took the usual, pathetically short American one-week vacation. In 1968 we spent the week camping, traveling by car between Boston and Nova Scotia, sleeping in a tent, and cooking over a Coleman stove. In 1988 we flew to Paris and spent the week driving around Normandy and the Loire Valley, staying in decent hotels and eating dinners in Michelin-starred restaurants. We added to our enjoyment, compared to 1968, by undertaking a much more goods-intensive vacation than we had when we were younger (and had much lower capacities to earn money). We could have chosen the camping week in 1988, but we didn't; that we chose the French vacation implies that we viewed it as more desirable. We were better off—but we were chasing around more, cramming more spending into the same amount of time.

We already saw that higher wage rates induce people to work more hours and to increase their labor force participation—the elasticity of labor supply is positive. The time spent on the other major uses of time must drop if people work more—there are only twenty-four hours a day. A headline in the *New York Times* of August 1, 1989, describing some early sleep research that a coauthor and I produced, blared, "Sleep? Why? There's No Money in It."[6] That research showed that an American male whose wage was twice the average slept twenty minutes less per night than a man whose wage was half the average. In the US in the early twenty-first century, going from someone whose earnings are at the tenth percentile among workers to someone whose earnings put him at the ninetieth percentile reduces sleep time by about fourteen minutes on a typical night—close to two hours less over an entire week, and a hundred hours less over an entire year. Sleep—people's number one activity—is costly.

When one's pay per hour increases one also cuts back on TV watching, just as nonworkers do when their household's income increases. Reducing TV watching and sleeping is the main way that higher-wage workers economize on time when the chance to earn more induces them to work more hours in the day. They also cut back on time spent on other leisure activities, but nowhere nearly as much as on sleep and television. Home production and grooming hardly decrease at all when the incentive of higher pay induces people to do more paid work.

The differences in spending time that result from increases in earning power or other sources of household income demonstrate that all nonwork time is not the same. The time spent on those activities that are most enjoyed when money is spent along with them—those that are most goods intensive—increases with higher unearned incomes and greater earnings ability relative to the time spent on activities that take a lot of time but little money per hour. With a higher hourly wage—the chance to earn more money by working more—we usually increase our work time, but in the remaining, reduced nonwork time, we spend our increased earnings or increased unearned incomes on things like expensive vacations, as my wife and I did in 1988, or on tickets to the Super Bowl or the opera. We also cut back on our sleeping, TV watching, and other time-intensive activities.

THE TOP 5 PERCENT—AND THE REST OF US

The effects of higher wage rates and household incomes exist even after we account for the many other differences among people that cause them to use time differently, such things as gender, marital status, having young children at home, age, race, and ethnicity. But that is not the same as answering the simple question of whether Hemingway was correct in stating that the rich merely have more money than the rest of us. And how people with different incomes, whatever the sources of income or their demographic characteristics, spend their time is both intellectually and pruriently interesting.

The differences in time use of all individuals in the top 5 percent of households in the US ranked by household income compared to that of the other 95 percent are presented in Figure 10.3. The solid bars show the additional (if above the zero line) or the lesser (if below) amount of time spent by the top income group compared to their less wealthy compatriots. The striped bars do the same for France. Clearly, today's rich are different from

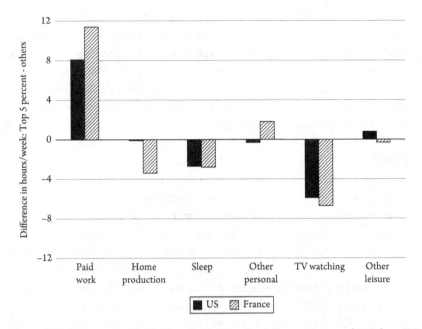

Figure 10.3 Difference in Weekly Hours by Activity, Top 5 Percent Compared to Others, US 2003–2015, France 2009–2010

the rest of us, and not just in having more money (*pace* Hemingway). They work more and make up for the additional time spent in paid work by cutting back on sleeping and especially on TV watching. Yes, the rich are different in how they use time, but they are different because their ability to earn more per hour leads them to work more than others and to do things outside work that allow them to economize on their scarce time while enabling them to spend their high incomes.

Further evidence for these tradeoffs is apparent by looking at attorneys, medical doctors, and college and university professors with doctorates. These professions are at the top of the educational ladder in the US. Each requires at least three years of schooling beyond college/university. Americans with advanced degrees earn 20 percent more than those with "only" a college degree. Doctors, attorneys, and professors even earn substantially more than other Americans who have more than a bachelor's degree. Bill Gates, a college dropout, earns much more than Americans with a doctorate, but on average people in these occupations are among the elites in the American labor market.

These elites, like other high earners, spend more of their time in paid work than other workers. Professors work six hours more each week than the average American worker, doctors ten hours more, and attorneys three hours more. Because of the limited time each week, these elites necessarily cut back on other activities, and the main thing they cut back on is TV watching. The average professor, doctor, or attorney watches only ten hours each week, far less than the sixteen hours that other American workers spend weekly watching television. Among professors this cutback exactly offsets the extra time that they spend working for pay, and for doctors it accounts for over half their additional working hours. Attorneys too watch less TV than the average American worker, only 13.4 weekly hours, and the decline from the average accounts for most of their extra work time.

Professionals in these three occupations all work a lot. But there are some remarkable differences between professors and members of the other two occupations. Professors perform much of their weekly work on weekends, around 12 percent (compared to the 28 percent they would do if they worked the same amount on weekend days as on weekdays). Doctors do a slightly smaller percentage of their total work on weekends, and attorneys do much less. These differences result from the nature of the work in each occupation. I can prepare and review lectures at any time and in any place, and I can do most of my research when and where the mood strikes me. A doctor typically sees patients only on weekdays, although hospital work is performed every day. An attorney can do some work at home, but appearing in court and seeing clients are typically weekday activities.

This nearly unique characteristic of the academic life—its temporal variety—is to me and many other academics one of its many attractions, perhaps the main one of which is not really having a "boss." Flexibility, the feeling of being free within some limits to do what one wants when one wants, is a characteristic of the job that makes it special. Whether every worker with an advanced degree, or workers generally, could flourish with such freedom is unclear, but those who choose this line of work are very much aware of this job characteristic.

Doctors and attorneys perform nearly one-fourth of their paid work over the three US summer months—June, July, and August. That is close to what we would see if people in those occupations worked the same amount each summer week as in other weeks. That's not true among university professors: they perform substantially less than one-quarter of their annual work time during the summer months.

The academic life generates more variability in work timing across the year than does work in other professions. This too makes this occupation more attractive than working in the other elite occupations. It allows more time to take vacations with the family when the weather is nice and when children are available to travel because their own schools aren't in session. Having chosen this profession, I'm obviously prejudiced, but I would paraphrase the Waylon Jennings/Willie Nelson song, "Let 'em grow up to be professors, and maybe also doctors and lawyers and such."[7] That professors earn less per hour of paid work than attorneys or doctors suggests that people generally are willing to pay—to give up some income—to enjoy the flexibility and freedom that the academic work life provides.[8]

VARIETY, ROUTINE, AND TIMING—WHO GETS THE "SPICE OF LIFE"?

If variety is "the spice of life," a good question is who gets to enjoy the spice, high- or low-income people. One definition of "variety" is "the quality or state of having different forms or types."[9] Here I'll use "variety" to mean doing more different things over a day, a week, a year, or a lifetime, and I'll define "routine" as having a less variable schedule from day to day when one is not working.

Increases in household income might lead people to alter the variety of activities that they undertake—the number of different things that they do with their time. Switching activities takes time and thought. We can think of time spent switching among activities as a fixed cost, something that we must do on a one-shot basis when we change from doing one thing to doing another. The cost might be time spent traveling between activities, or it might just be the time taken to think about what to do next. And we must incur this cost even if we plan to spend only a little bit of time in the activity that we might switch to.

Among people with higher incomes the fixed costs of switching activities might be less of an obstacle. Even with the same education, high-income people can afford the costs of switching. Although they spend more time than others in the single activity of paid work, in their reduced amount of nonwork time, more educated people do so many more different things than other people that in total they enjoy more variety. Using sets of time diaries for Australia, Israel, and Germany from the 1990s, one study showed that on average men in the top third of the distribution of educational attainment engaged in about 10 percent more different activities than men in the lowest third. Among women the differences were even larger, about 20 percent. With additional education leading to higher earnings and thus higher household incomes, this study demonstrated that high-income people do more different things than other people.[10]

Thanks to the larger, more recent time-diary surveys, we can consider how the variety of activities that people undertake is directly related to household incomes—how variety differs between households in the top

5 percent of income-receiving households and others. Even though people in those households spend more time in the single activity of paid work, and have less time outside paid work, on average in both the US and France they are engaged in about 5 percent more different non-work activities than people in other households.

Nonroutine behavior—having more temporal variety across days—rises with household income for the same reason, that is, the greater ease of altering schedules that leads people with higher incomes to enjoy a more variable schedule outside the workplace. Define "routine" across a pair of days as the fraction of time during which the exact same activity is performed at that same time on both days. Differences in this fraction based on data from the late 1990s for Australia, Germany, the Netherlands, and the US show that people in the top third of the distribution of education—who on average are in higher-income households—enjoy less temporally routine schedules than those in the middle third.[11] And people in the middle third have less temporally routine schedules than those in the bottom third. These differences exist even if we account for the fact that more educated people work more. They more than make up for their schedules of paid work by behaving much less routinely when not working for pay.

Work that is performed at unenjoyable times—nights and weekends—also disrupts the ability to maintain a desirable nonwork schedule and so pays a small premium over work at "standard" times. Workers who will be attracted to this extra pay are those who most feel that they need the extra income. That suggests that low-wage individuals, minorities, the less educated, and the young are more likely to be doing more of their paid work at these times. In the US in 2003–2015, workers in households in the top 5 percent of household incomes did only 9 percent of their weekly work on weekends; workers in less well-off households performed 11 percent of their total work on weekends. The same is true in the evening and at night: in the US such work is done disproportionately by low-skilled, young, and minority workers.

The widening of wage differences in the US over the last forty years suggests that we would expect to see an increased fraction of evening and night work being performed by workers whose hourly pay has risen least, those at the bottom of the pay distribution. Work at the fringes of the regular workday has indeed become increasingly the province of low-wage, less-skilled workers.[12] We have a stereotype of the high-paid financier working all night. No doubt some do, but night work is unenjoyable work and is performed disproportionately and increasingly by low-wage workers—the cleaning staff and food-deliverers, for example—not by financiers.

THE RICH HAVE IT EASY

The central theme of this chapter can be summarized by replacing "king" in Tom Petty's song "It's Good to Be King" with "rich," "educated," or "high skilled." It is true that the rich work longer hours and put in longer workweeks and work years than other people. They give up time in some activities, especially those like sleeping and television watching that take a lot of time and relatively little money. Instead, they enjoy leisure activities that are goods rather than time intensive. They spend their nonwork time in more different activities than other people, and they enjoy less routine schedules in how they spend time across the days.

The choices that high earners make are understandable results of the greater opportunity cost of their time, arising from the higher earnings that they can obtain and the incentives that those earnings provide them to do more paid work. The time of high earners is more valuable than that of people who have less capacity to earn by doing paid work. What is remarkable is that the time of people who have not worked and may never work—of nonworking spouses, of the unemployed, and of retirees—is also valuable. It is valuable because everyone has a choice of how to spend time, and those choices are more varied among people whose household incomes are higher, even if they contribute no funds to the family's exchequer.

All the ways that the rich spend their time differently from the rest of us are the results of their own free choices. Nobody forces a college graduate, a doctor, an attorney, or a professor to do more paid work than other people. Nobody forces their nonworking partners to sleep less or watch less television. Their choices about time are their own. And they choose to enjoy more different things, to have a more temporally varied life, and to work at more pleasant times of the day and week. These are enjoyable characteristics of life that accrue disproportionately to the economically well-off. It is "good to be king," and in Western society, especially in the US with its relatively high and increased income inequality, the rich and the well educated are nearly kings—and queens.

CHAPTER 11

ᴑᐧᴑ

Kvetching about Time

K vetch, a Yiddish word now widely used in English, means "to complain or gripe habitually." And a favorite complaint is that someone is stressed for time. One definition of stress is "a state of mental or emotional strain or tension resulting from adverse or very demanding circumstances."[1] It wouldn't seem that having only twenty-four hours in a day is an "adverse or very demanding" circumstance: it is a situation that every human being has always faced, just as we have faced the same oxygen content in the air we breathe. We don't find the air's oxygen content to be stressful and don't complain about limited air, unless we are at high altitude, deep-sea diving, or suffering from lung disease. Yet many of us find the limit of twenty-four hours in the day to be stressful. We feel stressed for time, rushed, harried, and hassled by what we perceive as a lack of time. We complain about the limitations on the hours in the day—we *kvetch* about time. We Americans seem to view kvetching as our national pastime. And complaining about time—feeling that we are "time-poor," even though we all enjoy the same amount of time—is a manifestation of our national pastime.

The reason for the kvetching about time is that there are things that we would enjoy doing if we had more time but that we can't currently do. For some of us the additional time might not make much difference—we're already doing everything we want to do in our limited time and with our limited incomes. For others—probably most of us—if we had more time, we would be able to spend it and our incomes in more satisfactory ways. That is especially likely to be true among people who are doing more different things and often rushing to complete each one. Having more time would relieve them from having to shoehorn their substantial income into the same limited time that is available to others who have less income.

The notion that the limited amount of time might create more pressure on those who have greater incomes gives a hint about whom we can expect to do the most kvetching: it is those people who have the highest incomes. High-paid workers have less time for nonwork activities than lower-paid workers, so they must crowd their higher earnings, which allow them to buy more things, into fewer hours of nonwork time during a week. But even nonworkers—retirees, nonworking partners of workers, nonworking students, and the unemployed—might be expected to kvetch more if their household incomes are higher, because they have more things to spend their money on than lower-income nonworkers but have the same twenty-four hours per day to spend it in. Even children might be stressed for time if their household incomes are higher. A Tom Cheney cartoon illustrated this for two eight-year-old boys, one of whom is kvetching, "So many toys—so little unstructured time."[2]

The apparent choice in life is to feel time-poor and income-rich, to be pressured for time but not for money, or to feel financial pressure but little time pressure. In the early 2000s, I applied for a grant from a foundation to work on time-stress. The social psychologists who were the foundation's program officers were terribly concerned about time pressure among well-off families. I thought: Tough; if you want to avoid feeling time pressure, take a job that pays only half your current earnings per hour of work. Or if you don't work for pay, donate half your unearned income to charity. You'll feel less time pressure, but you'll feel burdened by more financial pressure. I would be very happy to wager that most people would choose to feel time-poor rather than income-poor, and that is the choice that we make either explicitly or, more usually, implicitly and by default.

WHICH ACTIVITIES ARE STRESSFUL?

Before looking at the implications of the theory of kvetching in more detail, some background information showing differences in time-stress by gender, by the presence of children, and—most important—by the kinds of activities that we do, is helpful. Because American time-diary surveys contain no information on complaining about time, I use non-US and some other American data to examine some of these ideas. For France, Germany, and the UK, information on kvetching about time is available from the same people who provided time diaries.

An hour of paid work takes the same sixty minutes as an hour of sleep or an hour of home production, including cooking, cleaning, taking care of kids, and other activities. It also takes the same sixty minutes as going to a museum or listening to about one-half of *Hamilton*. You might then think that whether you spend an hour in one activity or another, you won't feel differently stressed for time. An old song went, "A dollar is a dollar most any old time."[3] The question is whether the phrase's analog, An hour is an hour most any old time, is correct.

The answer is a resounding no. Even though an hour in one activity has the same opportunity cost as an hour spent in another activity, people find spending an hour in some activities more stressful than an hour spent in others. The French survey asked people to rate whether they "feel pressed for time" on a 5-to-1 scale, and the German survey similarly asked if the person was "frequently under time pressure," also rating feelings on a 5-to-1 scale. The UK survey just asked whether the person "felt rushed."[4] Because its question was phrased differently from the French and German questions, and because 21 percent of the UK residents in the survey said that they felt rushed, I treat the French and German data similarly and include as "stressed" only those who say they are very pressed for time. This gave 23 percent "very stressed" in France, 16 percent in Germany.

Perhaps not surprisingly, any switch that increases time away from work reduces stress. This is apparent in Figure 11.1, which shows that making the switch away from paid work to another activity reduces the likelihood

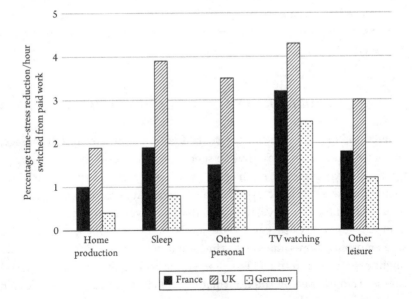

Figure 11.1 Percentage Cut in the Likelihood of Being Very Stressed When One Hour of Paid Work Is Switched to Another Activity, France 2009–2010, UK 2014–2015, Germany 2012–2013

that one feels rushed for time in all three countries. The solid bars measure reductions in the chance of being very stressed for time in France, the striped bars for the UK, and the dotted bars for Germany. In all, a switch from working for pay to TV watching is the biggest reducer of time-stress. Sleep is a close second in France and the UK, and in Germany switching from work to sleep also reduces time-stress. Performing one less hour of paid work and one more hour of home production generates the smallest reduction in time-stress in all three countries, with switches to other leisure and other personal care activities producing midsize reductions in time-stress.

Paid work is the most stressful activity in France, the UK, and Germany, and the effects are strikingly similar in these three countries. They account for differences in gender, marital status, region, and the presence of children of different ages. If we had the data to examine time-stress among people who completed time diaries, we would probably see the same effects in the US. Perhaps Eugene O'Neill was correct, "You can't be too careful about work. It's the most dangerous habit known to medical science."[5]

Some activities are more pleasurable than others; some generate more or lesser feelings of time-stress. The implications of the statistics depicted in Figure 11.1 can be described similarly to the simple description of the theory of relativity attributed to Einstein, "If you're sitting with a girl you love for two hours you think it's only one minute; but if you're sitting on a hot stove for one minute you think it's two hours. That's relativity."[6] Not all the ways that we spend an hour of time leave us feeling equally stressed for time.

GENDER, HEALTH, AND TIME-KVETCHING

Women and men have the same twenty-four hours in the day. On average, though, women have more time to spend over their lives. In the US today, female life expectancy at birth exceeds male life expectancy by nearly five years, and even at age forty-five the average American woman can expect to live nearly four years longer than the average forty-five-year-old man. The differences by gender are similar in other rich countries.[7] With women having more time—with time seemingly less scarce for them—we might expect women to feel less pressed for time than men. This expectation is strengthened by the information in Figure 11.1. After all, women do less paid work than men, and since paid work is the most stressful activity among the major uses of time in people's lives, women's lesser time performing paid work should lead us to expect that they will feel less stressed for time than men.[8]

This reasonable expectation is contradicted by data describing the US, Australia, and Germany in the early 2000s. Women were more likely than men in the same country to report that they are very stressed about time. They were also less likely to report that they are rarely or never stressed for time. These differences are not artifacts of something unusual that might have been occurring in the early 2000s in these countries. In the 2009–2010 French time-diary data, 24 percent of women but only 22 percent of men reported themselves as always being rushed for time. The comparable percentages in 2012–2013 in Germany were 18 and 14 percent; in 2014–2015 in the UK, they were 23 and 19 percent.

This conclusion does not change if we adjust for differences in where women and men live, their ages and education levels, and even the number of young children in their households. No matter how one cuts the data, then and now in each of several rich countries women who have the same demographic characteristics as men (except, obviously, gender) are more likely to say that they are stressed for time. The gender difference remains quite large when we compare women and men who spend the same amounts of time in paid work, home production, personal care, or leisure. Time-stress is particularly a woman's issue.

With this finding, the crucial question is why women are more stressed for time than men, even when they spend their time doing the exact same things. One reason might be something arising from women's doing more different things each day. It takes time to switch between activities, and women do more different activities—for example, in 2009–2010 in France, 5 percent more than men. This difference means that women incur greater costs because of the additional time that they spend switching activities and thinking about what to do next. In a real sense, that cost means women have less time at their disposal each day than men.

A more likely related possibility, but one that is difficult to prove, is that women are household managers, responsible for juggling more balls in the air each day. When our kids were little it was my wife more than me who rearranged her schedule to stay home with them if they were sick and had to miss school, or when there was a teacher-training day. And that was with a husband who was a professor, an occupation with a very flexible work schedule. In families where both partners work rigid schedules, the burden on wives of juggling household activities is often even heavier.

There is another related explanation that is independent of marital status and the division of the responsibilities for managing childcare. We saw that leisure activities, including TV watching, produce much less time-stress than other activities (except sleep). An Australian study showed that women's leisure is more likely to be simultaneous with nonleisure activities than men's, thus less likely to be pure leisure.[9] Consistent with women juggling activities, their leisure time is more likely to involve multitasking—doing other things simultaneously—which will make them feel more stressed for time.

All these explanations make sense. They suggest that women are more stressed for time than men because they do more different things, do more things at the same time, and feel responsible for the household, regardless of whether there are children to be managed and different activities to be undertaken and planned. This is "merely" a matter of feeling, but the feelings are strikingly different between men and women, and they do not arise from gender differences in how time is spent, how much is earned, or from any other economic factors. They appear to be inherent in Western societies regardless of any other differences between men and women.

Bad or even only fair health makes one less likely to be working, and it is associated with more TV watching. While doing less paid work reduces time-stress for the average person, the unhealthy person finds it more challenging to accomplish almost all activities other than the most sedentary, such as sleeping and TV watching. Home production is more difficult—it takes more time to shop, prepare food, or clean up if you are in bad health. Other leisure activities are also more difficult or even impossible, with some forms of exercising being obvious examples. If the unhealthy person is doing paid work, in many occupations work time is also more difficult. These greater challenges mean that the person whose health is poor essentially has less time to accomplish the same things that a very healthy person can. People coping with health problems will be more pressed for time because time is effectively scarcer for them.

In US data, people who said that their health was fair or poor were ten percentage points more likely to report being always or almost always stressed for time than healthy people of the same age, education, marital status, and so on. In French data, the 22 percent of people who report themselves as very healthy are nine percentage points less likely than others to say that they are stressed for time. Being in fair or poor health increases time-stress by as much as would switching four hours each day of sleeping to the activity that creates the most time-stress—paid work. One way of thinking about this fact is to infer that the unhealthy person really has only twenty hours in a day compared to the healthy person's twenty-four.

It's not just one's own health that determines time-stress—one's partner's health matters too. In Australian, German, and American data, people with an unhealthy partner who are doing the same amount of paid work and have the same demographic characteristics as others with a healthy partner report being more stressed for time. Their partner's time-stress spills over onto them, perhaps because caring for the partner is inherently stressful, perhaps just because of shared feelings. The same data also show that partners' feelings about time are generally shared: if your partner is more stressed for time, you are more likely to say you are stressed for time too.

Having a physical disability can make accomplishing many daily activities very time consuming, so that individuals with disabilities effectively have less time at their disposal. A Spanish study done in 2010 shows that the more severe the disability, the greater the feeling that time is scarce. Adjusting for differences in time spent on paid work, home production, and leisure activities, those Spaniards with severe disabilities reported being much more stressed for time than other people. Those with moderate disabilities were less stressed, but more stressed than those who had no disability.[10] There's a trite saying, that "when you've got your health, you've got everything." Having your health may not give you "everything," but when you've got your health, you do feel that you have more time in the day.

"INSANITY IS HEREDITARY. YOU CAN GET IT FROM YOUR CHILDREN."

Our children are not the cause of any insane behavior that my wife or I may exhibit—they are our biggest source of pride and our biggest achievements in our seventy-five years of life.[11] But the stress that they produced—our worries about them, whether or not these were based in reality—took up our time and occasionally still does. Children's roles in making us feel more stressed for time, the possibility that parents feel more time pressure when a child enters the family, and thinking about whether feelings of time pressure differ between mothers and fathers add another time dimension to the role of children in households.[12]

When she had two preschool children and a large house, my daughter-in-law kvetched, "With the kids and the house, I often feel that I have four hours of tasks and only two hours to do them in."[13] One study looked at Australians' feelings of time-stress, on a 5-to-1 scale, with 5 being most stressed, examining both husbands' and wives' feelings in the four years before and after the birth of a child. Figure 11.2 shows the patterns of time-stress for each spouse over this period, from four years before the birth to four years after. The solid line is for fathers, the dashed line for

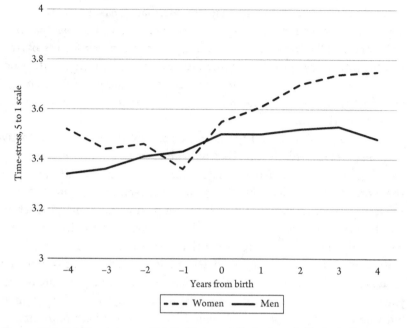

Figure 11.2 Relation between Child's Birth and Father's and Mother's Time Stress, Australia, 2001–2011.
Source: Adapted from Hielke Buddelmeyer, Daniel Hamermesh, and Mark Wooden, "The Stress Cost of Children on Moms and Dads," *European Economic Review* (2018), Figure 1.

mothers. The increase in mothers' feelings of time-stress after a birth is three times greater than the increase in fathers' time-stress, and it stays greater for at least four years after the child is born. The same figure based on German data shows a similarly larger rise in time-stress among mothers than fathers after a child is born.

In the year before the future mother gives birth she seems much less time-stressed than in previous years. In this era of controlled fertility this decrease in stress itself might lead future parents to have a child. Mothers, currently perceiving an absence of time-stress, may wish to have a child and decide with their partners that having the kid is a good decision, even with the additional time-stress that the child will eventually create.[14]

Children increase mothers' time-stress more than fathers', and that is not because mothers perform the majority of childcare. The lines in the figure account for differences in time spent in childcare and paid work, in age, education, and other characteristics. The difference in time-stress may stem from mothers' "managerial role" in the household and the burden a child adds to that role. There is also some evidence (in Germany) that young children, even ones who are long past being breastfed, disrupt parents' sleep patterns, especially mothers', which reduces their feelings of well-being (and presumably increases their time-stress).[15] This evidence should not surprise anyone who has been awakened at 3:00 a.m. by a screaming child.

The additional time-stress that mothers feel doesn't stem from the child being the firstborn or being one of many, as the increase in time-stress that accompanies the birth of a child is about the same for a first child as for a fourth or fifth. The old woman of nursery-rhyme fame "who lived in a shoe" may have had so many children that "she didn't know what to do," but each extra child added no more to her stress than any other kid living in the shoe with her.[16]

The data don't allow examining how long the extra time-stress persists or whether it ever dissipates—we can't examine parents' time-stress over the entire span between the child's birth and its entry into adulthood. But we can compare time-stress of other parents from the four years before to the four years after a child leaves the household. A figure like Figure 11.2 for Australia that looks at mothers' and fathers' time-stress through the years around a kid's departure—around the time that the parents become "empty-nesters"—looks much different. There is no abrupt drop in time-stress when the child leaves the household. Instead, both parents' time-stress drops steadily over these years. And the decline is not very large, far less than the increase felt by the mother after the child is born. The time-stress that a new child causes parents, and especially the mother, never totally disappears.

IS IT TOUGH TO BE RICH?

I doubt that most people would answer yes to this question. I certainly wouldn't. The amount that you can earn, and the other income brought into your household through a partner's earnings, through inheritances, interest, and other types of unearned income—will make you more stressed for time because you have more things to buy or do in your limited time. These effects suggest that being rich might be tough.[17] Among workers in the US, Australia, and Germany in the early 2000s, those people who were always or often stressed had the highest earnings. The sometimes stressed were next in income level; earnings among the rarely stressed were lower still; and earnings were lowest among the never stressed. Those who earn more per hour are more stressed for time.

Maybe high-earners' extra time-stress results from their spending more time doing paid work each week. In the recent French, German, and British time-diary data, adjusting for such demographic differences as marital status, age, location, and the presence of children of different ages, those workers who earned more per hour in the same length workweek were more likely to report being very stressed for time. High-wage people do more paid work than others, giving them less time in which to enjoy their extra income. But the extra amount that they can earn each hour adds further to their time-stress by enhancing the higher incomes that they then try to spend during their fewer nonworking hours.

That it is one's extra income itself, not only how one spends one's time, that alters time-stress can be seen by comparisons among nonworkers whose household incomes differ. These people are earning nothing, spending no part of their week working—they have twenty-four hours daily to enjoy the unearned income that they have access to. But even for them, the French data show that being in a household at the ninetieth percentile of the income distribution makes one 15 percent more likely to feel stressed for time than a person of the same age, education, and geographic location who resides in a household that is only at the tenth percentile of income. Those with more unearned income have more choices to make and more things to do in their limited time, and that makes them feel rushed.

This discussion might lead us to answer yes to this section's titular question. But what's causing the time-stress is the "need" to stuff a lot of additional spending into just twenty-four hours. Not having the wherewithal—the need—to spend more money would solve one's problem of time-stress, but it would create the opposite problem: feelings of financial stress. Surveys that ask people how stressed they are for income give results for both men and women, for all countries where they have been used, that are exactly opposite those on time-stress. Not surprisingly, higher earners are less stressed for income than lower earners, and even among nonworkers, people with higher household incomes feel less financial pressure than nonworkers in low-income households.

MAN IS BORN CRYING, LIVES COMPLAINING, AND DIES DISAPPOINTED[18]

Kvetching about time is ubiquitous in Western societies. In the US, it is often a signal of one's importance—if we can show that we are stressed for time and complain about that stress, others might view us as busy, very important people. If we judge importance by one's earnings or wealth, then the extra kvetching about time that economically well-off people do compared to others does reflect their economic advantages. Being stressed for time goes with the turf of being rich and/or a high earner. Cross-country studies comparing kvetching about time in wealthy Western nations to kvetching in poorer countries haven't been done, but I expect that in developing countries, where earnings and unearned incomes are lower, there would be much less griping about time and much more about incomes.

We can't always get what we want, and with little more time and much more income than our grandparents, spending our money, which takes time, makes us feel time-poorer than our grandparents. Mick Jagger also sang, "You get what you need." Even though he studied at the London School of Economics, Mick was wrong: we need more time, but we're not going to get it. So why kvetch about it?

CHAPTER 12

✧

Do We Have More Time Now?
Will We Get More Time?

It's true that we only have twenty-four hours in each of the 365 days of the year. It's also true that our incomes have grown much more rapidly than the expected lengths of our lives. Together, the small rise in longevity and the remarkably large rise in our incomes have made us better off—they have expanded the choices available to us, although they have increased the relative scarcity of time facing us. But perhaps other changes have freed up time for us, offsetting the limits on our time and the large relative increase in our incomes. Depending on the nature of the changes that give us more time, how we spend them—how we divide the extra time up among such uses as home production, sleep, grooming, and other activities—will differ. Each of us must choose how to spend any time gifts that we receive.

Some extra time is available very temporarily and unexpectedly when a planned activity doesn't materialize, such as when a work assignment gets canceled or a sporting event for which you had tickets is postponed. The several hours that are freed up must be reallocated on very short notice to other activities—one way or another, the time is going to be used. Even if we spend the freed-up time lying on the couch and staring at the ceiling, we have implicitly chosen how to spend it (in an activity classifiable as pure leisure).

Less temporary but usually unexpected is a spell of unemployment, for example, a layoff or an entire plant closing. In both cases, people are suddenly out of work and have time that must be spent on some nonwork activities. They are surely worse off—people are unlikely to have chosen to become unemployed, but they do have more time in which to spend their (reduced) income. With less money, they must choose how to spend this freed-up time, knowing that the time gift is not something that was wanted, and believing or at least hoping that the extra time will only be temporary.

Extra time could also be permanent. A worker or even all workers might find that employers just don't want them to work as many hours per week, or weeks per year, as before. Incentives that alter employers' choices about how many hours to require each employee to work might have changed. Perhaps technology might advance so much that people could obtain all the goods and services they might possibly desire while working many fewer hours per week. More likely, at least in the foreseeable future, and in some cases in the recent past, government might increase penalties on employers who require their employees to put in long work hours, leading to more free time for those workers as their employers decide not to work them so hard. In all these cases, the extra time must be spent on something.

Time can be and has been permanently freed up by improvements in the technology that we use in home production; automatic clothes washers and dryers, robot vacuum cleaners, power lawn mowers, microwave ovens, and other devices are standard examples. Technology has even made more efficient use of our leisure time possible. Exercise machines are a good example: one company advertises that its machine provides a complete workout in only fourteen minutes.[1] We could use this more efficient production of home activities and leisure to spend more time working for pay, or we could switch to other nonwork activities. These nonwork time gifts also give us more choice and require us to decide how to spend the time.

Understanding the impacts of all these examples of extra time requires knowing how much time each frees up. With that information we'll know whether the changes in our discretionary time have been sufficient to overcome the pressure to spend the increases in our incomes in the limited time that we have—whether the growth in opportunities produced by our higher incomes has been matched by growth in the time available in which to spend those incomes. We can also discover how people choose to spend the additional time that they have obtained, and that information would be a good guide for speculation about what people would do with any increases in extra time that might occur in the future.

"'TIS THE GIFT TO BE FREE"?

The simplest time gift is a sudden, temporary, brief, and unexpected cancellation of a commitment. In my work a meeting is canceled at the last minute; an ice storm shuts down the university, leading to classes being called off; or, as so commonly happens, a student fails to show up for an appointment. Unplanned shocks to planned home production might also occur: stores will shut down during a storm, canceling a shopping trip; or the dog might get his "business" done more rapidly than expected, leaving extra time after the dog walk. A fire engine siren screaming down the street might wake us up an hour earlier; there might be no hot water for a planned shower. These events free up time that we expected to spend in personal activities, sleep, and grooming; they're time gifts in personal care. A rained-out baseball game yields a time gift in leisure.

Some of these time gifts, particularly those resulting from freed-up work time, might make us better off, because we feel our income will remain unchanged while we now have additional time to spend on more enjoyable activities. These examples are gifts that are "a joy to be free." Others leave us worse off: we had planned to do something enjoyable—maybe going to a concert—and now our plans have gone awry. In these cases, it isn't a gift to be free. Regardless of whether the time gift is desired or not, common to all these temporary unexpected changes—these disruptions to our planned activities—is the need to decide how to spend the extra time.

There is no information on how people choose to spend unexpected temporary time gifts—no survey of time use compares what people had planned to do with what they actually do. We can only speculate, but the common behavior that I've shown throughout suggests some answers. The residual activities—what we do when we have nothing else to do—are TV watching and sleeping. Other leisure activities are also undertaken, as perhaps are some short-term home-production activities that might be accomplished in a less hurried fashion than otherwise—cooking dinner, for example. Unexpected time gifts are likely to be enjoyed, or at least spent, in the nonwork activities that we typically enjoy doing—the things that reduce our time stress the most—leisure and personal care.

TEMPORARY LONG-LASTING "GIFTS"

In the US we classify people as unemployed if they have made an explicit effort to look for work in the past four weeks but have not found a job or have not started one that they have already found. Similar definitions underlie statistics on unemployment around the world. An unemployed person is someone who would rather be spending some time working for pay than doing something else—engaging in home production, personal care, or leisure activities. In terms of measuring what the economy is producing, though, it matters how the unemployed person spends time. The burden of recessions or even depressions may be overstated, because those who become unemployed may be producing things at home—repairing their roofs, adding onto their homes, cooking meals instead of eating at restaurants—that would otherwise have been produced through a monetary transaction that required other people to spend their time on it. Some macroeconomists even argue that much of the rise in unemployment that occurs in recessions reflects some workers' choices to switch their effort from paid work to home production.[2]

We do paid work, which we find stressful, because the pain of working is less than the pleasure that we get from combining the additional money that we earn from working with our time in nonwork activities. We are worse off if we are unemployed.[3] Worse still, the extent of our loss if we become unemployed rises increasingly rapidly the longer we have been unemployed: the first week of unemployment might be spent on necessary minor home repairs (home production), but there are limits on how much additional useful home production one can do after being unemployed for many months.[4] There can only be so much house-painting or so much cooking of meals to be stockpiled for future dinners.

Long-term unemployment (defined in the US as being unemployed more than six months) rose to nearly half of all unemployed workers during the Great Recession; even after nine years of recovery it still constituted 20 percent of the much smaller number of unemployed workers.[5] Historically it has represented an even larger share of European unemployment than it has in the US. For many unemployed workers their unemployment spell is so long that they have few home-production activities that are worth doing. On a larger scale, it suggests that, when the national unemployment rate increases in a recession and more people have time on their hands, residents of a country will be spending more time at leisure and in personal care.

Since 1948, the first year in which the US issued official statistics on unemployment, the unemployment rate dropped below 3 percent of the labor force only during the Korean War (1950–1953). Some people are unemployed even when the economy is booming. Take an unemployed American who has the same characteristics as someone who is working—same gender, number of children, age, education, state of residence—all those characteristics that we have seen contribute to people's decisions about how to spend time independent of whether unemployed or working for pay. Let's say that a worker with the same demographic characteristics puts in forty hours per week; by definition, the demographically identical unemployed person works zero hours per week.

Making these assumptions, we can examine how a typical unemployed worker would spend the forty hours each week that are freed up by the period of unemployment. In the early 2000s in four countries, the US, Australia, Germany, and Italy, women used between 35 and 50 percent of the time freed up on home production. Men used between 10 and 35 percent on additional home production. The overwhelming majority of freed-up time was used for additional personal care and for leisure activities. That was especially true in Italy, where men usually spend very little of their time in home production whether they are doing any paid work or not.[6]

Compared to male unemployed workers, women who are unemployed do spend larger fractions of their freed-up time doing home-production activities. But even among unemployed women, in all four countries little more than half of the time gift was devoted to activities, such as cleaning and cooking, that are substitutes for things that the women could have bought had they been working for pay and earning some money. The unemployed, both men and women, do not just switch from paid work that generates goods and services valued in the market to unpaid work that produces things that substitute for their purchases. Instead, on average in rich countries, unemployed workers spend most of their time gifts choosing to do those nonwork activities that people generally find least stressful—personal care and leisure. Although they are less happy than if they were still holding a job, very sensibly they cope with the burden of unemployment by doing those things that they find most enjoyable.

Unemployed workers in the US spend only one-third of their freed-up time in home production. That leaves the remaining two-thirds to be spent among all the personal and leisure activities that people do. While there is tremendous diversity among the unemployed (and everyone else) in choosing how to use their time, US data for 2003–2015 show some common behavior. Unemployed men and women both spend about 15 percent of their freed-up time sleeping, but they spend no more time in other personal care—including grooming and washing up—than employed workers. Another 20 percent of their freed-up time is spent watching television, and about one-third is used in other leisure activities. As with choices made by retirees, by young nonworkers, and by other groups, sleeping and TV watching account for large shares of time, even when the time is a gift.

When an economy moves into recession, even those people who retain their jobs may find that the determinants of their choices about how to spend their time are affected. If nothing else, their weekly work hours are likely to drop, as employers cut back on paid hours of even those workers whom they don't lay off. In the US over the past fifty years, the average drop in the weekly work hours of employees who kept their jobs during

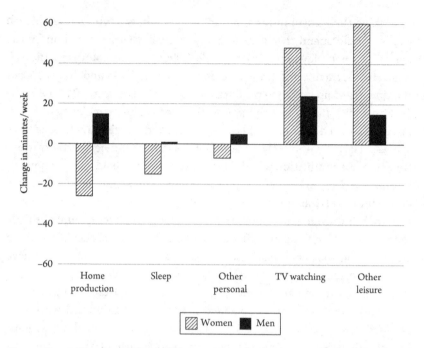

Figure 12.1 Effects of a One Hour/Week Cut in Work Time in the Great Recession, US, 2009–2010, Compared to Other Years, 2003–2015 (Minutes per Week)

the typical recession was about one hour per week. In the Great Recession, which reached a trough in 2009, work time dropped by two hours per worker compared to the period 2003–2008.

Examining how time was spent around the bottom of the Great Recession, the years 2009 and 2010, compared to the rest of the period 2003 through 2015, allows inferring the economy-wide effects on time use of higher national unemployment. Figure 12.1 presents comparisons of people during the recession years to their counterparts of the same age, education, and so on in the other eleven years of the period. A bar extending above the zero line shows that some of the lost hour of paid work was spent in the activity; a bar going below zero shows that the lost hour of work was accompanied by a reduction in the time spent in that activity.

Of each hour of work that the average worker lost in the US economy during the Great Recession, only a little was spent in extra home production and essentially none in sleep or other personal care. Instead, almost was all spent on additional TV watching and other leisure activities. There were differences between men (solid bars) and women (striped bars), though. Men added a quarter-hour of home production, while women did less home production during the Great Recession than in other years. Women added more TV watching and other leisure activities than men, but for both sexes leisure activities in total accounted for a large majority of the time freed up from paid work in the entire US economy.

We can't know for sure how people in other wealthy countries choose to alter their uses of time during recessions, but with all the evidence that, except for shorter work years, they make similar choices to those in the US about spending time, it is likely that the Great Recession saw people in other rich countries spending most of their freed-up time watching TV and engaging in other leisure activities.

PERMANENT GIFTS OF TIME OFF WORK

Among the few well-known lines penned by economists is John Maynard Keynes's comment in 1930:

> For many ages to come the old Adam will be so strong in us that everybody will need to do *some* work if he is to be contented. . . . we shall endeavor to . . . make what work there is still to be done as widely shared as possible. Three-hour shifts or a fifteen-hour week may put off the problem for a great while.[7]

Keynes also warned that it would be "at least another 100 years" before this happened. But barely ten years are left in the century of leeway that he gave himself, and we are by no means down to fifteen-hour workweeks. His forecast has not come to pass, nor has it even been approached. In the United States especially there is no evidence of any decrease in "the old Adam" over the past half-century; even in Western Europe, Japan, and other wealthy areas, the Adam is only slightly diminished.

In this same essay Keynes foresaw this diminution of people's fixation on working and earning incomes as a boon to society, with the permanent decline in work hours allowing for a more moral society, one concentrating less on money-grubbing and more on the "higher things" in life. We know that those higher things include the leisure and home-production activities that people find stress-reducing and which Keynes might have favored. The issue is whether a permanent reduction in work time would lead to this possibly desirable outcome, or whether instead people would make themselves happier by using their freed-up time to watch more television, primp/groom themselves more, or engage in other activities of which Keynes might have been less likely to approve. The general question is what people would do with a time gift resulting from a permanent cut in work hours.

No country has seen a decline in work time to fifteen hours per week. It's not even easy to find many cases when a cut in work hours represented a permanent time gift rather than a blip due to a temporary economic decline. There are two examples, though, where the average worker's hours were cut permanently due to circumstances arising from employers' decisions instead of workers'. In each case these cuts occurred while the economy was booming, so that they weren't just results of temporary drops in employers' demands on their workers' time.[8]

Until the mid-1980s, Japan penalized overtime work—required employers to pay higher hourly earnings—only on workweeks longer than forty-eight hours. Between the late 1980s and the mid-1990s the standard workweek—the workweek that didn't require any overtime pay—was dropped gradually by legislation from forty-eight to the same forty hours that has been the standard workweek in the US since 1938. An hour of work beyond forty hours each week began costing Japanese employers more than before.

A very similar series of changes played out in Korea more than a decade later. The standard workweek in Korea had been forty-four hours since 1991, with worktime beyond forty-four hours being penalized by requiring extra overtime pay. Between 2004 and 2008, the standard workweek was decreased to forty hours, so that employers were required to pay extra on an additional four hours of the workweek that had not previously required overtime pay.

These changes had their desired effects on the lengths of the workweeks in the two countries. Japanese employers reacted to the legislation by reducing the weekly hours required of their workers. The leftmost pair of bars in Figure 12.2, describing Japanese work time, shows the size of the decline in women's (striped bars) and men's (solid bars) weekly work hours in Japan from 1986 to 1996. For the average male worker, this cut in employers' demands for a longer workweek resulted in a time gift of over three hours per week, and for the average female worker a gift of nearly one hour. Looking at Koreans' time in paid work in 2009, shown by the next pair of bars moving rightward in Figure 12.2, men's work time dropped a lot—nearly four hours—while women's work time in Korea rose very slightly. The lesser drop in women's work time in both countries occurred because relatively few Japanese and Korean women had been working long hours before the legislation. It was not possible for very many women to have been affected by the new laws.

The other bars in Figure 12.2 show how Japanese and Koreans changed the time that they spend in the other main activities, home production, personal care, which includes sleep, and leisure, which includes TV

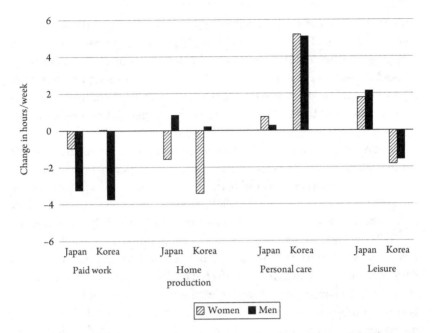

Figure 12.2 Changes in Time Use Resulting from Reductions in the Standard Workweek, Japan 1986–1996, Korea 1999–2009.
Source: Calculated from Jungmin Lee, Daiji Kawaguchi, and Daniel Hamermesh, "Aggregate Impacts of a Gift of Time," American Economic Association, *Papers and Proceedings* 102 (May 2012), Tables 1 and 2.

watching, during the decade when employers decreased (mostly men's) hours of work. Some of the changes are unlikely to have been related to the cut in work hours. Women decreased the time spent in home production, probably due to the spread of time-saving appliances and, especially in Korea, to the tremendous and precipitous drop in the birth rate that had occurred over the previous two decades.[9] Leaving aside home production, though, the best conclusion is that Japanese workers used the freed-up time to enjoy more leisure activities, while Koreans used it to sleep and engage in other personal care.

If we delve further into the specifics of how workers spent their gifts of time, the data show that over half of the extra leisure time in Japan was spent watching television. The extra time that Korean workers spent entirely on additional personal care wasn't mostly extra sleep—over half of it was spent on grooming and washing up. These are hardly the uplifting kinds of activities that Keynes predicted might become more important when people no longer felt the need or urge to work so many hours.

The permanent cuts in work hours in Japan and Korea were imposed by legislation that altered employers' incentives and reduced the length of the workweek in each country. They did not arise from workers' choices about how much to work, although the ways that the time gifts were spent were the results of people's own choices, presumably unencumbered by employers' wishes about their employees' nonwork time. The cuts in hours worked appear to have reduced workers' incomes, although by less than 2 percent, while giving them more time to spend away from work. Workers faced an imposed trade-off—more free time, at the cost of a reduction in income.

Looking at a random sample of employees in Korea before and after the cut in work hours, and the concomitant fall in earnings, we can infer whether the legislation made workers feel better off. Those who had worked between forty-one and forty-four hours in 1999—that is, those who were most likely to have been affected by the cut—were more satisfied with life in 2009 than in 1999 compared to other workers who were not directly affected—that is, those who worked fewer than forty hours per week. In Japan, the workers who were most likely to have been affected by the cut in work hours were also most likely to have reported the largest increases in overall happiness between the 1980s and the 1990s.[10] The trade-off that the legislation imposed on workers made them happier. At least in the range of work time that we observe in rich countries, the Japanese and Korean experiences suggest that people's well-being is raised by small permanent time gifts that are imposed on them and that lead them to switch away from paid work.

There is no way of knowing how people would spend the permanent gift of twenty-five hours each week that Keynes envisioned. If it were accompanied by some cuts in income, the demonstration that nonworkers with lower household incomes spend more time sleeping and TV watching implies that much of a huge time gift would be spent in additional sleeping and TV watching. But it's unlikely that people would accept very large reductions in incomes to obtain a lot more nonwork time each week. The evidence from Japan and Korea that people were happier after the cuts in work hours is based on how people responded to much smaller drops in work hours—and in earnings.

If humanity ever gets to the point where paid work becomes rare, we are unlikely to spend most of the time freed up from work on additional sleep. It's hard to imagine adding more than one extra hour per night to sleep time. The same for television: even Americans, already the rich-world champions of TV watching, would not be likely to spend most of a large time gift in front of the tube, perhaps even doubling their already large amount of TV watching. We can't know how people would spend a huge permanent time gift resulting from less paid work. But we do know that cutting work time a little and accepting small cuts in pay does make people better off. It does expand their opportunities.

PERMANENT GIFTS OF TIME OUTSIDE WORK

The tremendous improvements in the technology of production along with the increasing skills of the workforce have caused productivity in US business to more than double in the past fifty years; the increases in Western Europe have been about the same. Despite this, the higher earnings that the growth in productivity has fueled have led to essentially no freed-up work time in the US, and only to quite small decreases in work time in Western Europe. Outside of work it's harder to measure productivity, since we don't sell the purchases and time that we combine to enhance our enjoyment of home production, personal activities, and leisure. But in these nonwork activities, too, people have become more efficient due to improvements in technology.

The little more than three hours per day that Americans and others spend in home production are partly the results of the greatest improvements in technology outside the workplace. Inside one's home the availability of home appliances has saved time and allowed the enjoyment of arguably better products. Clothes washers and dryers produce cleaner clothes in much less time than it took to wash clothes by hand in a tub and hang them on a line to dry. Turning on the electric or gas oven is less time consuming and gives us more options for food preparation than did gathering wood, lighting and maintaining a fire, and torching some meat.

Examples of technological changes that have freed up time outside our homes abound. My younger son has been advantaged by a snowblower each winter, whereas I endured shoveling snow as a middle-aged resident of the northern US. The growth of the Internet and the rise of supermarkets and big-box stores have allowed people the opportunity to make fewer trips to obtain the same amount of goods, and Americans today are shopping less frequently than they did forty years ago.[11] In nearly every home production activity there has been some kind of technological improvement. Increases in the efficiency of home production have given people the opportunity to reallocate time within home-production activities and toward other activities that they might find more enjoyable.

With personal care accounting for around eleven hours of the typical day in rich countries, this near majority of the day presents the greatest opportunity for saving time through increased efficiency. Yet breaking down personal-care time suggests that relatively few technical improvements have occurred in our ability to economize on time in these activities. At best we are little more efficient at sleeping—can obtain the same restoration of our faculties with fewer hours sleeping—than we were several hundred years ago. One-third of our time—the amount we sleep—has hardly been amenable to major technical improvements. It takes about the same amount of time to enjoy sexual activities as it always has. We have become more efficient in grooming, cleaning up, showering, and other personal-care activities: hair dryers, electric shavers, running water, flushing toilets, and other improvements have created the possibility of freed-up time, even if most people have chosen to use this possibility to improve the quality of the personal care that they generate for themselves. Economizing on the bulk of the time spent in personal care does not seem likely any time soon.

There have been tremendous technological improvements in the enjoyment of leisure time. My first television, purchased in 1950, had a 12-inch (30-centimeter) screen, a black-and-white picture, and poor sound; our TV today has a 55-inch (140-centimeter) screen, incredibly detailed color, and surround sound. Today's TVs cost a smaller share of the average family's income than did their 1950 ancestors. The technological change in televisions has made everyone better off. What an improvement—but it hasn't saved me time. It takes two hours to watch the main part of *The Today Show*, as it did in 1952 when the show first appeared. Television watching remains the same time-intensive activity that it was in the 1950s.

Other leisure activities are much more high-tech and enjoyable than they were fifty or more years ago. The technology of museum exhibitions, with their interactive computerized displays and other attractions, makes museum-going more fun than it was to visit the static displays that preceded them. But there has been no time saving. I'm sure people would rather see a professional football match today, with the big screens allowing replays and close-up views of the action, than one in the 1950s. But a professional US football match still takes more than three hours, and a professional soccer match also is no shorter than it was fifty years ago. With TV watching accounting for about half of leisure time in the US and nearly that much elsewhere, and with few if any time-saving improvements in other leisure activities, time freed up in leisure activities through improved technology has been minimal. Advances in technology have improved our well-being and allowed for more enjoyment per minute, but they haven't saved us any time.

Considering all these possibilities, people have been able to save time because of improved technologies, but only in time spent on home production. These technological improvements have allowed us to enjoy more leisure than people did fifty or a hundred years ago. But work time in the US differs little from what it was fifty years ago, and little time has been freed up by improvements beyond those in home production. Taken together, citizens of wealthy countries do have somewhat more discretionary time at their disposal today than their grandparents had. But the increase in their discretionary time has been dwarfed by the increases in monetary living standards that have resulted from improved technologies within the workplace and increases in the skills that people bring to their jobs.

PROSPECTS FOR SAVING TIME

Think of the issue of time saving from the perspective of somebody with an income of $50 million per year, which would be the unearned income from wealth of $1 billion.[12] Even if this plutocrat, one of over 2,200 people worldwide, has his servant bathe and dress him, shave him, do all his shopping, cook all his meals and clean up afterward, and do all the childcare in the household, he still will sleep at least six hours per day. Reading, watching television, and attending sporting or cultural events will take him the same amount of time that it takes you and me, although having his personal jet plane always available might allow him a wider range of choices among leisure activities. With so much income, and because paying people to do so many things for him doesn't save him much time, he will be much more rushed than the rest of us. Like the rest of us, unless he cuts back on his work time, he has been and will for the foreseeable future be faced with the prospect of not having a lot of time to enjoy all the "things" that he can purchase. Even if he does no paid work, he must cram his vast spending into his twenty-four hours per day.

Maybe the next hundred years will see time-saving improvements in our nonwork activities. Perhaps a pill will be created that will allow the average person to obtain a refreshing sleep in only four hours per day. Another time-saving possibility in a time-intensive personal-care activity would be the "Orgasmatron" in Woody Allen's *Sleeper*. But without improvements that are currently in the realm of science fiction, we are unlikely to obtain much more time freed up for discretionary purposes. Modern people in wealthy countries are "cursed" by the lack of time and the historically large and growing spending power at their disposal. They are not going to get more free time in which to spend and enjoy their incomes any time soon. The answer to the questions that form the title of this chapter is No, not much!

CHAPTER 13

✧

What Is to Be Done?

L ife is hectic. And despite the permanent gifts of time that we have received over the past hundred years, particularly the increase in efficiency in home production, the growth in our incomes has far outpaced growth in the time available to us outside of work. Partly this is because we have chosen to use the time that has been freed up to live better, to enjoy more varied leisure activities, to groom ourselves better, and—most important—to live more interesting lives. These choices, while making us better off, have done nothing to increase the amount of discretionary time that we feel we have. We are rushed for time—we often feel that we lack the time needed to enjoy our purchases in the way we would like to. Barring such very unlikely changes as large increases in the efficiency of how we use our nonwork time or a complete halt to growth in incomes, the relative shortage of time will only get worse. Our time will become more valuable as it becomes relatively scarcer. Even today, although few people implicitly value an hour of their time as much as the hourly wage that they could earn, they do value it, perhaps at half of their hourly wage. With rising living standards, and the increasing relatively scarcity of time, people will value their time even more highly in the future.

The question is what to do about this continuing and probably worsening predicament, one that will see us having more opportunities—being increasingly financially well-off—but even more stressed for time. We might make decisions at several levels that will enable us to have more time or at least feel that we do. As individuals we might change our behavior to alter our feelings of time pressure. Presumably the only reason that we would make such changes is that we decide that they will make us better off. As part of a community we might agree with our neighbors, the others in our community, to change our living conditions—the local institutions that govern our lives—in such ways as to enhance our well-being. Our employers might offer more time-friendly working conditions. Finally, and much more generally, we can ask the governments that we have created to institute policies that alter the incentives that affect how we use time so that we may become better off.

WHAT AN INDIVIDUAL CAN DO

The crucial phrase for what individuals can do to spend their time more sensibly is the opening of a Simon and Garfunkel song: "Slow down, you move too fast."[1]

As individuals there are options that can enable us to reduce our feelings of being very rushed. My personal advice on this may be no better than anyone else's, but I do have the advantage of having thought about this issue in depth and having lived a long time. So here are a few actions that have helped this American workaholic to relax a little and perhaps generate some time gifts, or at least to make my use of time less stressful. Most of these have involved imposing rules that function as self-control mechanisms.[2]

Exercise—do something that you find to be intrinsically enjoyable. Aside from the enjoyment it brings, it might even generate a time gift: an analysis of a large group of studies of the impact of running as exercise suggests that one hour of running added much more than one hour to one's life span.[3]

"Bathing is time-wasting," says the hero of a recent novel.[4] Showering is clearly faster than a bath, but a two-minute shower is less relaxing than a ten-minute bath. Allocating more time to some personal activities is a pretty good way to reduce time stress. After all, they are among the least time-stressing activities that we do.

Impose routines that prevent work from interfering with less stressful nonwork activities. The spillover of work onto leisure is a real problem for people who control their own schedules, typically higher earners who are already more time-stressed than others. For example, impose a rule that you won't do any work between 9:00 p.m. and 6:00 a.m. Or, as in my household, if you can't control yourself, have your partner impose such a rule on you.

If you live within three miles (five kilometers) of your workplace, try walking to or from work occasionally. It is amazing how refreshing walking can be, as by its nature it forces you to relax. It's much different from sitting in your auto dealing with traffic or being frustrated by a bus driver's dawdling or by delayed trains.

It's very easy to let work and even leisure become solo activities such that togetherness with family and friends falls by the wayside. With people in rich countries spending remarkably little time together, imposing a rule that you will eat breakfast and dinner with your partner and children (if you have them) can go a long way toward relieving time stress. It's difficult to work when at table with one's family, so this is also a way to decrease the stress of paid work.

Force yourself to slow down in nonwork activities. Racing to eat, to prepare food, and to clean up after meals reduces the enjoyment from those uses of time and makes things that are inherently relaxing more stressful.

All these suggested changes are small. Some require imposing self-control, which may be difficult given the pressures to "get ahead" at one's job. But ask yourself whether you would like to look back on your life and conclude that it has mirrored the life of the hero of Harry Chapin's song, "Cat's in the Cradle," who was so busy working that he missed all the major events of his son's childhood and young adulthood, a failure that redounded upon him in old age.[5]

Beyond these suggestions, there is another, quite easy way to reduce time pressure: renounce the race to earn more and accept a lower-paid job that requires fewer hours of paid work each week. While small reductions in work time and the accompanying small cuts in earnings increase people's satisfaction with life, I doubt that most people will be willing to sacrifice a lot of income to obtain a lot more nonwork time. That kind of sacrifice is especially unlikely to be desirable if most of one's colleagues, workmates, and friends are unwilling to do the same. Again, we are thrown back on the problem that a change that might be desirable for a community may not be attractive to individuals making the change on their own.

WHAT COMPANIES AND COMMUNITIES CAN DO

We can do things on a community- or company-wide basis that allow each of us to reduce our feelings of being stressed for time and that can also contribute to familial or even community togetherness. Occasionally we see news stories about some company's efforts to allow its workers more control over their work schedules, typically within a workweek of the same length as the standard workweek. For example, in 2014, financial giant Merrill Lynch was reported to be requiring its low-level executives to spend four days each month away from the office. Some innovative small companies discourage workers from putting in more than forty hours per week. Others have tried to impose limits on the timing of workers' emails to prevent them from bothering each other at all hours of the day and night. Still others try to allow for greater smoothing of work time over their employees' lives by facilitating work by their older employees.[6]

These attempts to intervene directly by putting restrictions on workers' workaholic behavior are laudable. What a wonderful world it would be if all companies and governments were to create similar policies of their own accord, to allow their workers more freedom to schedule their work time, and to limit workers' hours. But it's not going to happen for a variety of reasons. Given the vagaries of people's nonwork lives and companies' needs to have workers interacting and being productive together, allowing employees complete freedom to schedule their work time can only succeed in environments where one worker's productivity doesn't depend on others'. In workplaces where cooperation is essential, allowing workers complete freedom to choose their own work times would lower productivity. No company wants to be the only one in its industry experiencing a productivity drop, out of fear that the higher costs which the decrease in productivity generates would jeopardize its competitive position.

Company-imposed limits on weekly hours and working days per month or year sound good to workers—as long as there is no cut in the pay that the worker receives each month. But even the last hour worked in a day, week, or month is at least somewhat productive, so that cutting hours will cut the total amount that is produced. The decline in productivity produced by cutting work hours will create the same cost disadvantage for the company that institutes this policy as would allowing its workers complete flexibility in their scheduling—unless pay is cut commensurately. Again, few companies will want to institute such policies on their own for fear of placing themselves at a disadvantage vis-à-vis their competitors.

These explanations for the rarity of company-imposed limits on work time and of policies allowing workers freedom in scheduling argue from the viewpoint of the employer, but workers—particularly high-skilled, high-wage workers—are also partly responsible for the near absence of company-based limits. Workers who can earn a lot per hour want to work more. This translates into the substantial number of high-skilled American workers, and the somewhat smaller number of high-skilled workers in other rich countries, who are putting in more than forty hours per week. Moreover, because these workers are central to their companies' success and have substantial impacts on others' work lives, their interest in working long hours spills over to the decisions that less-skilled workers make about their work time. This is the kind of behavior that makes workaholism not merely a personal issue but one that affects all of society.

The news media will keep reporting stories about "enlightened" companies that allow workers more freedom of work time and work scheduling than what are standard in the US and other wealthy countries. These changes may work well for a few companies that have unusual structures of production. For most companies, though, the desire to be competitive in the products and services that they sell makes it unlikely that these commendable policies will be very widespread. For most high-wage workers—those who work long hours and engage in workaholic behavior—these changes will also not be attractive. Sadly, the free market in a modern economy, especially one with increasingly unequal earnings, provides few incentives to limit work time or to allow substantially greater flexibility in the timing of work.

If it is unlikely that we will see widespread privately initiated limits on work time and timing, perhaps private initiatives outside the workplace will create an environment that increases incentives to allow more flexibility and fewer hours at work. Sometimes we see parents, worried about their teenagers' tight schedules of school, music lessons, soccer, and other sports, getting together to take a town-wide "time-out" to allow for more familial togetherness. This kind of behavior too is unlikely to become very widespread for the same general reasons that company-imposed limitations will not: each aspiring soccer player and musician has incentives to work harder to succeed—to "cheat" on limits on spending time in the activities that they are interested in. With these incentives, even the most well-meaning town-wide limits on time use will be circumvented by families and children seeking to "get ahead."

WHY GOVERNMENTS SHOULD FIDDLE WITH PEOPLE'S SPENDING TIME

With individuals and companies unlikely to be able to reduce the time stress that rising incomes, and desires and ability to have and do more things, impose, and with company- and town-based private initiatives also unlikely to reduce the time stress facing people at work and in their private lives, there is only one alternative: government action. Such action will be anathema to free-market ideologues and to the minority of high-skilled, high-earning people who fail to see themselves as workaholics, those who are so caught up in a rat race that their behavior is beyond their conscious control. But there is a panoply of changes in public policy that can reduce the extent of stress about time that pervades wealthy countries.

Social scientists, including economists, love to suggest new policy ideas and to argue for changes in existing government policies that they feel will improve people's well-being. Their efforts stem from their beliefs that their own research has important things to say about policy and from their desire to see their ideas adopted. This behavior is altruistic and narcissistic at the same time. It is easy to argue for some social or economic policy; it is harder to justify one's arguments by making it clear that the policy is something that wouldn't be undertaken privately—without government interference. That should be the criterion for government policy. Simply pointing to undesirable societal outcomes does not mean that governments must become involved. The fundamental justification for a government policy must be the externalities that have led some individuals' or groups' behavior to create negative outcomes for others or even for an entire society.

The justification for government policies dealing with time use is that society has gotten itself into a situation where a few individuals altering their behavior will not lead others to do so, and that failure will leave the first group of individuals worse off. That being the case, nobody has an incentive to undertake changes that will make society as a whole better off. Either we all do something because we are compelled or face new incentives to do so, or nobody changes their behavior. In the case of time use, the American rat race—the long work years, and the work lives that are compacted into only part of adulthood—fits this bill. Few companies have an incentive to cut back on their employees' work hours, because they fear losing workers to other companies that offer longer hours and more earnings. No store can afford to shut down on Sundays or evenings when it believes that its competitors will stay open and draw business away, both at those times and, more important, even permanently. This rat race in the workplace spills over to family life, reducing togetherness and serving to loosen family ties. Because togetherness is something that makes people better off—that expands their opportunities in life—policies that foster togetherness are also desirable.

That these externalities have created a rat race in time use justifies policies to get the "rats" off their treadmills. With most government policies that affect time use regulating time at work, and with paid work time essentially unchanged over the last forty years in the US, changes in policies that deal with work time provide the biggest scope for improving well-being.

Outside the workplace, policies aimed at other aspects of behavior might also indirectly affect how we spend time. They too need to be looked at so that their side effects do not alter time use in ways that speed up the rat race that people increasingly find themselves in.

WHAT GOVERNMENT POLICY CAN DO
TO ALTER NONWORK TIME

Discussing policy in the context of time away from work is important. No government policies have the explicit goal of altering the amount of time that people spend in household production, personal care, or leisure. But large numbers of policies have side effects, often substantial ones that alter people's incentives to choose among these major nonwork types of activity. A few of these policies aim explicitly at changing the amount and timing of people's work activities, but in doing so they must also alter nonwork time (since there are only twenty-four hours in most days). Even policies that might not appear to have any impact on how we use our time, such as some sales taxes or requirements that limit the kinds of subsidies that people receive under food assistance programs, will alter how people spend their nonwork time.

Blue laws—limiting shop-opening hours and, today in some American states, still limiting times when alcohol may be sold—were originally imposed in colonial America to induce people to attend church. Other countries imposed these "Sunday-closing laws" for the same reason as the US.[7] By the late twentieth century, however, these laws were weakened in most Western countries. In any case, the usual rationale for their existence, at least in Europe, became that of protecting workers, typically in retail outlets, from being required to work at times when most other people were not working.

Blue laws could limit or alter nonwork time by forcing shoppers to crowd their buying onto weekdays. When I lived in the Netherlands in 1994, I could not shop on weekends or after 6:00 p.m. on all but Thursday evenings. Most stores had to be closed at these times. I was forced to leave work early to shop, or to concentrate my shopping on Thursday evenings. An evaluation of the Dutch blue laws that were relaxed in the late 1990s examined how people's shopping timing and total time spent shopping changed. With the lessened restrictions on shop-opening hours, people did spread their shopping more over the week. That's no surprise, but what is a little surprising is that they spent more time shopping each week, not just on the days when stores had previously been closed. But this comes at a cost of increased work for retail workers, both more individuals working and longer hours among those who do work.[8]

The evidence suggests that relaxing blue laws does enhance shoppers'/consumers' well-being, allowing them to spread their purchasing time without restriction. Shoppers benefit from the increased freedom to schedule their time. Whether workers benefit is a different question. Some workers who might have wanted to work evenings and Sundays can do so once the laws are repealed, so they are better off. Others, who would prefer not to work evenings or Sundays, may be required to do so to keep their jobs. As with so many policies, many people (shoppers) gain a little, while a few (those workers compelled to work at times when they would prefer not to be working for pay) are substantially harmed. Given the extremely long annual work hours and their unusual timing in the US, a return to mandated retail closing times is an attractive option.

Many countries offer families payments based on the number of children in the household, as did the US until 2018 through personal exemptions in the federal income tax. To the extent that this pro-natalist policy enhances fertility, as the evidence suggests it does, it will also shift time toward home production (childcare) and away from some of the other general categories of time use, including perhaps even paid work.[9] Recognizing that childcare takes time, the United States, like many other countries, subsidizes it through the federal income tax system with a childcare tax credit. The purpose is to encourage people, especially women who provide most of the childcare time that is included in home production, to enter the workforce or, if already working for pay, to increase their weekly work hours. To the extent that it does so—and the evidence is positive on this—the extra work time is especially likely to be taken from time otherwise spent in home production by encouraging hiring nannies and putting children in childcare facilities.

It might make sense to eliminate this policy, eliminating its side effects of reducing nonwork time. With men's and women's time spent in home production becoming more equal, abolishing subsidies for childcare will create increasingly equal incentives for both women and men to reduce the amount of paid work that they seek. These can be enhanced if, as in some European countries, paid family leave is offered and can be shared by both partners when a child is born.

General sales taxes can alter how people spend their time. Taxes on specific goods will do this to the extent that people can avoid the tax by purchasing less of the good that the tax has made more expensive and by using more of their own time instead. In 2007, a worldwide rise in the price of corn, the main ingredient in the Mexican staple tortillas, imposed a burden on Mexican families, especially lower-income ones. To counteract its impact, the Mexican government ended tariffs (border taxes) on imported corn.[10]

Without the tariff reduction one can imagine that Mexican homemakers would have had to spend more time grinding corn themselves rather than purchasing pre-ground corn.

Whether people really switch from buying things to using more of their own time when goods become more expensive depends on the activity and the goods that are used during that activity. For the broad commodity of food, the evidence suggests that people can substitute some of their own time when food generally becomes more expensive, but not very much.[11] But when a specific commodity becomes more expensive, it is much easier than for food generally to buy a less-processed substitute and spend time in home production making the final product. If, for example, the price of cheese sticks rises, some people will buy whole cheese and then spend a little extra time in home production cutting the cheese into sticks to obtain something like the manufactured product.

Government policy can have especially large effects on how we use our time when the kinds of things that we can buy, not just their prices, are altered. In the early 2000s, the US government, under its Food Stamps (SNAP) program, began basing the amount of assistance that it offers poorer households on a minimally nutritious diet that could be produced using raw rather than processed foods. This saves the taxpayer money— raw food materials are less expensive than processed food. With a smaller federal budget for this purpose, beneficiaries of the program could attain the same nutritional level as before the change.

The difficulty is that this restriction altered how the program's beneficiaries, especially women, who constitute the majority of recipients and who do the majority of food preparation, spend their time.[12] Low-income women, many of whom also faced increased work requirements imposed under welfare programs, found that their nonwork time had to be shifted toward home production in the form of food preparation, since making a meal out of raw food products took them more time than preparing meals using more processed foods. Together with requirements that SNAP recipients find paid work, this restriction added greatly to the time pressure on low-income women. This conjunction of policies shows that we need to structure policies that affect time outside the workplace to account for their interactions, often negative, with policies affecting paid work time and the pressures of nonwork time.

HOW TO CHANGE THE TIMING OF WORK

Most countries have national policies that are explicitly designed to change the timing of work.[13] Such policies as limits on the standard workweek and premium pay for overtime work do so implicitly: by altering the amount of work performed they lead employers to alter its timing. But some overtime laws, although not the US federal law, explicitly target days worked. California and a few other western states have overtime laws that go beyond setting the standard workweek at forty hours to also requiring premium pay for workers putting in more than eight hours on any single day. Similar daily overtime-pay requirements exist in many rich countries.

The additional requirement of daily overtime pay does reduce the fraction of employees working more than eight hours per day, as we would expect. But because it raises the cost of a day when a worker is on the job for more than eight hours, it gives employers an incentive to spread work over more days in the week, further reducing average hours worked each workday.[14] Evidence on the ease of substituting additional days in place of fewer hours per day suggests that, although this substitution occurs, the effects are very small. Even when an extra daily hour of workers' time becomes more expensive to them, employers find it hard to add extra days to the workweek. This difficulty means that a public policy that reduces work hours per day does not have the negative side effect of increasing the number of days when employees work. Instead, some of the reduction in total work time stemming from the cut in daily hours is made up for by an increase the number of jobs offered. Spreading work across more people, with new jobs being created and with each worker doing a bit less paid work, is an attractive way to create a slight reduction in the time pressure facing the average person.

The amount of evening, night, or weekend work that is performed will be affected by overtime legislation or by any other legislation that targets the amount of work and that penalizes work beyond some level. In most countries, although again not in the US, governments have enacted policies that explicitly aim to limit the amount of work at these unusual times. In many countries, including such large economies as France and Germany, extra hourly pay must be offered for work outside what are defined as "normal" working times. Many other countries impose explicit limits on the amount of work that an employee can perform at these times.

An interesting illustration of the complexity of these laws is provided by Portugal. Payment for overtime hours worked after eight hours per day or forty hours per week is required, and there are absolute limits on the number of overtime hours that can be worked in a year. Portugal also mandated a 25 percent wage premium for work performed between 8:00 p.m. and 7:00 a.m. on weekdays, a 100 percent premium for work done on weekend days, and up to a 150 percent wage premium for weekend night work. The complexity of these laws indicates the kinds of restrictions and mandates operating in many European labor markets but completely absent in the US.

With Americans working more than Europeans in evenings, nights, and on weekends, a European-style penalty on such work, for example, requiring a 50 percent pay premium for any hours worked at these times, might be a way of reducing the amount of work at times that most people find undesirable. One study showed that requiring employers to pay premium wages for work performed at these unusual times does reduce the share of work performed then.[15] But the effects are small, so that only a 2 percent reduction in work at these times would result if a Portuguese-style set of restrictions were imposed on American employers who currently face no government-mandated premium pay for work performed outside normal hours. A similar conclusion follows from Australia's expansion of wage penalties for retail work performed on Sundays, an attempt to induce shops to reduce opening hours then. This legislation did reduce hours per worker, but the impact was also very small.[16]

Imposing penalties on employers who schedule extra work or work at unusual times does not appear to be a promising approach to reducing the burden of paid work, although it will help a little. If we want to shift the timing of work, we should simply outlaw work at unusual times, mandating that no work be performed during certain hours, perhaps midnight to 5:00 a.m., and none on Sundays. This mandate, essentially a return to blue laws, would do the job. It wouldn't greatly reduce the amount of paid work, but at least it would to some small extent allow greater family togetherness.

Occasionally observers propose mandating a thirty-two-hour work-week.[17] Cutting the workweek to thirty-two hours would undoubtedly create more jobs, but those would hardly be enough to prevent a huge drop in the total amount of paid work performed. While the fifth eight-hour day each week may not be as productive as any of the first four days—and there is no evidence on this—it is at least somewhat productive. Cutting one day of work without altering work time on the other four days would undoubtedly decrease GDP and decrease per-capita incomes. It may be worth doing if we value having a three-day weekend each week very highly, but it would come with substantial costs in the amount that we produce, and thus in our incomes. It would be far from costless.

Another possibility is flextime, mandating that companies allow their employees to choose their work timing, within the requirement that workers put in a given number of hours each week. Many workers find this idea attractive—after all, from most workers' viewpoints the freedom to choose one's timing, the same freedom that describes most of my work life as an academic, seems very appealing. To some extent this already characterizes work timing in certain occupations and industries, such as among some hospital workers, and airline pilots and flight attendants. Offering flextime should enable employers to cut costs per hour paid, since workers, desiring this benefit of their jobs, will be willing to work for less per hour. Offset against this cut in labor cost is a possible rise in costs resulting from a reduction in workplace productivity as workers' schedules can no longer be as carefully synchronized.

Flextime is not mandated in the US and is not likely to be required any time soon. It is available in some workplaces; the sparse evidence suggests that it does reduce profits, but that much of the reduction can be mitigated by more careful attention to human-resource policies.[18] Given the diversity of the structure of production across industries and companies, a national flextime mandate would be a clumsy approach to reducing the burden of paid work.

Except when we play the lottery or otherwise gamble, we do not like uncertainty. Uncertainty about work timing is especially disturbing, as anyone with a suddenly sick young child whose illness requires rescheduling work time knows. Some workers, especially those in retail outlets, experience the same unpleasantness when they are informed that their services are suddenly needed on a morning when they had expected to stay at home, or are suddenly not needed and will not be compensated on a day when they had planned to be working. People's aversion to uncertainty should make mandating that schedules be adhered to, at least over some pre-announced limited period, very attractive to workers. It might even be attractive to companies. The reduction in uncertainty about scheduling will increase people's willingness to work for companies that offer it. That might then lower the hourly wage that workers are willing to accept by enough to more than offset the cost of the reduction in employers' flexibility in scheduling.

A few cities, including New York, San Francisco, and Seattle, have passed ordinances that require employers, particularly in fast-food and similar retail outlets, to provide workers with announced schedules two weeks ahead of the work date.[19] If employers don't adhere to the schedule, they are required to pay premium wages should shifts be changed on short notice. These laws will not alter work timing, but they will reduce uncertainty about it, making workers better off by allowing them to schedule their nonwork time in a more satisfying way. With proper planning, these ordinances are unlikely to raise labor costs greatly, and they might even reduce them by making these jobs attractive to more workers.

Policies mandating this kind of reduction in workers' uncertainty seem very desirable. We saw that most workers' schedules do not vary and are not subject to the vagaries of employers' perceptions of the demand for their products, but some are, especially among retail workers and even more among female retail workers. The laws do not represent a win-win proposition, but they do to combine a big win for a few people with a very small loss for employers and stockholders.

With six different time zones the US economy is dis-coordinated. That will be increasingly true as the economic center of gravity shifts steadily away from the Northeast. Time zones are artificial, not God-given, and there is no reason not to change them if that would be economically beneficial. One simple change would be to create just two zones, two hours apart from each other, covering the entire contiguous forty-eight states. A dividing line running at the western end of the current Central time zone would demarcate these two proposed zones. Making this change would allow more coordination of schedules and timing of activities across the country and foster more social cohesion than is currently possible. For frequent flyers it would reduce the psychological and perhaps even the physiological effects of jet lag produced by coast-to-coast travel.

POLICIES TO DEAL WITH LONG WORKING HOURS

The excess work time of Americans compared to citizens of other rich countries is substantial, and it is not explainable by any of the commonly offered stories for it, including tax policy, extreme consumerism, and others. It is a manifestation of what economists call a "low-level equilibrium," a situation in which a group, or a society, finds itself in an inferior situation that internal incentives prevent it from ameliorating. What can be done to spring the American workforce from this low-level equilibrium trap?

In addition to this goal of reduced work time, spreading work time across people and across people's lifetimes is desirable. People benefit from variety—we buy more different goods and services and do more different things with our time as our incomes increase and provide us the opportunity to do so. With a reduction in total annual work time for workers, but a greater spread of work time across the population and across our lives as we age, we will be happier. The appropriate policy should accomplish one or both goals—reducing average work time per person over the year, while allowing people a greater chance to spread work over their lives. Enabling people to mix time spent in paid work and other time spent in leisure and personal care over more days and years would make them better off on average over their adult lives.

A remarkable variety of government policies directly affect the amount of time that Americans and others spend working for pay. Altering them to reduce work time to a level that would be predicted from looking at work time and productivity in other rich countries seems especially attractive in the relatively workaholic US. And although Americans tend to retire later than workers in other rich countries, most still have substantial periods of time late in life when they are doing no paid work.

One policy that can affect work time directly is the overtime law—time-and-a-half for overtime—which in the US was originally embodied in the Fair Labor Standards Act. Forcing employers to pay extra for hours beyond forty per week gives them an incentive to keep weekly hours below what they otherwise would be. Although it raises employers' labor costs, which is why employers' groups and right-leaning politicians are vehemently against its extension, it almost certainly also increases total employment, spreading work across the population. It thus meets the dual criteria of reducing work time per worker while spreading work among more workers and potential workers, as is clear from research evaluating its impacts.[20]

While the US overtime law was extended to additional industries over the first forty years of its existence, since the 1970s its impact on work time has been reduced because an increasing fraction of American workers have been treated as presumptively exempt from the requirement that employers offer overtime pay. In 1974, salaried workers had to earn 150 percent of the median weekly pay before they were assumed exempt from protection under the federal overtime law; in 2018 that limit was 50 percent. An effort to reverse this decline was made by the Obama administration in 2016, but it was blocked by the courts and will almost certainly not be reinstituted for at least several years.

Income taxes are mostly taxes on people's work, since paid work time generates most of the income that Americans and others receive. As such, they can affect how much we wish to work. Payroll taxes—Social Security and Medicare taxes in popular American parlance—can have similar effects. Economists have studied the impacts of higher income and payroll taxes on hours of work nearly ad nauseam. While there is no definitive conclusion about their effects, the evidence seems strongly to favor the conclusion that the effects are there, but that they are not very large.[21] In any case, raising taxes, even in a country like the US where they are low by international standards, has been political anathema since the 1980s. Even if they were raised, the evidence suggests that they would lead to only small reductions in hours of work and would do little to spread work more evenly across more people and over a greater share of people's adult lives. Changing taxes is unlikely to have important effects in changing the amount of time pressure that people feel.

The structure of pension plans, both private and public, alters the amount that we work, particularly in later life. Defined-benefit pensions—offering a certain predetermined amount of monthly income at some age, with the lifetime amount often declining if not claimed at that age—provide strong incentives that reduce labor force participation and work hours among older people. Defined-contribution pension plans, such as 401(k) plans in the US, which offer pension payments based on accumulated investments in the plan, have negative effects on work time among the elderly insofar as they provide sufficient income to finance purchases only during old age. In general, pension policies, especially defined-benefit plans, create incentives to compress working time into our earlier years and work against spreading leisure more evenly over our lives.

The major impact of public policy on work among the elderly in the US and elsewhere is through public pensions—in the US through the Social Security Act of 1935. When the Act became effective it offered retirement pay at age sixty-five—that at a time when the average sixty-five-year-old could expect to live to age seventy-eight. The retirement age was raised to sixty-six by 2009, and by 2022 full Social Security pay will be offered only at age sixty-seven—but at a time when a sixty-seven-year-old can expect to live to age eighty-four. American public pensions have been modified to increase incentives to continue working in older age, but the growth in life expectancy has far outpaced the changing incentives, so that we now expect public pensions to support us for seventeen instead of the thirteen years that our great-grandparents could have expected in the late 1930s. Even with some small increases in the age when public pensions in Europe can be claimed, the amount of time that people are collecting pensions and doing almost no paid work has also risen there.

The incentive to move from full-time work to full-time nonwork—to compress our lifetime of work into our earlier years and stuff nonwork time into our later years—should be reduced by raising the age of eligibility for full Social Security benefits in the US. Gradually raising it to age seventy throughout the 2020s and 2030s would achieve this end and would have the desirable effect of ensuring the financial integrity of the Social Security program. But the argument here is not financial—it is that by raising the age of eligibility for full benefits we could reduce people's incentives to compartmentalize work earlier in life and nonwork when they are older. We could enhance the variety of people's experiences as they age.

Over the years the US Social Security system has reduced the disincentives against working while receiving benefits. In its early days an "earnings test" was imposed that required recipients of Social Security to forgo some benefits if they earned more than a certain low amount. The changes in this requirement, which was repeatedly eased and in 1999 abolished, provided older workers more incentives to continue working. The evidence suggests that relaxing the earnings test did increase hours of work among the elderly.[22] While it does not meet the goal of reducing work hours per worker, it does encourage people to spread work more evenly over their lifetimes.

Despite these difficulties and the incentives that public pensions create to reduce spreading work over the lifetime, the US is still far ahead of most European countries in minimizing the disincentives that currently crowd work out of one's later years. Since 1987 there has been no mandatory retirement age in the US, a work-life extending policy that is only recently being adopted in a few European countries. In most European economies, public and private pensions also provide very strong incentives for leaving work well before age seventy and thus for minimizing the variety of activities over a lifetime (as well as leading to tremendous fiscal imbalances). Those countries could do well by adopting and even going further than the American pension system in encouraging work into late middle age and even into old age up through the early seventies.

HOW TO MAKE A MAJOR CHANGE IN TIME USE

All the policy changes that I have suggested would help to achieve the goal of spreading reduced annual work time over a longer working life, but all are marginal: none would have a big effect. Even worse, all these changes require altering policy regimes that have been debated continually over the past seventy years and on which people hold very different and strongly entrenched opinions. Their likely minor effects and the political difficulties of adopting them militate against relying upon them as ways of solving growing feelings of time deprivation.

American labor force participation rates differ little from those in Europe, and weekly hours when people are working also don't differ much. But annual hours of paid work are much greater in the US than in Europe, and higher now than in other rich countries too, because Americans work more weeks per year than others. To have a major impact on work time, and to enable people to feel less pressured on each day and throughout their lives, a successful policy must operate along the dimension of reducing the number of weeks that people work each year.

To address the issue of work time directly—to cut the Gordian knot of labor market policy—the US needs to embark in a new direction, namely mandating minimum paid annual vacation time. Mandating four weeks of paid vacation would still leave the US behind many Western countries, but a good estimate is that it would double the average amount of paid vacation time that American workers receive. As such, it would reduce hours worked per year for the typical worker; coupled with some of the existing policies designed to spread work more over the lifetime—to enhance variety in life—it would help to achieve the dual goals that I have outlined. It would go a long way to springing the US labor market from its low-level equilibrium trap.

Additional paid vacation and public holidays do not offer society an unalloyed gain of more leisure time. They are not costless; they are not a "free lunch." If people are working fewer hours per year because they are enjoying more vacation and public holidays, they will produce less. With more time off and less production, total earnings will fall. Living standards—GDP per capita, the dollar amount produced per person—will not be so high. Like most things in life, the choice between more or fewer vacations and holidays represents a trade-off—additional leisure and lower living standards, or less leisure and more income. The best choice in this trade-off that society can make depends on the cost of additional leisure in terms of income—on what we would have to give up and how we value the leisure that will be gained compared to the lost income—on our preferences for leisure and income.

Based on research on people's productivity over the working day, we can get a bit of an insight into the nature of this trade-off between GDP and nonwork time. We are generally most productive in our first few hours at work on a given day. This fact was demonstrated back in the days of scientific management in the 1920s. It has been shown in similar studies recently and is demonstrated too by research using the American time-diary data.[23] Studies of the impacts of strikes offer similarly suggestive evidence: much of the production lost during a strike is made up by additional unexpected production before and afterward.[24]

Taking the small amount of evidence together, we just don't know exactly what the leisure–output trade-off is in this case—how much income Americans (or people in other wealthy countries) would have to give up in exchange for an additional day or week of vacation or holiday time. But we can be pretty sure that the lost production—the cut in per-capita GDP—would be less than proportional to the cut in hours of work. For example, if Americans averaged four instead of two weeks of paid vacation per year (a decrease in work time of 4 percent), GDP per capita would fall by less than 4 percent. Say that the cut in work time of 4 percent would cut output by 2 percent—a one-for-two trade-off.

In 2017 that would have meant that the additional leisure would have reduced GDP from around \$59,500 per capita to around \$58,300 per capita. Even that decline probably overestimates the reduction in living standards. As employers adjust to shorter annual hours by hiring more workers, including older workers, the additional employment would cushion the drop in GDP.

Enacting this novel (for the US) and sweeping change will take some political will. But the arguments for it are strong, and it would be the simplest way to make a major difference in how people spend their time and how they live their lives. It would enable them to balance paid work and non-work time more easily and to mitigate the increasing pressures that are generated by rising purchasing power with no commensurate increase in available time.

THE FUTURE OF TIME USE

The drop in the percentage of adults working or seeking work in the US since 2000 and the small drop in hours spent in paid work each year are welcome developments. They suggest that America has taken a small step back from what by international standards has for the past thirty years been an unusually large amount of time spent doing paid work. The US has also seen an increase in older Americans working or seeking work. This too is a welcome step in the ability to enjoy variety—to mix work and leisure and other nonwork activities more over our lifetimes.

Despite these changes, Americans still have a long way to go until they enjoy the leisure that you would think the tremendous productive power of the American economy would allow. The policies that I have discussed, particularly the requirement of mandating substantial paid vacations, would go a long way to increasing the well-being of American society. It's not that other rich economies are in any sense more admirable than the American economy. But unless one believes that the human purpose is to spend time working for pay, which seems an antiquated belief if it was ever correct, providing increased incentives for people to enjoy more leisure and enjoy more work-leisure variety over their lives is a sensible path to take.

What if we don't do anything to alter the incentives that have people working long hours and concentrating their paid work in their thirties, forties, fifties, and early sixties? The answer seems clear from the discussions throughout: if economic growth continues even at a diminished rate of barely 1 percent per year, the purchasing power of our grandchildren will double ours. If our grandchildren haven't reduced the amount that they work each year and haven't altered the timing of work over their lifetimes, they will feel even more rushed than we do now. They will have more things to buy and more different things to do, but they will have little or no more time in which to do them. This is a very unappealing prospect.

Instituting sensible policies, such as mandating minimum paid vacations, will go a long way toward preventing people from winding up in increasingly hurried and pressured societies. Changing public policies on work time and timing will not be done quickly, in the US, Europe, or elsewhere. It will require substantial debate. Even though many of the policies exist in other rich countries, some have barely been mentioned in the US. Similarly, American-style policy on pensions has not been discussed sufficiently in Europe. But all these changes make sense, and all would go a long way to solving people's problems of shortages of time—of time stress. It is time to begin talking about them now.

NOTES

PREFACE

1. http://apps.webofknowledge.com.ezproxy.lib.utexas.edu/Search.do?product =WOS&SID=3BBRXuHA4JLLDMJHMpo&search_mode=GeneralSearch&prI D=1de537b3-bc81-488e-bb55-18dbfce1ac96 is the URL for the *Web of Science* for this search, conducted on August 24, 2017.
2. Just a few of these are Rachel Connelly and Jean Kimmel, *The Time Use of Mothers in the United States at the Beginning of the 21st Century* (Kalamazoo: W. E. Upjohn Institute for Employment Research, 2010); Jean Kimmel, ed., *How Do We Spend Our Time? Evidence from the American Time Use Survey* (Kalamazoo: W. E. Upjohn Institute for Employment Research, 2008); and Daniel Hamermesh and Gerard Pfann, *The Economics of Time Use* (Amsterdam: Elsevier, 2005).
3. John Robinson and Geoffrey Godbey, *Time for Life: The Surprising Ways Americans Use Their Time* (University Park: Pennsylvania State University Press, 1997) did use a few small American surveys to focus on how time was spent in the US.
4. Martin Luther King Jr., "Letter from a Birmingham Jail," April 16, 1963.
5. These are Jeff Biddle and Daniel Hamermesh, "Sleep and the Allocation of Time," *Journal of Political Economy* 98 (Oct. 1990): 922–43; and Daniel Hamermesh, "Shirking or Productive Schmoozing? Wages and the Allocation of Time at Work," *Industrial and Labor Relations Review* 43 (Feb. 1990): 121S–133S.

CHAPTER 1

1. The case is *Federal Trade Commission v. Amazon.com, Inc.*, Case No. 2:14-cv-01038-JCC.
2. Luca Zamparini and Aura Reggiani, "Meta-Analysis and the Value of Travel Time Savings: A Transatlantic Perspective in Passenger Transport," *Networks and Spatial Economics* 7 (2007): 377–96, summarizes a huge number of studies of the willingness to pay to reduce commuting time.
3. Jeff Dominitz and Charles Manski, "Using Expectations Data to Study Subjective Income Expectations," *Journal of the American Statistical Association* 92 (Sept. 1997): 855–67, demonstrated the strong relationship between income expectations and outcomes.
4. The Federal Reserve Board Survey of Consumer Expectations is described at https://www.newyorkfed.org/microeconomics/sce.
5. Daniel Hamermesh, "Expectations, Life Expectancy, and Economic Behavior," *Quarterly Journal of Economics* 100 (May 1985): 389–408, showed how people's

beliefs about how long they would live, and the chances of living to age sixty or eighty, were fairly well aligned with the population statistics on these outcomes.

6. John Leeds, *The Household Budget, with a Special Inquiry into the Amount of Value of Household Work* (Philadelphia: Leeds, 1917).
7. A very good popular discussion of how biology affects our time use is "The Tyranny of Time," *The Economist*, December 18, 1999, p. 72.

CHAPTER 2

1. Richard T. Ely, *An Introduction to Political Economy* (New York: Hunt and Eaton, 1891), 22.
2. The idea of home production was initially proposed by Margaret G. Reid, *The Economics of Household Production* (New York: Wiley, 1934).
3. The Sipress cartoon appeared in the *New Yorker*, Dec. 24 and 31, 2007.
4. Richard Wrangham, *Catching Fire* (New York: Basic Books, 2009), provides evidence on the tremendous amount of time that primitive people (almost exclusively women) spent or still spend in food preparation.
5. Garey Ramey and Valerie Ramey, "The Rug-rat Race," *Brookings Papers on Economic Activity* (Spring 2010): 129–76.
6. A comparison of food time is from Daniel Hamermesh, "Time to Eat," *American Journal of Agricultural Economics* 89 (Nov. 2007): 852–63.
7. This is based on Elena Stancanelli and Leslie Stratton, "Maids, Appliances, and Couples' Housework: The Demand for Inputs to Domestic Production," *Economica* 81 (July 2014): 445–67.
8. Richard Freeman and Ronald Schettkat, "Marketization of Household Production and the EU-US Gap in Work," *Economic Policy* 41 (Jan. 2005): 5–39.
9. The data are from Jeremy Greenwood, Ananth Seshadri, and Mehmet Yorukoglu, "Engines of Liberation," *Review of Economic Studies* 72 (Jan. 2005): 109–33.
10. Jeff Biddle and Daniel Hamermesh, "Sleep and the Allocation of Time," *Journal of Political Economy* 98 (Oct. 1990): 922–43, was the first to examine the role of the value of time in this unusual activity.
11. Edward Laumann, John Gagnon, Robert Michael, and Stuart Michaels, *The Social Organization of Sexuality: Sexual Practices in the United States* (Chicago: University of Chicago Press, 1994), Tables 3.4 and 3.5.
12. The distribution of grazing time in relation to primary eating was investigated in Daniel Hamermesh, "Incentives, Time Use, and BMI: The Roles of Eating, Grazing, and Goods," *Economics and Human Biology* 8 (March 2010): 2–15.
13. Meg Sullivan, "Our Ancestors Probably Didn't Get 8 Hours a Night, Either," *UCLA Newsroom*, Oct. 15, 2015, http://newsroom.ucla.edu/releases/our-ancestors-probably-didnt-get-8-hours-a-night-either.
14. Alan Krueger and David Schkade, "The Reliability of Subjective Well-Being Measures," *Journal of Public Economics* 92 (Aug. 2008): 1833–45, Table 6, provides evidence on this from subjective responses that time diarists have offered about the activities they have engaged in.
15. See the calculations in Mark Aguiar and Erik Hurst, "Measuring Trends in Leisure: The Allocation of Time over Five Decades," *Quarterly Journal of Economics* 122 (Aug. 2007): 969–1006.
16. https://www.nytimes.com/2016/07/01/business/media/nielsen-survey-media-viewing.html, June 30, 2016. On average, American adults are *watching* five hours and four minutes of television per day. The bulk of that—about four and

a half hours of it—is live television, which is television watched when originally broadcast.

17. Fernando Lozano, "The Flexibility of the Workweek in the United States: Evidence from the FIFA World Cup," *Economic Inquiry* 49 (April 2011): 512–29, provides evidence on the role of televised sporting events.

CHAPTER 3

1. See Daniel Hamermesh, "The Labor Market in the United States, 2000–16," IZA World of Labor, https://wol.iza.org/articles/the-labor-market-in-the-us-2000-2016, for a discussion of these and related statistics.
2. Thomas Kniesner, "The Full-time Workweek in the United States, 1900–1970," *Industrial and Labor Relations Review* 30 (Oct. 1976): 3–15, presents the history of the US workweek over much of the twentieth century.
3. Peter Kuhn and Fernando Lozano, "The Expanding Workweek? Understanding Trends in Long Work Hours among US Men, 1979–2006," *Journal of Labor Economics* 26 (April 2008): 311–43, examines changes in the percentage of Americans working long hours, with some information going back to 1940.
4. A table listing paid leave time by country can be found at https://en.wikipedia.org/wiki/List_of_minimum_annual_leave_by_country. One survey about vacation time is reported at https://www.bloomberg.com/news/articles/2017-05-23/americans-are-taking-more-paid-vacation-days.
5. A very careful study by Joseph Altonji and Jennifer Oldham, "Vacation Laws and Annual Work Hours," Federal Reserve Bank of Chicago, *Economic Perspectives* (Fall 2003): 19–29, shows how additional mandated annual leave reduces annual work hours.
6. Joseph Altonji and Emiko Usui, "Work Hours, Wages, and Vacation Leave," *Industrial and Labor Relations Review* 60 (April 2007): 408–28, provides the evidence for the US. Ali Fakih, "Vacation Leave, Work Hours, and Wages: New Evidence from Linked Employer-Employee Data," *Labour* 28 (Dec. 2014): 376–98, is the Canadian study.
7. Joachim Merz and Lars Osberg, "Keeping in Touch—A Benefit of Public Holidays Using Time Use Diary Data," *Electronic International Journal of Time Use Research* 6 (Sept. 2009): 130–66, demonstrates how in those German states with more public holidays people spend more time enjoying leisure together.
8. The role of unions in affecting paid holidays and vacations is examined by Laszlo Goerke, Sabrina Jeworrek, and Markus Pannenberg, "Trade Union Membership and Paid Vacation in Germany," *IZA Journal of Labor Economics* 4 (2015).
9. *Reserve Bank of Minneapolis Quarterly Review* 28, July 2004, with some evidence for it in Naci Mocan and Luiza Pogorelova, "Why Work More? The Impact of Taxes, and Culture of Leisure on Labor Supply in Europe," National Bureau of Economic Research Working Paper No. 21297, June 2015.
10. This argument was made by Juliet Schor, *The Overworked American: The Unexpected Decline of American Leisure* (New York: Basic Books, 1991).
11. Daniel Hamermesh and Joel Slemrod, "The Economics of Workaholism: We Should Not Have Worked on This Paper," *B.E. Journal of Economic Analysis and Policy* 8 (2008), presents a theory of workaholism and some tests for its presence. George Akerlof, "The Economics of Caste and of the Rat Race and Other Woeful Tales," *Quarterly Journal of Economics* 90 (Nov. 1976): 519–617, illustrates how everybody in a workplace, or a society, might work harder than

they really wish to in order to demonstrate to the employer how qualified they are. Some evidence on this is offered by Renée Landers, James Rebitzer, and Lowell Taylor, "Rat Race Redux: Adverse Selection in the Determination of Work Hours in Law Firms," *American Economic Review* 86 (June 1996): 329–48.

CHAPTER 4

1. For example, stories at http://www.cnn.com/2013/06/24/opinion/drexler-four-day-workweek/index.html and http://www.businessinsider.com/why-we-should-have-a-4-day-work-week-2016-5.
2. Jens Bonke, "Do Morning-Type People Earn More than Evening-Type People? How Chronotypes Influence Income," *Annals of Economics and Statistics*, 105/106 (Jan./June 2012): 55–72, examines the simple question whether those who are working in the morning earn more than those who work the same total hours but do not work mornings. A study relating mortality to the timing of sleep, covering nearly one-half million Britons, suggested that morning types have lower mortality rates: Kristen Knutson and Malcolm von Schantz, "Associations between Chronotype, Morbidity, and Mortality in the UK Biobank Cohort," *Chronobiology International*, published online April 11, 2018.
3. The link between violent crime and work at nights in large cities is demonstrated in Daniel Hamermesh, "Crime and the Timing of Work," *Journal of Urban Economics* 45 (March 1999): 311–30.
4. Ana Rute Cardoso, Daniel Hamermesh, and José Varejão, "The Timing of Labor Demand," *Annals of Economics and Statistics* 105/106 (Jan./June 2012): 15–34, presents information underlying a similar figure for Portugal, showing a larger pucker over the usual lunchtime hours.
5. Daniel Hamermesh, "The Timing of Work over Time," *Economic Journal* 109 (Jan. 1999): 37–66, shows the changing timing of work between 1973 and 1991. The statistics on timing in 1973 are from this source.
6. https://www.osha.gov/dep/fatcat/dep_fatcat.html details the time path of workplace fatalities.
7. Peter Kostiuk, "Compensating Differentials for Shift Work," *Journal of Political Economy* 101 (Jan. 1990): 1054–75; and Matthew Shapiro, "Capital Utilization and the Marginal Premium for Work at Night," unpublished paper, University of Michigan, 1995, present evidence on the wage premium that employers must offer for unusual work times.
8. Daniel Hamermesh and Elena Stancanelli, "Long Workweeks and Strange Hours," *Industrial and Labor Relations Review* 68 (Oct. 2015): 1007–18, tabulates data on the incidence and amount of night work in various countries.
9. Juliane Scheffel, "Compensation of Unusual Working Schedules," unpublished paper, SFB649, Humboldt University—Berlin, 2011, shows how work at various unusual times of the day is compensated in Germany.
10. Gerald Oettinger, "An Empirical Analysis of the Daily Labor Supply of Stadium Vendors," *Journal of Political Economy* 107 (April 1999): 360–92; Colin Camerer, Linda Babcock, George Loewenstein, and Richard Thaler, "Labor Supply of New York City Cabdrivers: One Day at a Time," *Quarterly Journal of Economics* 112 (May 1997): 404–41; M. Keith Chen, Judith Chevalier, Peter Rossi, and Emily Oehlsen, "The Value of Flexible Work: Evidence from Uber Drivers," NBER Working Paper No. 23296, 2017.

11. Marie Connolly, "Climate Change and the Allocation of Time," IZA World of Labor, Jan. 2018, https://wol.iza.org/articles/climate-change-and-the-allocation-of-time.
12. Hamermesh and Stancanelli, "Long Workweeks and Strange Hours."

CHAPTER 5

1. Jungmin Lee, "Marriage, the Sharing Rule, and Pocket Money: The Case of South Korea," *Economic Development and Cultural Change* 55 (April 2007): 557–81, examines how Korean couples determine the amount of pocket money that each spouse receives. Shelly Lundberg, Robert Pollak, and Terence Wales, "Do Husbands and Wives Pool Their Resources?," *Journal of Human Resources* 32 (Summer 1997): 463–80, demonstrates how clothing purchases vary when one spouse rather than the other receives money from the government. The indirect evidence is in, among many others, Martin Browning and Pierre-André Chiappori, "Efficient Intra-Household Allocations: A General Characterization and Empirical Tests," *Econometrica* 66 (Nov. 1998): 1241–78.
2. Leora Friedberg and Anthony Webb, "The Chore Wars: Household Bargaining and Leisure Time," unpublished paper, University of Virginia, Dec. 2005.
3. *OECD Labor Force Statistics, 2006–15* (Paris: OECD, 2016).
4. Holger Bonin and Rob Euwals, "Participation Behavior of East German Women after German Unification," IZA Discussion Paper No. 413, 2001.
5. Michael Burda, Daniel Hamermesh, and Philippe Weil, "The Distribution of Total Work in the EU and USA," in *Working Hours and Job Sharing in the EU and USA: Are Europeans Lazy? Or Americans Crazy?*, ed. Tito Boeri et al. (New York: Oxford University Press, 2008).
6. Charlene Kalenkoski, David Ribar, and Leslie Stratton, "The Influence of Wages on Parents' Allocations of Time to Childcare and Market Work in the United Kingdom," *Journal of Population Economics* 22 (April 2009): 399–419, uses data from around the year 2000 to examine how spousal differences in wage rates affect the time each spends in childcare and home production.
7. James Andreoni, Eleanor Brown, and Isaac Rischall, "Charitable Giving by Married Couples: Who Decides and Why Does it Matter?," *Journal of Human Resources* 38 (Winter 2003): 111–33, presents data on how American couples determine their charitable contributions.
8. Cristina Borra, Martin Browning, and Almudena Sevilla, "Marriage and Housework," IZA Discussion Paper No. 10470, 2017.
9. Michael Burda, Daniel Hamermesh, and Philippe Weil, "Total Work and Gender: Facts and Possible Explanations," *Journal of Population Economics* 26 (Jan. 2013): 239–61, proposes the existence of iso-work, presents the data depicted in Figure 5.2, and discusses reasons why this phenomenon has arisen.
10. These are the same countries that were included in Figure 2.2, excluding Mexico, in which women and men both reported performing much more total work than any of the other countries.
11. Mark Aguiar and Erik Hurst, "Measuring Trends in Leisure: The Allocation of Time over Five Decades," *Quarterly Journal of Economics* 122 (Aug. 2007): 969–1006, shows that this increasing equality exists even when one makes substantial changes in what is viewed as home production.
12. Sarah Fleche, Anthony Lepinteur, and Nattavudh Powdthavee, "Gender Norms and Relative Working Hours: Why Do Women Suffer More than Men from Working Longer Hours Than Their Partners?," *American Economic Association, Papers and Proceedings* 108 (May 2018): 163–8.

13. Alan Krueger and David Schkade, "The Reliability of Subjective Well-Being Measures," *Journal of Public Economics* 92 (2008): 1833–45, Table 6.

14. Aguiar and Hurst, "Measuring Trends in Leisure," shows that this increasing equality exists even when one makes substantial changes in what is viewed as home production.

15. These issues are discussed at length in a report by a panel of National Academy of Sciences: Katharine Abraham and Christopher Mackie, eds., *Beyond the Market: Designing Nonmarket Accounts for the United States* (Washington, DC: National Academies Press, 2005).

16. Alan Jay Lerner and Frederick Loewe, "A Hymn to Him," 1956.

17. Daniel Hamermesh, *Beauty Pays: Why Attractive People Are More Successful* (Princeton, NJ: Princeton University Press, 2011), offers a general discussion of the issues and provides evidence on the role of beauty in earnings. One study of young American adults, Jaclyn Wong and Andrew Penner, "Gender and the Returns to Attractiveness," *Research in Social Stratification and Mobility* 44 (June 2016): 113–23, suggests that much of the differences among women's perceived looks arise from their grooming, but a study that explicitly measured money spent on grooming by Chinese adult women, Daniel Hamermesh, Xin Meng, and Junsen Zhang, "Dress for Success—Does Primping Pay?," *Labour Economics* 9 (Oct. 2002): 361–73, suggests only a small effect.

18. Daniel Hamermesh and Jason Abrevaya, " 'Beauty Is the Promise of Happiness'?," *European Economic Review* 64 (Nov. 2013): 351–68.

19. Issues in measuring the size of the homosexual population are discussed by Dan Black, Hoda Makar, Seth Sanders, and Lowell Taylor, "The Earnings Effects of Sexual Orientation," *Industrial and Labor Relations Review* 56 (April 2003): 449–69.

20. Michael Martell and Leanne Roncolato, "The Homosexual Lifestyle: Time Use in Same-Sex Households," *Journal of Demographic Economics* 82 (Dec. 2016): 365–98, makes similar calculations using these data, and, because the study restricts the age range to twenty-five to fifty-four, it produces even smaller samples of people whom they can identify as homosexual.

21. Marie-Anne Valfort, *LGBTI in OECD Countries*, OECD Working Paper No. 198, 2017, surveys the literature on economic outcomes, including work time, for gays, lesbians, and other sexual minorities in wealthy countries.

22. Calculated from waves of the World Values Survey in the 1990s.

23. Rob Walker, "It's a Man's World: Men's Grooming Breaks New Ground," *Global Cosmetic Industry Magazine*, Feb. 23, 2014, http://www.gcimagazine.com/marketstrends/consumers/men/Its-a-Mans-World-Mens-Grooming-Breaks-New-Ground-246591491.html.

CHAPTER 6

1. Gary Becker, *A Treatise on the Family* (Cambridge, MA: Harvard University Press, 1981).

2. William Haefeli, *New Yorker*, June 2, 2014.

3. Joan García-Román, Sarah Flood, and Katie Genadek, "Parents' Time with a Partner in a Cross-National Context: A Comparison of the United States, Spain, and France," *Demographic Research* 36 (Jan. 2017): 111–44, uses time-diary data from these three countries to examine togetherness, as measured by our stylized Sections B + C + D in Figure 6.1.

4. Simon George-Kot, Dominique Goux, and Eric Maurin, "Following the Crowd: Leisure Complementarities Beyond the Household," *Journal of Labor Economics* 35 (Oct. 2017): 1061–88.

5. García-Román, Flood, and Genadek, "Parents' Time with a Partner in a Cross-National Context."

6. Cahit Guven, Claudia Senik, and Holger Stichnoth, "You Can't Be Happier than Your Wife: Happiness Gaps and Divorce," *Journal of Economic Behavior and Organization* 82 (2012): 110–30, presents the German evidence; and Ariel Kalil and Mari Rege, "We Are Family: Fathers' Time with Children and the Risk of Parental Relationship Dissolution," *Social Forces* 94 (2015): 833–62, provides Australian evidence on shared eating time.

7. OECD, "What Are Equivalence Scales?," http://www.oecd.org/eco/growth/OECD-Note-EquivalenceScales.pdf presents a brief discussion and a list of alternative measures of equivalence scales. Edward Lazear and Robert Michael, *Allocation of Income within the Household* (Chicago: University of Chicago Press, 1988), analyzes these issues in detail.

8. Based on https://www.census.gov/data/tables/time-series/demo/income-poverty/historical-poverty-thresholds.html, and http://www.oecd.org/eco/growth/OECD-Note-EquivalenceScales.pdf.

9. Hélène Couprie and Gaëlle Ferrant, "Welfare Comparisons, Economies of Scale, and Equivalence Scale in Time Use," *Annals of Economics and Statistics* 117/118 (June 2015): 185–210.

10. This point has been made forcefully in a regrettably neglected study by Patricia Apps, "Gender, Time Use, and Models of the Household," IZA Discussion paper No. 796, 2003.

11. Katie Genadek, "Same-Sex Couples' Shared Time in the United States," unpublished paper, University of Colorado, 2017, presents evidence on these issues.

12. Sarah Flood and Katie Genadek, "Time for Each Other: Work and Family Constraints among Couples," *Journal of Marriage and Family* 78 (2016): 142–64.

CHAPTER 7

1. As reported in Quartz https://qz.com/311360/students-in-these-countries-spend-the-most-time-doing-homework/, based on the OECD's analysis of data from the Program for International Student Assessment (PISA).

2. Reported in Mark Perry, "2016 SAT Results Confirm Pattern That's Persisted for 50 Years—High School Boys Are Better at Math than Girls," *AEIdeas* (blog), Sept. 27, 2016, http://www.aei.org/publication/2016-sat-test-results-confirm-pattern-thats-persisted-for-45-years-high-school-boys-are-better-at-math-than-girls/.

3. Sol Lim, Cheol Han, Peter Uhlhaas, and Marcus Kaiser, "Preferential Detachment during Human Brain Development: Age- and Sex-Specific Structural Connectivity in Diffusion Tensor Imaging (DTI) Data," *Cerebral Cortex* 25 (June 2015): 1477–89.

4. Jeff Biddle and Daniel Hamermesh, "Sleep and the Allocation of Time," *Journal of Political Economy* 98 (Oct. 1990): 922–43, builds a model that illustrates the dual role of sleep as consumption and investment.

5. An exhaustive survey on the impact of changing school starting times is Anne Wheaton, Daniel Chapman, and Janet Croft, "School Start Times, Sleep, Behavioral, Health, and Academic Outcomes: A Review of the Literature," *Journal of School Health* 86 (May 2016): 363–81. Jinseok Shin, "Sleep More and Study Less

in the Morning: The Impact of Delayed School Start Time on Sleep and Academic Performance," unpublished PhD chapter, University of Texas at Austin, 2018, provides the results on sleep timing, sleep time, and achievement in Korea.

6. Calculations of the distribution of educational attainment among twenty-five- to twenty-nine-year-olds in 2016 are based on statistics calculated from the Current Population Survey, Merged Outgoing Rotation Groups, for that year.

7. Calculated from Mark Aguiar, Mark Bils, Kerwin Charles, and Erik Hurst, "Leisure Luxuries and the Labor Supply of Young Men," NBER Working Paper No. 23552, 2017.

8. This was initially demonstrated in detail by Alan Gustman and Thomas Steinmeier, "A Structural Retirement Model," *Econometrica* 54 (May 1986): 554–84. A good survey of the literature is Sergi Jimenéz-Martin, "The Incentive Effects of Minimum Pensions," IZA World of Labor, https://wol.iza.org/articles/incentive-effects-of-minimum-pensions/long.

9. Elena Stancanelli and Arthur van Soest, "Partners' Leisure Time Truly Together upon Retirement," *IZA Journal of Labor Policy* 5, no. 12 (2016), demonstrates this using the kinks at various ages that exist in the French public pension system. See also the survey by Laura Hospido, "Pension Reform and Couples' Joint Retirement Decision," IZA World of Labor, https://wol.iza.org/articles/pension-reform-and-couples-joint-retirement-decisions/long.

10. Corry Azzi and Ronald Ehrenberg, "Household Allocation of Time and Church Attendance," *Journal of Political Economy* 83 (Feb. 1975): 27–56, reports this from other researchers' random surveys of the US population.

11. David Blanchflower and Andrew Oswald, "Is Well-Being U-Shaped over the Life Cycle?," National Bureau of Economic Research, Working Paper No. 12935, Feb. 2007.

12. John Bound, "Self-reported versus Objective Measures of Health in Retirement Models," *Journal of Human Resources* 26 (Winter 1991): 106–38.

13. The extent and sex composition of widows in the US population is based on calculations from the Current Population Survey, Merged Outgoing Rotation Groups, 2012–16.

CHAPTER 8

1. I categorize anyone listing his or her race as African American, or as African American and other, as African American; and anyone listing his or her race as Asian American, or Asian American and other, but who does not list him/herself as Hispanic, as Asian American. A white or Asian American who views her/himself as Hispanic is classified as Hispanic, while I classify other whites as non-Hispanic whites.

2. The size of the immigrant population over the last 150 years is documented at http://www.migrationpolicy.org/programs/data-hub/charts/immigrant-population-over-time?width=1000&height=850&iframe=true.

3. https://www.bls.gov/opub/reports/race-and-ethnicity/2015/home.htm presents unemployment rates by racial/ethnic group for 2015.

4. Daniel Hamermesh, Katie Genadek, and Michael Burda, "Racial/Ethnic Differences in Non-Work at Work," National Bureau of Economic Research, Working Paper No. 23096, 2017, presents these results and offers and tests several explanations for them.

5. Hamermesh, Genadek, and Burda, "Racial/Ethnic Differences in Non-Work at Work."

6. Brian Resnick, "The Black-White Sleep Gap," *The Atlantic*, October 23, 2015, https://www.theatlantic.com/politics/archive/2015/10/the-black-white-sleep-gap/454311/ discusses this laboratory research on sleep time.

7. That sleep is relatively time intensive is shown for the US and Israel by Reuben Gronau and Daniel Hamermesh, "Time vs. Goods: The Value of Measuring Household Technologies," *Review of Income and Wealth* 52 (March 2006): 1–16.

8. Evidence on the excess prices paid by minorities is provided by Ian Ayres and Peter Siegelman, "Race and Gender Discrimination in Bargaining for a New Car," *American Economic Review* 85 (June 1995): 304–21. Some of the subsequent literature is summarized by John Yinger, "Evidence on Discrimination in Consumer Markets," *Journal of Economic Perspectives* 12 (Spring 1998): 23–40.

9. http://cmhd.northwestern.edu/wp-content/uploads/2011/06/SOCconfReportSingleFinal-1.pdf presents evidence on these racial/ethnic differences.

10. These are calculations based on questions in successive waves of the US General Social Surveys, 1996–2010.

11. Victoria Reitig and Andreas Muller, "The New Reality: Germany Adapts to Its Role as a Major Migrant Magnet," Migration Policy Institute, Aug. 31, 2016, http://www.migrationpolicy.org/article/new-reality-germany-adapts-its-role-major-migrant-magnet?gclid=EAIaIQobChMIycD7lOqx1gIVjrbACh1XBwsAE AAYASAAEgL2o_D_BwE for Germany; and https://www.thelocal.fr/20141201/immigration-in-france-10-key-stats for France.

12. Barry Chiswick, "The Effect of Americanization on the Earnings of Foreign-born Men," *Journal of Political Economy* 86 (Oct. 1978): 897–921. The leading technical volume on immigration in the US is George Borjas, *Immigration Economics* (Cambridge, MA: Harvard University Press, 2014), while the leading nontechnical book is his *We Wanted Workers* (New York: Norton, 2016).

13. Daniel Hamermesh, "Immigration and the Quality of Jobs," in *Help or Hindrance? The Economic Implications of Immigration for African-Americans*, ed. F. Bean and D. Hamermesh (New York: Russell Sage, 1998), demonstrates this for the US, while Osea Giuntella, "Do Immigrants Squeeze Natives out of Bad Schedules? Evidence from Italy," *IZA Journal of Migration* 1, no. 7 (2012), shows a similar result based on Italian data.

14. Daniel Hamermesh and Stephen Trejo, "How Do Immigrants Spend their Time? The Process of Assimilation," *Journal of Population Economics* 26 (April 2013): 507–30, demonstrates the importance of English-language proficiency. Andres Vargas, "Assimilation Effects beyond the Labor Market: Time Allocations of Mexican Immigrants to the US," *Review of Economics of the Household* 14 (Sept. 2016): 625–68, makes the comparisons for Mexican immigrants.

15. Immigrant-native differences in economic outcomes in France and Germany are documented by Yann Algan, Christian Dustmann, Albrecht Glitz, and Alan Manning, "The Economic Situation of First- and Second-Generation Immigrants in France, Germany, and the United Kingdom," *Economic Journal* 120 (Feb. 2010): F4–30. That immigrants, at least in France, pay more than natives for the same consumer products, is demonstrated by Arthur Acolin, Raphael Bostic, and Gary Painter, "A Field Study of Rental Market Discrimination across Origins in France," *Journal of Urban Economics* 95 (Sept. 2016): 49–63.

CHAPTER 9

1. Roland Fryer and Matthew Jackson, "A Categorical Theory of Cognition and Biased Decision Making," *Berkeley Electronic Journal of Theoretical Economics* (2008), discuss how people classify others' group identities in ways that lead to treatment of people as group members rather than individuals.

2. Joe Jones, "California Sun," 1960.

3. Definitions taken from the *American Heritage Dictionary of the English Language*, and from the *Merriam-Webster Dictionary*.

4. Some stereotypes about suburbia are listed at https://thepilver.com/2009/05/03/top-7-suburban-stereotypes/. They are epitomized by the Malvina Reynolds song "Little Boxes," https://www.google.com/search?q=%22Little+Boxes%22&ie=utf-8&oe=utf-8&client= firefox-b-1. Eric Jaffe, "Why People in Cities Walk Fast," *The Atlantic Citylab*, March 21, 2012, discusses studies of this possible phenomenon.

5. The term "New York minute" appears to have originated in Texas around 1967. A New Yorker does in an instant what a Texan would take a minute to do: http://www.urbandictionary.com/define.php?term=New%20York%20Minute.

6. R. A. DeMarchi, "New Time Zones: Fixing the Current Economic Crisis," https://www.docs-archive.net/New-Time-Zones%3A-Fixing-the-Current-Economic.pdf. A good discussion of the bases for time zones is Todd Rakoff, *A Time for Every Purpose* (Cambridge, MA: Harvard University Press, 2002).

7. Daniel Hamermesh, Caitlin Myers, and Mark Pocock, "Cues for Coordination: Latitude, Letterman, and Longitude," *Journal of Labor Economics* 26 (April 2008): 223–46, Table 2, presents evidence on the effect of time zones on the timing of work and sleep.

8. https://www.timeanddate.com/news/time/venezuela-change-timezone.html discusses the history of the changing Venezuelan clock time.

9. Osea Giuntella and Fabrizio Mazzonna, "Sunset Time and the Economic Effects of Social Jetlag: Evidence from US Time Zone Borders," unpublished paper, University of Pittsburgh, April 2017, provides evidence on the linkage among sunlight, sunset time, and sleep time in the US. Pavel Jelnov, "Economics of the Time Zone: Let There Be Light," unpublished paper, 2017, Leibniz University Hannover, discusses the roles of time zones in Russia.

10. Hamermesh, Myers, and Pocock, "Cues for Coordination," examines how TV broadcast timing alters TV watching, sleep, and work timing. The origins of this American peculiarity are discussed by Brian Winston, *Media, Technology, and Society—a History: From the Telegraph to the Internet* (London: Routledge, 1998).

11. A history of DST in the US is at http://www.webexhibits.org/daylightsaving/e.html. https://www.usnews.com/news/best-states/articles/2017-10-27/massachusetts-may-leave-eastern-time-zone documents a proposal to put Massachusetts on DST year-round, equivalent to its entering the Canadian Atlantic time zone.

12. US Department of Transportation, *The Daylight Saving Time Study: A Report to Congress from the Secretary of Transportation*, 1975, summarized early studies. Matthew Kotchen and Laura Grant, "Does Daylight Saving Time Save Energy? Evidence from a Natural Experiment in Indiana," *Review of Economics and Statistics* 93 (Nov. 2011): 1172–85.

13. The original study is Mark Kamstra, Lisa Kramer, and Maurice Levi, "Losing Sleep at the Market: The Daylight Savings Anomaly," *American Economic Review* 90 (Sept. 2000): 1005–11. The extension is by Russell Gregory-Allen, Ben Jacobsen, and

Wessel Marquering, "The Daylight Saving Time Anomaly in Stock Returns: Fact or Fiction?," *Journal of Financial Research* 33 (Winter 2010): 403–27.

14. Daniel Hamermesh, "Timing, Togetherness, and Time Windfalls," *Journal of Population Economics* 15 (Nov. 2002): 601–23, examined the Dutch data for 1990.

15. The evidence on tests and road deaths is summarized in Yvonne Harrison, "The Impact of Daylight Saving Time on Sleep and Related Behaviours," *Sleep Medicine Review* 17 (2013): 285–92, while Austin Smith, "Spring Forward at Your Own Risk: Daylight Saving Time and Fatal Vehicle Crashes," *American Economic Journal: Applied Economics* 8 (2016): 65–91, examined changes in fatalities in relation to the presence or absence of DST in Indiana.

16. Lawrence Jin and Nicolas Ziebarth, "Sleep, Health, and Human Capital: Evidence from Daylight Saving Time," unpublished paper, Cornell University, 2017.

17. Yiannis Kountouris and Kyriaki Remoundou, "About Time: Daylight Saving Time Transition and Individual Well-being," *Economics Letters* 122 (2014): 100–3, studies well-being in Germany just before and after the shift to Summer Time.

CHAPTER 10

1. "'The Rich Are Different' . . . The Real Story behind the Famed 'Exchange' between F. Scott Fitzgerald and Ernest Hemingway," *Quote/Counterquote* (blog), July 12, 2014, http://www.quotecounterquote.com/2009/11/rich-are-different-famous-quote.html.

2. George Johnson and John Bound, "Changes in the Structure of Wages in the 1980s: An Evaluation of Alternative Explanations," *American Economic Review* 82 (June 1992): 371–92, and Chinhui Juhn, Kevin M. Murphy, and Brooks Pierce, "Wage Inequality and the Rise in Returns to Skill," *Journal of Political Economy* 101 (June 1993): 410–42, were among the first to document this profound change in the American labor market.

3. The underlying historical data are in Bureau of the Census, *Current Population Reports*, P60–259. Peter Gottschalk and Robert Moffitt, "The Growth of Earnings Instability in the US Labor Market," *Brookings Papers on Economic Activity*, 1994, was among the first to document this. Thomas Piketty, *Capital in the 21st Century* (Cambridge, MA: Harvard University Press, 2014), gained worldwide fame by documenting the especially sharp rise in incomes among the very well-off and trying to explain its causes. A good discussion of changes in the income shares of the top 1 percent of families in several countries is Facundo Alvaredo, Anthony Atkinson, Thomas Piketty, and Emmanuel Saez, "The Top 1 Percent in International and Historical Perspective," *Journal of Economic Perspectives* 27 (Summer 2013): 3–20.

4. These summaries include John Pencavel, "Labor Supply of Men: A Survey," in *Handbook of Labor Economics*, vol. 1, 3–102, ed. Orley Ashenfelter and Richard Layard (Amsterdam: North-Holland, 1986); Mark Killingsworth and James Heckman, "Female Labor Supply: A Survey," in *Handbook of Labor Economics*, 103–204; Richard Blundell and Thomas MaCurdy, "Labor Supply: A Review of Alternative Approaches," in *Handbook of Labor Economics*, vol. 3, 1559–1695; and Michael Keane, "Labor Supply and Taxes: A Survey," *Journal of Economic Literature* 49 (Dec. 2011): 961–1075.

5. Reuben Gronau and Daniel Hamermesh, "Time vs. Goods: The Value of Measuring Household Technologies," *Review of Income and Wealth* 52 (March 2006): 1–16, estimates the relative goods and time intensities of various activities for the US and Israel.

6. Peter Passell, *New York Times*, Aug. 2, 1989, p. 1, discussing Jeff Biddle; and Daniel Hamermesh, "Sleep and the Allocation of Time," *Journal of Political Economy* 98 (Oct. 1990): 922–43.
7. The song is "Mamas Don't Let Your Babies Grow Up to Be Cowboys," written and performed by Ed and Patsy Bruce in 1975–1976 but made famous two years later by Willie Nelson and Waylon Jennings.
8. Daniel Hamermesh, "Why Are Professors 'Poorly Paid?,'" *Economics of Education Review* 66 (2018): 137–41.
9. The definition is from https://www.merriam-webster.com/dictionary/variety.
10. Reuben Gronau and Daniel Hamermesh, "The Demand for Variety: A Household Production Perspective," *Review of Economics and Statistics* 90 (Aug. 2008): 562–72, presents the evidence on variety and education in these countries.
11. The discussion of temporal routine is from Daniel Hamermesh, "Routine," *European Economic Review* 49 (Jan. 2005): 29–53.
12. Daniel Hamermesh, "Timing, Togetherness, and Time Windfalls," *Journal of Population Economics* 15 (Nov. 2002): 601–23, demonstrates who works evening and nights and documents the increase in the relative amount of total work performed at night by low- compared to high-wage workers.

CHAPTER 11

1. The word *kvetch* is now in most English-language dictionaries, e.g., https://www.merriam-webster.com/dictionary/kvetch. The definition of stress is from https://www.google.com/search?q=stress+definition&oq=stress+deinition&aqs=chrome..69i57j0l5.4319j0j7&sourceid=chrome&ie=UTF-8.
2. Tom Cheney, *The New Yorker*, Sept. 23, 2002, 60.
3. Nathan Bivins, "Get the Money," *ca.* 1900.
4. The French question asks whether the individual feels pressed for time (*l'individu se sent pressé par le temps*). I treat as stressed those who respond "every day" (*tous les jours*). The German question asks whether the respondent is frequently under time pressure (*häufig unter Zeitdruck*). I use "agree completely" (*stimme voll und ganz zu*) as the stressed category.
5. Eugene O'Neill, *The Iceman Cometh*, 1939.
6. *Wenn man mit dem Mädchen, das man liebt, zwei Stunden zusammensitzt, denkt man, es ist nur eine Minute; wenn man aber nur eine Minute auf einem heissen Ofen sitzt, denkt man, es sind zwei Stunden—das ist die Relativität.* https://www.gutzitiert.de/zitat_autor_albert_einstein_thema_relativitaet_zitat_2753.html.
7. The data on life expectancy are for 2015 from https://www.ssa.gov/oact/STATS/table4c6.html.
8. Much of the discussion in this section is based on Daniel Hamermesh and Jungmin Lee, "Stressed Out on Four Continents: Time Crunch or Yuppie Kvetch?," *Review of Economics and Statistics* 89 (May 2007): 374–83.
9. The Australian study is Lyn Craig and Judith Brown, "Feeling Rushed: Gendered Time Quality, Work Hours, Nonstandard Work Schedules, and Spousal Crossover," *Journal of Marriage and the Family* 79 (Feb. 2017): 225–42.
10. Ricardo Pagán, "Being under Time Pressure: The Case of Workers with Disabilities," *Social Indicators Research* 114 (2013): 831–40.
11. Sam Levenson, *In One Era and Out the Other*, 3rd ed. (New York: Pocket Books, 1981).
12. Much of the discussion in this section is based on Hielke Buddelmeyer, Daniel Hamermesh, and Mark Wooden, "The Stress Cost of Children on Moms and Dads," *European Economic Review* 109 (2018): 148–61.

13. The quote is from Hannah Ebin Hamermesh, phone call on July 5, 2002.
14. Germaine Louis, Kirsten Lum, Rajeshwari Sundaram, Zhen Chen, Sungduk Kim, Courtney Lynch, Enrique Schisterman, and Cecilia Pyper, "Stress Reduces Conception Probabilities across the Fertile Window: Evidence in Support of Relaxation," *Fertility and Sterility* 95 (June 2011): 2184–89, shows that even when fertility is not controlled, fecundity is greater when a woman is less stressed.
15. Joan Costa-Font, Sarah Flèche, and Ricardo Pagán, "Sleep Costs of Having Children," unpublished paper, London School of Economics, 2017, provides the evidence on sleep patterns and well-being in Germany.
16. The rhyme goes back to at least the seventeenth century: https://en.wikipedia.org/wiki/There_was_an_Old_Woman_Who_Lived_in_a_Shoe.
17. Here too, much of the discussion is based on Hamermesh and Lee, "Stressed Out on Four Continents"; Sanford DeVoe and Jeffrey Pfeffer, "Time Is Tight: How Higher Economic Value of Time Increases Feelings of Time Pressure," *Journal of Applied Psychology* 96 (July 2011): 665–76, demonstrates some of the findings on time pressure and income in a laboratory context.
18. Samuel Johnson. https://www.brainyquote.com/quotes/samuel_johnson_118274.

CHAPTER 12

1. http://www.bowflex.com/max-trainer/.
2. The view that unemployment as measured reflects people's choices to substitute home for market production is associated with real business cycle theory, of which the most prominent exponents are Nobel Prize winners Robert E. Lucas and Edward Prescott.
3. Rainer Winkelmann, "Unemployment and Happiness," *IZA World of Labor*, https://wol.iza.org/articles/unemployment-and-happiness, 2014, reviews evidence demonstrating this for Germany and other countries.
4. Michael Hurd, "A Compensation Measure of the Cost of Unemployment to the Unemployed," *Quarterly Journal of Economics* 95 (Sept. 1980): 225–43, demonstrates how the burden of a spell of unemployment rises with its duration.
5. Calculated from www.bls.gov.
6. Michael Burda and Daniel Hamermesh, "Unemployment, Market Work, and Household Production," *Economics Letters* 107 (May 2010): 131–33.
7. John Maynard Keynes, "Economic Possibilities for Our Grandchildren," in *Essays in Persuasion* (New York: W. W. Norton, 1930).
8. These legislated changes and their detailed impacts are discussed in Daiji Kawaguchi, Jungmin Lee, and Daniel Hamermesh, "A Gift of Time," *Labour Economics* 24 (Oct. 2013): 205–16.
9. The fertility rate in Korea was an already low 1.63 in the mid-1990s, having fallen from well above 2.0 in the early 1980s; by 2005 it was nearly the lowest in the world, 1.08. https://fred.stlouisfed.org/series/SPDYNTFRTINKOR.
10. The examination of happiness in Japan and Korea before and after the legislated changes in standard workweeks is in Daniel Hamermesh, Daiji Kawaguchi, and Jungmin Lee, "Does Labor Legislation Benefit Workers? Well-Being after an Hours Reduction," *Journal of the Japanese and International Economies* 44 (June 2017): 1–12.
11. Olivier Coibion, Yuriy Gorodnichenko, and Dmitri Koustas, "Consumption Inequality and the Frequency of Purchases," NBER Working Paper No. 23357, 2017.

12. "The Billionaires 2018," *Forbes*, March 6, 2018, https://www.forbes.com/billionaires/#7325ce60251c.

CHAPTER 13

1. Simon and Garfunkel, "59th Street Bridge Song," 1966.
2. An excellent discussion of issues in self-control is Jon Elster, *Ulysses and the Sirens: Studies in Rationality and Irrationality* (New York: Cambridge University Press, 1979).
3. Gretchen Reynolds, "An Hour of Running May Add 7 Hours to Your Life," *New York Times*, April 12, 2017.
4. Bernhard Schlink, *Die Frau auf der Treppe* (Zurich: Diogenes, 2014), 170.
5. Sandy and Harry Chapin, "Cat's in the Cradle," 1974.
6. *New York Times*, Jan. 11, 2014; Cody C. Delistraty, "To Work Better, Work Less," *The Atlantic*, Aug. 8, 2014. https://www.monster.com/career-advice/article/32-hour-work-week is one of many reports about this kind of experiment in work scheduling. Attempts to impose restrictions on workers' hours in a few companies are also described by John Gapper, "Bankers and Lawyers Are on an Unhealthy Treadmill," *Financial Times*, Jan. 15, 2014; and "Turning Boomers into Boomerangs," *The Economist*, Feb. 18, 2006, 65.
7. A good discussion of blue laws in the US is David Laband and Deborah Heinbuch, *Blue Laws: The History, Economics, and Politics of Sunday-Closing Laws* (Lexington, MA: Heath Lexington Books, 1987).
8. The Dutch evidence is based on Joyce Jacobsen and Peter Kooreman, "Timing Constraints and the Allocation of Time: The Effects of Changing Shopping Hours Regulations in the Netherlands," *European Economic Review* 49 (Jan. 2005): 9–27. The Canadian study is Mikal Skuterud, "The Impact of Sunday Shopping on Employment and Hours of Work in the Retail Industry: Evidence from Canada," *European Economic Review* 49 (Nov. 2005): 1953–78.
9. Joshua Gans and Andrew Leigh, "Born on the First of July: An (Un)natural Experiment in Birth Timing," *Journal of Public Economics* 93 (Feb. 2009): 246–63, shows how fertility subsidies can alter fertility. Susan Averett, H. Elizabeth Peters, and Donald Waldman, "Tax Credits, Labor Supply, and Childcare," *Review of Economics and Statistics* 79 (Feb. 1997): 125–35, demonstrates the positive effects of the US childcare tax credit on women's labor supply.
10. "Mexico Cuts Tortilla Tax," *New York Times*, Jan. 13, 2007, http://www.nytimes.com/2007/01/13/world/americas/13mexico.html, discusses the Mexican reaction to the increased corn price, which occurred in part because of the US push to devote corn production to expanding the supply of ethanol.
11. Daniel Hamermesh, "Direct Estimates of Household Production," *Economics Letters* 98 (Jan. 2008): 31–34, analyzes the extent to which food in general, and household time, can be substituted.
12. US Department of Agriculture, Food and Nutrition Service, *Characteristics of Supplemental Nutrition Assistance Program Households: Fiscal Year 2013*, Table A.28.
13. Daniel Hamermesh, *Labor Demand* (Princeton, NJ: Princeton University Press, 1993), discusses the economics literature on the impacts of overtime legislation. Dora Costa, "Hours of Work and the Fair Labor Standards Act: A Study of Retail and Wholesale Trade, 1938–1950," *Industrial and Labor Relations Review* 53 (July 2000): 648–64, examines specifically how its extension to new industries altered hours typically worked in companies in those industries.

14. Daniel Hamermesh and Stephen Trejo, "The Demand for Hours: Direct Evidence from California," *Review of Economics and Statistics* 82 (Feb. 2000): 38–47.

15. Ana Rute Cardoso, Daniel Hamermesh, and José Varejão, "The Timing of Labor Demand," *Annals of Economics and Statistics* 105/106 (Jan./June 2012): 15–34.

16. Serena Yu and David Peetz, "Non-Standard Time Wage Premiums and Employment Effects: Evidence from an Australian Natural Experiment," *British Journal of Industrial Relations*, 2018.

17. "The Case for the 32-Hour Workweek," *Atlantic Documentaries*, June 22, 2015, https://www.theatlantic.com/video/index/396527/case-32-hour-workweek/, discusses one company's efforts along these lines.

18. The evidence on this is in Byron Lee and Sanford DeVoe, "Flextime and Profitability," *Industrial Relations* 51 (April 2012): 298–316.

19. The New York ordinance is described at http://mobile.reuters.com/article/idUSKBN18Q2IR.

20. See Charles Brown and Daniel Hamermesh, "Wages and Hours Laws: What Do We Know? What Is to Be Done?," unpublished paper, University of Michigan, 2018.

21. Richard Blundell and Thomas MaCurdy, "Labor Supply: A Review of Alternative Approaches," in *Handbook of Labor Economics*, vol. 3, ed. Orley Ashenfelter and David Card (Amsterdam: North-Holland, 1999), 1559–1695; and Michael Keane, "Labor Supply and Taxes: A Survey," *Journal of Economic Literature* 49 (Dec. 2011): 961–1075, summarize most of the immense literature on the impact of higher net incomes, and lower taxes, on the amount of paid work that people wish to do.

22. Leora Friedberg, "The Labor Supply Effects of the Social Security Earnings Test," *Review of Economics and Statistics* 82 (Feb. 2000): 48–63, examines the impact of changing the earnings test on the work time of older Americans.

23. See P. Sargant Florence, "Past and Present Incentive Study," in *Productivity and Economic Incentives*, ed. J. P. Davidson (London: Routledge, 1958), chapter 1; Marion Collewet and Jan Sauermann, "Working Hours and Productivity," *Labour Economics* 47 (Jan. 2017): 96–106; and Michael Burda, Katie Genadek, and Daniel Hamermesh, "Not Working at Work: Loafing, Unemployment, and Labor Productivity," National Bureau of Economic Research Working Paper No. 21923, Jan. 2016.

24. The classic study on this issue is George Neumann and Melvin Reder, "Output and Strike Activity in US Manufacturing: How Large Are the Losses?," *Journal of Labor Economics* 2 (Jan. 1984): 197–211.

INDEX

Figures are noted by an italic *f* following the page number.

activities
  categories of, 16
  enjoyment of, 19
  intensity of, 15
  switching between, 155
  timing of, 11, 15–16
age
  labor force participation rate and, 34
  religious activity and, 99
  role of, in time spent, 12
  sleep and, 25
  togetherness and, 79–80
American Time Use Survey, viii
appliances, home production and, 22–23
    (*see also* technology)
assortative mating, 74, 75
attorneys, time use by, 145–46
ATUS. *See* American Time Use Survey
Australia
  activity-switching in, 147
  annual hours worked in, 39*f*
  Daylight Saving Time in, 129
  labor force participation rate
    in, 37–38
  nonroutine scheduling in, 148
  paid holidays and vacation in, 40–41
  time stresses in, 155–59
  time use in, 9
  TV shows' broadcast times, in, 128
  unemployment in, 167
  wage penalties in, 187

bathing, stress reduction and, 178
beauty, earnings and, 202n17

blue laws, 183–84, 187
Brazil
  employment in, by gender, 57
  life expectancy in, 4

California, time use in, 120–21
Canada
  annual hours worked in, 39*f*
  childcare and education in, 20
  labor force participation rate in, 38*f*
  paid vacations in, 41
Candide (Voltaire), 113
Carson, Johnny, 123
Chapin, Harry, 179
Chávez, Hugo, 127
Cheney, Tom, 152
childcare, 18, 19–20 (*see also*
    parenthood)
Chile, employment in, by gender, 57
China, time zones in, 127
chore wars, 56, 67
cities, stereotypes about, 122
climate change, work and, 53
cohabitation, togetherness and, 81
college students, time use by, 93–94
committees, gender and, 58
commuting, time changes in,
    responses to, 6
comparative advantage, 74
construction projects, time and, 6
consumerism, weekly work hours
    and, 42
culture, gender work roles and, 64–65
customer service, time and, 5

Daylight Saving Time, 128–31
defined-benefit pension plans, 191
defined-contribution pension plans, 191
demography, time and, 12
disabilities, time stresses and, 157
discrimination, affecting time use,
    103–4, 106, 108–9, 114–15
divorce, 80–81
doctors, time use by, 145–46
domestic partnership, 85–86
DST. *See* Daylight Saving Time

earnings
  education and, 145
  inequality of, 8 (*see also* income
    inequality)
eating
  gender and, 67
  time spent on, 26–27
economic development, iso-work
    and, 64
economies of scale, 84
education
  career length and, 96
  childcare and, 19–20
  earnings and, 7, 137–41, 145
  labor force participation and, 138
  partnering and, 75
  togetherness and, 77
Einstein, Albert, 154
Emergency Daylight Saving Time Energy
    Conservation Act of 1973 (US), 129
Energy Policy Act of 2005 (US), 129
equivalence scales, 82–83, 84
Estonia, total work and gender in, 64
ethnicity. *See* race/ethnicity
Europe (Western; *see also individual*
    nations)
  immigration into, 105
  mandatory retirement age in, 192
  night work in, 51
  productivity in, 173
  unisex labor market in, 57–58
exercise, 29, 72, 178, 179
externalities, 44

Fair Labor Standards Act (US), 36, 190
financial planning, 7
Fitzgerald, F. Scott, 133

flexible workers (flextime),
    52–53, 187–88
FLSA. *See* Fair Labor Standards Act
food preparation and clean-up, 17, 18*f*
France
  activity-switching in, 148
  annual hours worked in, 39
  daily hours in major time use
    categories, 30*f*
  home production in, 20, 59, 60
  immigration to, 110, 113–15
  labor force participation rate in,
    37, 38*f*
  les vacances in, 41
  night work in, 51*f*
  nonworkers in, activities of, 142
  overtime pay in, 186
  paid holidays and vacation in, 40, 47
  retirement ages in, 97
  seniors' time use in, 99–100
  sleep in, 23
  spouses' age differences in, 75
  time stresses in, 152–54, 156, 159–60
  time use in, 9, 10
  togetherness in, 78–79, 81
  total work and gender in, 64
  TV watching in, 69
  weekend work in, 47
  work for pay in, 46–47
Franklin, Benjamin, 133

Garfunkel, Art, 178
gay marriage, 85–86
gay men
  time and, 69–71
  togetherness and, 84, 85
GDP (gross domestic product),
    measurement of, 66
gender
  eating and, 67
  grooming and, 67–68
  home production and, 59–62, 65–66
  homework and, 90
  industry and, 58
  leisure and, 68, 72
  life expectancy and, 154–55
  maturity and, 90, 93
  pay differences and, 66–67
  personal care and, 72

sleep and, 67
teens' time use and, 88–90
television and, 68–69
time use and, 56
total work by, 62–65
gender roles, 55–56, 58–59
Germany
  activity-switching in, 147
  daily hours in major time use
    categories, 30*f*
  home production in, 20–21, 59, 60
  hours worked in, annual, 39
  immigration to, 110, 113–14
  iso-work in, 63
  labor force participation rate in, 38, 59
  night work in, 51*f*
  nonroutine scheduling in, 148
  overtime pay in, 186
  paid holidays and vacation in, 40, 42
  religious activities in, 29
  seniors' time use in, 99–100
  sleep in, 23
  Summer Time in, 131
  teens in, schooling time of, 90
  time stresses in, 152–60
  time use in, 9, 10
  TV watching in, 29, 69
  unemployment in, 167
  weekend work in, 47
  work schedules in, 52
gig economy, 52–53
globalization, 49
global warming, work and, 53
government, policies of, for reducing
    time stress, 181–86, 193–95
grooming, 72
  gender and, 67–68
  race/ethnicity and, 108
  teens and, 91–92
  time spent on, 26, 67–68

Haefeli, William, 76
happiness, desire for, 7
health
  effect of, on activities, 156–57
  partners', 156–57
  seniors' time use and, 100–101
  time stresses and, 156–57
Hemingway, Ernest, 133

holidays, paid, 40–41
home production, 30
  as activity, 16–23, 59
  culture and, 65
  desirability of, 56, 62, 65
  economies of scale in, 84
  GDP and, 66
  gender and, 59–62, 65–66
  income per capita and, 21–22
  lesbians and, 70
  opportunity cost and, 61
  outsourcing of, 18–21
  partnering and, 73–75
  race/ethnicity and, 107*f*, 109
  supplemental national accounts
    for, 66
  technology and, 173
  time distribution for, 20–21
homework, 89–90
household management, 18
Hungary, total work and gender in, 64

immigration
  impacts of, on native population, 112
  night work and, 112
  time use and, 104–5, 110
incentives
  sleep and, 11
  time use and, 31
  work and, 11
incidence, 15, 33–34
income (*see also* money)
  education and, 7
  effects of, on purchases, 12–13
  expectations for, 7–8
  home production and, 21–22
  increases in, 3*f*, 4–5
  sacrificing, 179
  time and, 12–13
  time stresses and, 152
  togetherness and, 77–78
  unearned, 134–35
income inequality, 21–22, 136, 140
income subsidies, 82–83
income taxes, 190–91
intensity, 15, 33–34
Iolanthe (Gilbert and Sullivan), 25
iso-leisure, 67
iso-work, 63–64, 72

Israel
  activity-switching in, 147
  iso-work in, 64
Italy
  daily hours in major time use
    categories, 30f
  home production in, 20–21, 59–60
  leisure time in, 31
  night work in, 112
  personal care time in, 31
  time use in, 9
  total work and gender in, 64
  unemployment in, 167

Jagger, Mick, 161
Japan
  annual hours worked in, 39
  employment in, by gender, 57
  labor force participation rate
    in, 37–38
  taxation in, 42
  time use in, 9
  workweek reduced in, 170–72
Jennings, Waylon, 147
job safety, 50

Keynes, John Maynard, 169
Korea
  time use in, 9
  workweek reduced in, 170–72
  kvetching, 151

labor force participation rate, 34, 37, 192
  changes in, 35–38
  education and, 138
  gender and, 57, 59
  international, 37–39
  race/ethnicity and, 105–6
  wages and, 139, 143–44
labor market, unisex, 57–59, 66
labor supply, elasticity of, 139, 143
leisure, 27–30
  as activity, 16–17, 27–28
  contracting for, 17
  economic choices about, 87–88
  gender and, 68–69, 72
  technology and, 174–75
lesbians
  time and, 69–71
  togetherness and, 85

les vacances, 41
life expectancy, 3–4, 8, 154–55, 191
life stages, changes in, 87–88
living standards, rising, 7
London, time use in, 124–25
low-level equilibrium, 189

marriage
  decisions made within, 55–56
  economic theory of, 68, 74
  sleep and, 24
  time investment of, 85
  TV watching and, 69
men (see also gay men)
  hours worked, 56–57
  power of, in the household, 66
  time and, 69–71
  time stresses for, 154–55
  unemployed, 167
Merrill Lynch, 180
Mexico
  employment in, by gender, 57
  life expectancy in, 4
money
  affecting time use, 133–36
  spending of, 8
morning people, 46, 200n2
multitasking, 10

Nelson, Willie, 147
Netherlands
  blue laws in, 183–84
  home production and gender in, 59
  iso-work in, 63, 64
  night work in, 51f
  nonroutine scheduling in, 148
  religious activities in, 29
  sleep in, 24
  Summer Time in, 131
  time diaries in, 24
  time use in, 9
  TV watching in, 29
  weekend work in, 47
New York City
  culture of, 123–24
  time use in, 124, 125
New York minute, 123–24, 206n5
night work, 48–51, 112, 148
nonstudents (young adults), time use
  by, 94–95

nonwork activities
 choices of, among the
  nonworking, 141–44
 government policy and, 183–84
 incentives and, 31
 variations in, 15
Norway
 iso-work in, 64
 paid vacation in, 40

Obama administration, 190
O'Neill, Eugene, 154
opportunity cost, 5, 56, 153
 home production and, 61
 nonworking and, 134
 sleep and, 108
 wages and, 143
 wealth and, 133
outsourcing, 16
 fixed costs of, 19
 home production, 18–21
 income inequality and, 21–22
 overtime laws, 186–87, 190

paid work. *See* work
parenthood
 sleep and, 67
 time stresses and, 157–59
 togetherness and, 80
Paris, time use in, 124–25
partnering (*see also* togetherness)
 age difference and, 74–75
 assortative mating
  and, 74, 75
 education and, 75
 health and, 156–57
 home production and, 73–75
 reasons for, 73
 specialization and, 74
pay premiums, 50, 52
payroll taxes, 190–91
pension plans, 97, 99, 191 (*see also* Social
  Security)
Perry et al. v. Schwarzenegger et al., 85
personal care
 as activity, 16, 23
 gender and, 72
 race/ethnicity and, 107
 time spent on, 23–27
personal time, 30, 67–68

Portugal
 overtime laws in, 186–87
 time use in, 9
productivity, 46, 193
professors, time use by, 145–47
pro-natalist policies, 184
Proposition 8 (California; 2008),
public holidays, 41
public policy, for reducing time str
  181–86, 193–95

race/ethnicity (US), 103, 109–10, 11
 work productivity and, 106–7
 home production and, 109
 labor force participation and, 105–6
 nonwork time and, 107–10
 sleep and, 108–9
 time use and, 103–4, 115
 TV watching and, 109
recessions, time expenditures
  during, 167–69
regions
 identification with, 117–18
 time use and (US), 118–19
relationships, time and, 12
religious activities, time spent in, 29, 99
retirement, 87–88
rich, the. *See* wealthy, the
rural residents, time use by, 122
Russia, time zones in, 128

scarcity, 2
schooling, 87, 89–90, 91 (*see also*
  education)
senior citizens
 nonwork and, 97
 paid work by, 95–98
 time use by, 95–101
sex, reporting on, 25–26
sexual orientation, time and, 69–71
shopping, 17–18, 20
Simon, Paul, 178
Sipress, David, 17
sleep
 categories of, 10
 choice of, 24–25
 cost of, 142–44
 gender and, 67
 incentives and, 11
 opportunity cost of, 108

sleep (*cont.*)
  race/ethnicity and, 107*f*, 108
  teens and, 90–91
  time spent in, 10–11, 23–25, 67
  time zones and, 127–28
  togetherness and, 78
Sleeper (dir. Woody Allen), 175
sleeplessness, 25
Slovenia, total work and gender in, 64
slowing down, 179
Social Security, 97, 191–92
Social Security Act of 1935 (US), 191
South Africa, total work and
     gender in, 64
Spain
  daily hours in major time use
     categories, 30*f*
  time stresses in, 157
  time use in, 9
  togetherness in, 78
  total work and gender in, 64
spending power, time and, 3*f*, 4–6
sports, 29, 72
  teens and, 92
  watching of, on TV, 69
stereotyping, 117–18, 120, 122, 124
stock market returns, DST and, 130–31
stress, time-related, reducing, 178–95
suburbanites, time use by, 123
Summer Time, 128, 131 (*see also*
     Daylight Saving Time)
Sunday-closing laws, 183
Sweden
  annual hours worked in, 39*f*
  employment in, by gender, 57
  labor force participation rate in,
     37, 38*f*
Switzerland, paid holidays and
     vacation in, 40

taxation
  affecting time spent on certain
     activities, 184–85
  weekly work hours and, 42
technology
  effect of, on time, 164, 173–75
  home production and, 22–23
  leisure activities and, 174–75
  personal care and, 173–74
  productivity and, 173

teenagers
  grooming and, 91–92
  paid work by, 90
  sleep and, 90–91
  sports and, 92
  time use of, 87, 88–92
  TV watching and, 92
television watching, 11, 28–29
  cost of, 143, 144
  gender and, 68–69
  immigrants and, 111
  race/ethnicity and, 107*f*, 109
  seniors and, 100
  teenagers and, 92
  timing of, effecting behavior
     change, 128
Texas, time use in, 120, 121–22
third-party criterion, 16
time
  attitudes toward, 1–2
  choices about, 2–3
  classification of, 10
  cost of, 4–5
  demographic differences and, 12
  discretionary, changes in, 164
  economic approach to, 2
  economizing on, 83–84
  effects of, altering of, 13
  extra, use of, 163–75
  income and, 12–13
  interest in, vii
  measurement of, 8, 13
  outsourcing and, 20
  relationships and, 12
  scarcity of, 2–6, 8
  sexual orientation and, 69–71
  spending of, 8
  stress over, 151–61, 178
  use of, vii, 2 (*see also* time use)
  value of, 4, 7, 20, 135, 141, 149
time diaries, viii–ix, 9 (*see also*
     time use)
  listings in, 10
  purposes for, 28
time use, 9–10
  categories of, 10
  discrimination and, 103–4,
     106, 108–9
  gender and, 56
  money's effect on, 133–36

organizing of, 16
switching activities and, 147–48
time zones, 13, 118, 125–28, 189
togetherness, 179
   age and, 79–80
   cohabitation and, 81
   education and, 77
   gay men and, 84, 85
   income and, 77–78
   lesbians and, 85
   meaning of, 75–77
   parenthood and, 80
   perception of, 78–79, 81–82
   sleep and, 78
   time for, 77
   time savings and, 83–84
   well-being and, 82–84
Turkey
   employment in, by gender, 57
   total work and gender in, 64
Twain, Mark, 13
twenty-four-hour economy, 49

uncertainty, aversion to, 188
unearned income, 134–35
   incentive to work and, 136, 140–41
   time's value for, 141
unemployment, 34, 35, 163–67
United Kingdom
   daily hours in major time use
      categories, 30f
   home production in, 20–21
   labor force participation rate in, 38f
   life expectancy in, 4
   night work in, 51
   paid vacation in, 40
   religious activities in, 29
   seniors' time use in, 99
   sleep in, 23
   time stresses in, 152–54, 159–60
   time use in, 9, 10
   TV watching in, 29, 69
   weekend work in, 47
   working time spent in, 11, 39
United States
   childcare subsidies in, 184
   daily hours in major time use
      categories, 30f
   demographics of, 104
   DST in, 128–31

eating in, 26–27
gender and home production
   in, 59, 60
gender and work in, 56–57, 59, 60
girls' educational achievement in, 90
grooming in, 26
holidays in, paid, 40
home production in, 17–23, 59, 60
household income in, 135–36
immigration and, 104–5, 110–15
income inequality in, 136
iso-work in, 63
labor force participation rate in, 34–
   38, 105–6, 192
labor market in, 42, 57
leisure in, 28–30
life expectancy in, 4 (*see also* Social
   Security)
nonroutine scheduling in, 148
nonworkers in, activities of, 141–44
outsourcing in, 21
overtime laws in, 190
productivity in, 173
race/ethnicity in, 103, 109–10, 115
regional differences in, 118–22
religious activities in, 29
second-generation Americans
   in, 112–13
seniors' paid work in, 95–98
sex in, 25–26
sleep in, 10–11, 23–25
SNAP (Food Stamps) program in, 185
spouses' age differences in, 74–75
time stresses in, 155, 156–57,
   159, 160
time use in, 9
time zones in, 126–28, 189
togetherness in, 78–81
TV watching in, 28–29, 68–69,
   100, 128
unemployment in, 105–6, 166, 167
urban/rural differences in, 122–24
vacations in, 39–40, 193–95
volunteering in, 29–30
weekend work in, 47–48
work ethic in, 41–42
work sought in, changes in, 194
work time in, 11, 38–39, 41–44,
   48–53, 189
workweek in, 36–37

United States v. Windsor, 85
urban residents, time use by, 122

vacation time
  mandated, 193–95
  paid, 39–41
Venezuela, time zones in, 127
volunteering, 29–30

wages
  differences in, reasons for, 140
  education and, 137–41
  incentive to work and, 136, 138–41
  labor force participation and,
      139, 143–44
  opportunity costs and, 143
Warner, Charles Dudley, 13
wealth
  opportunity costs and, 133
  source of, 136–37
wealthy, the
  night work and, 148
  time stresses and, 159–60
  time use by, 144–49
widows, time use by, 101
women (*see also* lesbians)
  hours worked, 56–57
  multitasking by, 156
  roles for, 58–59 (*see also* gender roles)
  time and, 69–71
  time stresses for, 154–56
  unemployed, 167
  workforce participation of, 35
work (work for pay), 30
  as activity, 16
  categories of, 10
  climate change and, 53

conditions for, improvements in, 50
costs of, 97–98
defining, 33, 62
desire for more, 180–81
enjoyability of, 65
GDP's measurement of, 66
gender pay differences and, 66–67
global warming and, 53
incentives and, 11, 136, 138–41
incidence of, 33–34
intensity of, 33, 34, 105
lesbians and, 70
necessity of, 33
opportunity cost of, 56
productivity of, 106–7
seasonal variations in, 46
spreading of, across time and
      population, 189–92
stress of, 154–55
taxation and, 42
time spent in, 11
timing of, 45–53, 178, 180–81, 188–89
total, by gender, 62–65
uncertainty of, 188–89
workaholism, 43–44, 97, 180–81
work schedules (*see also* work: timing of)
  desirability of, 50
  variability of, 52–53
work time, reductions in, 169–72
workweek
  changes to, 180, 185–86, 187
  length of, 36–37
  in Western Europe, 39–40

young adults
  maturity of, 93–94
  time use of, 92–95